THE INVENTION OF MONOLINGUALISM

THE INVENTION OF MONOLINGUALISM

David Gramling

BLOOMSBURY ACADEMIC
NEW YORK • LONDON • OXFORD • NEW DELHI • SYDNEY

BLOOMSBURY ACADEMIC
Bloomsbury Publishing Inc
1385 Broadway, New York, NY 10018, USA
50 Bedford Square, London, WC1B 3DP, UK

BLOOMSBURY, BLOOMSBURY ACADEMIC and the Diana logo are
trademarks of Bloomsbury Publishing Plc

First published 2016
Reprinted 2018

Cover design: Nick Evans
Cover image © Matthew Thorsen

Names: Gramling, David, 1976- author.
Title: The invention of monolingualism / David Gramling.
Description: New York : Bloomsbury Academic, 2016. | Includes bibliographical
references and index.
Identifiers: LCCN 2016009638 (print) | LCCN 2016024009 (ebook) | ISBN
9781501318054 (hardback) | ISBN 9781501318047 (paperback) | ISBN
9781501318061 (ePub) | ISBN 9781501318085 (ePDF)
Subjects: LCSH: Languages, Modern–Study and teaching. | Languages,
Modern–Scholarships, fellowships, etc. | Language experience approach in
education. | Interdisciplinary approach in education. | Education,
Bilingual. | BISAC: LITERARY CRITICISM / General. | LITERARY CRITICISM /
Semiotics & Theory. | LANGUAGE ARTS & DISCIPLINES / Linguistics / General.
Classification: LCC PB36 .G55 2016 (print) | LCC PB36 (ebook) | DDC
418.0071–dc23
LC record available at https://lccn.loc.gov/2016009638

ISBN: HB: 978-1-5013-1805-4
       PB: 978-1-5013-1804-7
       ePub: 978-1-5013-1806-1
       ePDF: 978-1-5013-1808-5

Typeset by Deanta Global Publishing Services, Chennai, India
Printed and bound in Great Britain

To find out more about our authors and books visit www.bloomsbury.com
and sign up for our newsletters.

For Louise
(1911–2010)

CONTENTS

FOREWORD AND ACKNOWLEDGMENTS

A desire to write this book first set in during the Vermont winter of 1994–5, in the form of a vague shiver. I was immersed in an undergraduate liberal arts culture that prized foreign language learning, as a matter of pride as much as one of profit.[1] When other strategies for late-teenage living faltered, I tended over those winters to warm myself against found language objects—from German, Spanish, French, dance choreography, musical notation, other languages when they were lent to me, and even some English when held at the right angle. At that moment in my education, "foreign affairs," "global studies," and "intercultural competence" were still quizzically aerial concepts, meant for other people with clearer goals than mine. Even linguistics (let alone *applied* linguistics!) sounded too optimistic to have room for my suspicious, gangly movements around language. But I'd never yet had cause to doubt the poetic and political promise of multilingual language learning itself, which had made the world so livable for me since age ten onward.[2]

It was during that winter, while reading Eve Kosofsky Sedgwick's book *The Epistemology of the Closet*, that I first read a scholarly account of how certain structures in North Atlantic modernity had been able to ensure crucial, unearned triumphs for geopolitical brinkmen like U.S. President Ronald Reagan, thanks alone to their *mono*lingualism. Right there on its opening pages, Sedgwick's book was making an intervention about "monolingualism"—just without naming it for us in that fashion. "Knowledge, after all, is not itself power," she wrote, "although it is the magnetic field of power. Ignorance and opacity collude and compete with knowledge in mobilizing the flows of energy, desires, goods, meanings, persons" (2008: 4).

The logic was simple and saddening, there on the page. Hadn't everything else in my educational life urged me toward a contrary

1. On pride versus profit as motivations for learning foreign languages, see Alexandre Duchêne and Monica Heller (eds), *Language in Late Capitalism: Pride and Profit* (2012): 1–21.

2. On identity in multilingual foreign language learning, see for instance Claire Kramsch, "Authenticity and Legitimacy in Multilingual Second Language Acquisition" (2012).

and passionate conviction? Certainly, being multilingual opens up the borders, debunks the lies, and makes the friendships! Certainly, everyone deep down strives to meet the fecund and recalcitrant world in its own tones and terms—and not through some empire's addled Phraselator![3] Certainly, if Mr. Reagan had been so routinely able to manhandle the world by "dilating in his native [language]" (Sedgwick 2008: 4), such a scandal couldn't simply be chalked up—could it?—to *c'est la vie* or *it is what it is*. Something must have been, or become, quite amiss.

But why was I learning about adverse multilingualism and the structural privileges of the monolingual speaker from a primer on queer theory, and not from scholarship more squarely interested in language learning?[4] If I had myself been raised multilingually, I'd have surely encountered the brute power of monolingual privilege by my first morning of kindergarten, as several of the other girls and boys in my Central Massachusetts elementary school had done. But I had not. The closest I'd come to "foreign languages" in childhood was hearing my mother's stories about conjugating Latin for the nuns at Holy Family School in the 1950s—amo, amas, amat—punching each final syllable like a faulty brake pedal. These multigenerational memories of hangdog and inspirationless foreign language non-learning became, in a sense, my own *mother language.*

Neither did my wondrous college professors of foreign languages and literatures, afire as they were with philological, post-structuralist, and reflexive anthropological lines of thought, care much to talk about the former president and his disconcertingly effective monolingualism. For young researchers in language studies like me, there were few books, classes, or essays to turn to about monolingualism, and today still there are almost as few. Monolingualism's persistent non-place in humanities and social science research methodology—even amid the boom in multilingualism and translation studies today—portends that students of monolingual phenomena will need, for the time being, to

3. On Phraselators, see Mary Louise Pratt, "Harm's Way: Language and the Contemporary Arts of War" (2009): 1515-31.

4. On adverse multilingualism, see Aline Gohard-Radenkovic, "Le plurilinguisme, un nuveau champ, ou une nouvelle idéologie: Ou quand les discours politiquement corrects prônent la diversité" (2012): 1-14. See also Ulrike Jessner-Schmid and Claire Kramsch (eds), *The Multilingual Challenge: Cross-Disciplinary Perspectives* (2015): 1-18. On the notion of speaker privilege in multilingual contexts, see Claire Kramsch, "The Privilege of the Non-Native Speaker" (1997): 359-69.

"keep our treasures hidden in our neighbor's house," as my dear translator friend Aron Aji says.

In other words, critics of monolingualism (as opposed to criticizers of it, who are always and everywhere *à votre service*) will continue to forge our tools in the neighboring houses of literary studies, applied linguistics, political theory, linguistic anthropology, foreign and additional language pedagogy, classical, medieval and Renaissance studies, jurisprudence and legal studies, critical race studies, information technology, translation studies, psychology, mathematics, music history, and indeed queer theory. This is good, and it reminds us to be good guests—visitors who don't misuse, misinterpret, or run off with things our disciplinary hosts hold dear. A number of scholars have already done this well, dedicating a great portion of their writing lives to the explicit and sustained study of "monolingualism." They are few enough that I can thank almost all of them by name, for their profound and palpable influence on this book: Wolfgang Butzkamm, Elizabeth Ellis, Ingrid Gogolin, Brian Lennon, Till Dembeck, Thomas Paul Bonfiglio, Mary Louise Pratt, Rey Chow, Anjali Pandey, and Yasemin Yildiz. Though it feels immodest to thank Jacques Derrida for anything, there is also genuine gratitude in these pages for his indelible work, in and before *Monolingualism of the Other* (1996).

While writing this book, I have been guided, advised, cheered, and offered critical friendship by many treasured friends. I thank them here not from *a* to *z*, but in accordance with the simple ways they come to mind every day, always just in time. Thanks to my wise, big sisters in scholarship Chantelle Warner, Sarah Richardson, and Alison Phipps; thanks to my co-translators İlker Hepkaner, Kristin Dickinson, and Aron Aji for their generous *sohbet* about translating Turkish poetry and fiction; thanks to my advisers and mentors Claire Kramsch, Deniz Göktürk, Anton Kaes, Nikolas Euba, and Roman Graf for taking a longer view than I could; thanks to my supportive and forbearing departmental colleagues in German Studies at the University of Arizona; thanks to my graduate and undergraduate researcher colleagues for their vision, commitment, and rejuvenating conversation over the course of this project, particularly to Tara Taylor, Kerry Marnell, Lana Baeumlisberger, Judith Menzl, Nicholas McNutt, Kyung Lee Gagum, Summar Alsemeiry, Osman Can Örnek, Diane Richardson, Charles Norton, Nurulhude Baykal, Christina Butler, Kristen Michelson, Keri Miller, Mija Sanders, Patrick Ploschnitzki, Carolin Radtke, and Benjamin Horn; thanks to my enlightening comrades in multilingualism scholarship Katja Frimberger, Till Dembeck, Glenn Levine,

Gameli Tordzro, Naa Densua Tordzro, Ganyamatope Tawona Sithole, Jerry Won Lee, Peter Ecke, Malena Samaniego, Kamakshi Murti, Bethany Wiggin, Giulia Radaelli, and Martina Schwalm; thanks to my beautiful mother and very handsome brother, Kathryn Gramling and Robert Gramling, whose dissertations in nursing and public health were the only ones I'd read before writing my own; thanks to those who stuck by me as best they could "when it don't come easy": Russell Wagner, Elena Taylor-Garcia, Anne Moore, Julie Koser, Don Eggert, Jamilah Shubeilat, Susan Stryker, William Coker, Tes Howell, Aurora Choi, Bruce Cole, Ben Reynwar, Liz Crockett-Hixon, Samuel Ace, TC Tolbert, Lindsay Slabich and Kristen Mara, Benj Lipchak, Joseph Watson and Michael Warner, Rich and Beth Nobile, Mehtap Söyler, Ginny and George Lewis, Flint Freeman, Graziano Paolicelli, Christopher Moes, and Heike Fahrenberg. I would like to thank the supportive colleagues at Fakenham Prepress and Bloomsbury, most whom I'ver never met, who helped get this manuscript ready for reading: Haaris Naqvi, Mary Al-Sayed, Kim Storry, Andrew Mikolajski, and James Tupper.

Many institutions have encouraged this project along, and I relish the opportunity to thank them here. These are institutions whose working personnel—whether through financial, intellectual, or intangible means—have reminded me of the importance of the endeavor and have left me cairns of guidance, dialogue, and possibility: the Arts and Humanities Research Council of the United Kingdom's Translating Cultures Programme, the University of Arizona Confluencenter for Creative Inquiry, the Fulbright Commission of Germany, the Berkeley Language Center, the American Research Institute in Turkey, the University of Luxembourg Laboratoire de linguistique et de littérature allemande, the Pasqua Yaqui and Tohono O'odham Nations, the University of Iowa Translation Masters of Fine Arts Program, the National Endowment for the Arts, the Middlebury College German School, the American Literary Translators Association, and of course my home department at Arizona, the Department of German Studies. This book grew from a notion into a project, thanks in part to Arizona's Second Language Acquisition and Teaching Students Association (SLATSA), whose members kindly invited me in 2011 to present portions of Chapter 1 at their annual SLAT Roundtable in Tucson. Early drafts of short sections of Chapter 4 appeared in *Die Unterrichtspraxis / Teaching German* 42.2 and in Dembeck & Minnaard (2014), as did a short portion of Chapter 3 in *The American Book Review* (July 2014). Particular gratitude is due to the American Council of Learned Societies, and to the efforts of Niklaus Largier, Susana Ruiz, Chantelle Warner, Mary Wildner-Bassett, Linda Waugh, and Barbara Kosta, who helped me get more than my fair shot at a scholarly career.

Thanks to that "invisible college" called Researching Multilingually at Borders, which sets out daily from the Glasgow Lighthouse toward Durham, Bristol, Brussels, Nijmegen, Tucson, Sofia, and Gaza City. Thanks to Nazmi Al-Masri of the Islamic University of Gaza for reminding me that, perhaps tomorrow, there will be no siege between us. Thanks to my teachers of foreign languages (including music, dance, and often English, too) who've helped me through dry seasons from childhood to now: Genevieve Brechtl, Elizabeth Newell, Joanna Kulis, Ken Mammone, Grace Reidy, Jessica Roemischer, Vanessa van Ornam, Kalin Johnson, Manfred and Helga Fahrenberg, Peter Schmitz, Selim Kuru, Bev Mahlke, Maryanne Newman, Jayson Carver, Özlem Oğut, Mine Demiralp, George Lewis (of Freehold Theater Lab Studio), Ayla Algar, and Hicham Assaoui. Thanks to my grandmother Louise McEnelly, my father Paul Gramling, and my first friend in adulthood, the blues guitarist John-Alex Mason, who parted with us during the writing of this book. Mostly, thanks to Mohammad. See you tomorrow morning at 4:45.

DJG
Tucson
December 2015

INTRODUCTION

The monochrome remains [...] the reminder
of the culture we have not been able to create.
                    —Aleksander Rodchenko (Batchelor 2000: 153)

Some human inventions turn out to be disasters for almost everyone. If, and where, monolingualism is one of these disasters is not yet a settled matter. For the moment, I'd like to suggest that the "inventions" of monolingualism, taken to hand in this book, deserve an honest measure of credit for several unlikely achievements. Upon its scientific discovery in the seventeenth century, monolingualism became a vehicle for European Enlightenment, for mass literacy and organized anti-absolutism, for populaces who have at least a fighting chance at understanding their governments and laws, for the coalescence of modern scholarly disciplines, for coordinated and liberal market economies, for certain forms of internationalist solidarity and cognitive capitalism, and now for global logics of data transfer, content circulation, and the "internet unconscious."[1] In its self-effacing manner, monolingualism has been able to steady these platforms ever since for a vast superstructural constellation of aesthetic repertoires and epistemic paradigms, from which it is now more than inconvenient for us to divest—whether from the modern *book* as we know it, or from a canon of world literature that takes the translated monolingual book as its most granular integer of political appearance. Even in the most iconoclastic arenas of cultural production—whether surrealist, theocratic, deconstructivist, cybernetic, or anarchic—monolingualism is afoot,

---

1. I use "scientific" here in the broad French or German sense of a rational and methodical pursuit of knowledge, rather than in the narrower (U.S.) Anglophone sense of natural sciences. On the "internet unconscious" and its monolingualism, see in particular the section "I read my spam," in Sandy Baldwin, *The Internet Unconscious: On the Subject of Electronic Literature* (2015): 89–91. On "cognitive capitalism" and its effects on symbolic economies, see Yann Moulier Boutang, *Cognitive Capitalism* (2011): 2.

triaging what can be predictably communicated, marketably translated, politically operationalized, internationally distributed, rightfully
claimed, and even privately remembered.

But rather than hunting down monolingualism like a white-collar
crook on the run, this book seeks to venerate it, however briefly,
as a scientific-aesthetic invention that, in its time, first made the
Mercatorian notion of countable global cultures and languages at
least provisionally thinkable.[2] Early monolingualism gave seventeenth-
century scholars in Europe a way to yoke all of the propositional and
social ambitions of Language (*langage*) under the proprietary roof of
any single language (*langue*)—a powerful and imaginative act of what
we today might call (macro-)optimization.[3] In converting Language
from God's unwieldy prerogative into humanity's own, pluralizable,
panfunctional grid of rational extension, early modern thinkers from
Martin Opitz and Antoine Arnauld to Thomas Sprat and Gabriel
de San Buenaventura bequeathed to eighteenth-century speakers a
unified, possessible object called "a" language, whose essence inhered
in its promise to know everything, say everything, and translate everything—and to do all these things without "vicious excess of phrase."[4]

2. On Mercatorian logic in world-making and world-mapping processes,
see Pheng Cheah, "World against Globe: Toward a Normative Conception of
World Literature" (2014): 307. On the development of a systematized perception
of linguistic foreignness, see William Jervis Jones, *Images of Language: German
Attitudes to European Languages from 1500 to 1800* (1999): 85–214.

3. See for instance Chapter 1 of Anthony Pym, *The Moving Text* (2004). For
new critical perspectives on langage/langue, see for instance Beata Staworska,
*Saussure's Philosophy of Language as Phenomenology: Undoing the Doctrine of
the* Course in General Linguistics (2015).

4. This *historical* process was not of great interest to Noam Chomsky in
his book about the seventeenth century, *Cartesian Linguistics*, in which a
commitment to the notion of deep structure rested on the presumption that
perfectible generative panfunctionality always already inhered in so-called
"well-designed" individual languages. Chomsky writes confidently, for instance,
that "The use of the names of classical cases for languages with no inflections
implies only a belief in the uniformity of the grammatical relations involved,
a belief that deep structures are fundamentally the same across languages,
althought the means for their expression may be quite diverse" (88). Chomsky's
analyses were thus relatively unconcerned about the *political* process by which
independent "well-designed" languages come to the fore and are recognized as
such, a process I regard as *monolingualization*. See Noam Chomsky, *Cartesian*

These men could not have known that their zealous projections would culminate in the Globalization, Internationalization, Localization, and Translation (GILT) industries of the twenty-first century, though their works indeed suggest as much: namely, that today's instantaneous, multilingual, corpus-driven cross-language fuzzy algorithms of big-data traffic were not far from their own horizons of imagining.[5] Super-sized to fit the globe—and thus too big to fail—their invented "monolanguages" were no longer the vernacular mother tongues of the thirteenth to sixteenth centuries.[6] The matrices of home, hearth, soil, intrafamilial love, heritage, and indeed nation were too modest in their ambitions to keep astride of the inventions of monolingualism.

It is for this reason that the current book has little choice but to regard its object of inquiry with at least a little veneration. Whether we opt to call it a myth, a pathology, a paradigm, a relic, or a sham, monolingualism is woven into modernity's most minute and sophisticated political structures, and it is clearly not yet inclined to be waved off the stage by a university professor, nor even by a "multilingual turn"

Linguistics: A Chapter in the History of Rationalist Thought (2009). On the countability of languages, see in particular Sinfree Makoni and Alastair Pennycook, *Disinventing and Reconstituting Languages* (2006): 1–13. On Antoine Arnauld, see Robert Stockhammer, *Grammatik: Wissen und Macht in der Geschichte einer sprachlichen Institution* (2014): 127–37. On Martin Opitz, see for instance Esther Kilchmann "Monolingualism, Heterolingualism, and Poetic Innovation: On Contemporary German Literature, with a Side Glance to the Seventeenth Century" (2014): 74. On Thomas Sprat and "vicious excess of phrase," see Stockhammer (2014): 139, and on the purification of thought and language in the seventeenth century, see Jürgen Trabant, *Mithridates im Paradies: Kleine Geschichte des Sprachdenkens* (2003): 122–56. On Gabriel de San Buenaventura and his *Arte de la lengua Maya* (1684), see William Hanks, *Converting Words: Maya in the Age of the Cross* (2010): 222–41.

5. On fuzzy cross-language algorithms, see for instance Valerie V. Cross and Clare R. Voss, "Fuzzy Queries and Cross-Language Ontologies in Multilingual Document Exploitation" (2000): 641–6.

6. Rey Chow's Derridian usage of "monolanguage" is helpful, particularly for this historical threshold in the development of a pluralized language order. See Rey Chow, *Not Like a Native Speaker: On Languaging as a Postcolonial Experience* (2014): 29–31. On the historical construction of "mother tongue," see Thomas Paul Bonfiglio, *Mother Tongues and Languages: The Invention of the Native Speaker* (2010) and Yasemin Yildiz, *Beyond the Mother Tongue: The Postmonolingual Condition* (2012).

in one or another discipline (May 2013). Certainly, accounts differ on whether monolingualism can even exist as a category of experience or evidence, and—if or where it does—what its effects have been. Taking a radical stance on linguistic and language preservation and justice, researchers like the Finnish linguist Tove Skutnabb-Kangas have spent decades sounding the alarm about the epistemicidal effects of monolingualism on indigenous and settler languages alike (Skutnabb-Kangas and Dunbar 2010; see for a critique Chamberson 2008). In one of the first-ever books about monolingualism as such, the German education theorist Ingrid Gogolin (1994) offered, in turn, a detailed historical account of how the German school system came to acquire its "monolingual habitus," and why—as a consequence of Germany's civic habituation to monolingualism over the course of the nineteenth century—German schools are now ill-equipped to meet the needs of learners in a multilingual immigration society (Lau 2006a).

In contrast, eminent applied linguists like Alastair Pennycook find the word monolingualism to be not much more than an elite ruse, distracting us from the diverse, centrifugal linguistic practices in evidence everywhere we turn (Pennycook and Otsuji 2015: 16–20). Africanists in applied linguistics like Sinfree Makoni suggest further that focusing on "lingualism" of any particular sort—whether mono, multi, metro, bi or otherwise—unduly draws attention away from living, breathing speakers, who competently select languages (or parts of languages) to match a range of shifting, emergent purposes that are important to them in each new setting (Makoni and Trudell 2006: 17). Indeed, for many teachers of English to speakers of other languages (TESOL), the word "monolingual" represents little more than the fetishized, delusional abstraction of linguistic nativism. The applied linguists Jasone Cenoz and Durk Gorter write for instance that "[M]ultilinguals and learners who are in the process of becoming multilingual should not be viewed as imitation monolinguals in a second language or additional language, but rather they should be seen as possessing unique forms of competence, or competencies, in their own right" (Cenoz and Gorter 2011: 340; see also V. Cook 2007, Canagarajah 2007). This unfavorable image of the "imitation monolingual"—as a methodological mistake, a social strawperson, or a kind of subjectivity gone wrong—is tone-setting in most contemporary writings in the social sciences and humanities that invoke the word "monolingual."

The Indonesian applied linguist Setiono Sugiharto (2015: 2), ultimately unimpressed with the current "multilingual turn" in applied linguistics and Second Language Acquisition (May 2013), suspects that the bravura with which scholars have pilloried monolingualism over recent decades ultimately exaggerates the normativity of the monolingual in social life, overlooking centuries-old multilingual norms in contexts throughout the Global South (see also Mufwene and Vigouroux 2008: 5–21). Amid Europeans' technocratic zeal for multilingual civic planning since 1995, scholars and policy makers—so Sugiharto's argumentation—fail to acknowledge how multilingual subjectivity has been utterly unexceptional, at least outside of the cradle of Enlightenment philosophy (Sugiharto 2015: 3–4). These objections notwithstanding, the specter of a "monolingual prejudice within Second Language Acquisition" studies has been on the docket for remediation now for almost a quarter-century (V. Cook 1997, see also Sridhar 1994; Kachru 1994; Ortega 2007, 2008; Auer 2007).

Back in literary studies Michael Holquist, the eminent Slavic comparatist and translator of Mikhail Bakhtin, holds monolingualism to be a logical fallacy in a linguistically heterogeneous world (Holquist 2014: 7–8), while the Romance philologist Brigitte Jostes—herself a multiple-language user and researcher—has taken the opportunity in a recent essay to "come out" as a monolingual. "Deep down in my soul," writes Jostes,

> I am a monolingual person. While I am at it, I might as well come out of a second closet and admit that I am not actually mobile in a way that befits a modern European. Of course I get itchy feet once in a while; I am interested in other countries; I like to travel. Nevertheless, I suffer from chronic homesickness. And since the education-policy documents of all European institutions now link the praise of multilingualism with the advantage of mobility, I increasingly suspect that both stigmata—monolingualism and homesickness—are somehow connected. (Jostes 2010: 28)

Coming out of the shadows of language ideology, with her tongue in cheek, Jostes's affective performance—of disclosure, retrenchment, expropriation, and institutional perplexity—will find many kindred figures throughout this book, from Franz Kafka to Michigan congressman John Conyers, to various protagonists of contemporary world literature.

Turning from individual speakers' self-conceptions to broader paradigms of knowledge, Yasemin Yildiz's groundbreaking book *Beyond the Mother Tongue* (2012) has offered us the idea of a "postmonolingual condition," challenging scholarship to decide whether human

speakers have ever naturally come bearing a single "mother tongue."
In a similar vein, the Melbourne-based applied linguist Michael Clyne
(2008) suggests the term "monolingual mindset" for the misalignment
between Australian societal diversity in language and a state apparatus
disinclined to recognize it.[7] Michael Silverstein (1996), from a linguistic
anthropological point of view, and Jan Blommaert (2010), from sociolinguistics, have likewise been leading voices calling critical attention
to "monoglot standardization" and the history of language "uniformity"
respectively. It is however Elisabeth Ellis's work in sociolinguistics
over the past fifteen years that has striven most committedly toward
addressing the "unmarked" nature of monolingualism in research
paradigms and policy spheres alike (2006).

On the cultural politics of monolingual text

The literary comparatist Brian Lennon's *In Babel's Shadow* acknowledges in erudite detail how the trade publishing industry colludes in
tamping down multilingual literatures to conform to the governing
logics of monolingual states (2010: 141–3). The postcolonial theorist
Rey Chow, reading Derrida's jeremiad on colonial French, describes
monolingualism as "less the exclusive sign of imposition by political
force or cunning than [...] the promise of the singular, a promise that
remains open-ended and thus messianic in character" (2014: 29). In
Chow's account, monolingualism recommends itself to us not in the
garb of supremacy and dominance but in the accommodating and
sonorous tones of opportunity, advancement, and accessibility.

Some literary critics find monolingualism to be but a surface-level
conceit, which allows otherwise multilingual writers to house their
unconstrained, customary range of language use within a conventional, monolingualized repertoire acceptable to trade publishers
and accessible to diverse audiences. Monolingualism works, in this
account, as the entry-level lingua franca of literary traffic, a meta-
formal constraint that nonetheless avows the most various forms of
multilingual expression, shimmering in wait between the lines of an
apparently monolingual book. Hana Wirth-Nesher, reflecting on the
works of Henry Roth and Mary Antin, goes to inspired lengths to detect
"echoes of another language and culture [...] in so-called monolingual

---

7. See also Eades (2003): 115 on Aboriginal interpreters in monolingualist
Australian courtrooms. See also Lo Bianco 1999.

prose" (2008: 6). Wirth-Nesher points out how Israel Isodore Elyashev, regarded as one of the first modern Yiddish literary critics, had already a century ago issued just such a claim (in Yiddish): "Don't our finer critics carry within them the spirit of the German language? And among our younger writers, who were educated in the Russian language, isn't it a possible to discern the spirit of Russian?"[8] The very title of Elyashev's tract to this effect in the *Petrograder Tageblatt* in 1918, "Tsvey shprakhen: eyn eyntsiker literatur" ("Two Languages—Only One Literature"), foreshadows what is now a common stance in matters of monolingualism—namely that, after all, artists' and rhetoricians' choice for a single language is merely the necessary turnstile into an always close-at-hand, unruly world of multilingual heteroglossia.

Though Wirth-Nesher and other kindred readers delight in shoring up such communion between present and absent languages in manifest text, the cultural politics of such projects are often somehow ambivalent. Finding solace in the present absence of another language (say, Yiddish) in a monolingual (say, English) text is cold comfort for those who might like to be reading new literature in Yiddish instead, a language all but drummed out of literary existence by National Socialism. Indeed, the apophatic gesture can serve to exonerate the English text of both its monolingual privilege and its monolingualizing effects. In such cases, analytic recourse to the "depth" and "multilayeredness" of language celebrates a humanistic spirit of heteroglossia and interrelation, while nonetheless depoliticizing the very monolingualism of the text and its means of production. It will be of primary concern throughout Chapters 2 and 3 to query the mutual *political* accountability between the "translingual imagination" (Kellman 2000) and the manifest textual monolingualism expected of publishable manuscripts and their authors.[9]

Further along the disciplinary spectrum, there is humbling irony for modernists (like myself) in some medievalists' heuristic recourse to the notion of a "monolingual sociolinguistics" for the Romance language(s) of the early Middle Ages (Wright 1995: 483). "Monolingual" is, for some working in this research context, the term considered best equipped among potential alternatives to account for the rugged,

8. See Israel Isodore Elyashev, "Two Languages—Only One Literature," trans. Hana Wirth-Nesher, in Hana Wirth-Nesher (ed.), *What is Jewish Literature* (1992).

9. For an enlightening view on the relationship between multilingual authors and their monolingual literary production, see Komska (2015).

disorderly continuum of speech practiced clear across Southern Europe from Iberia to Asia Minor until the mid-eleventh century. This usage of "monolingualism" aims to house the range of radically divergent yet unbordered semiotic phenomena, unimaginable to most Euro-American moderns, that constituted medieval interculturality—a range of practices that Peter Trudgill (1986) has also called "inter-dialect." Absent any hard-and-fast systemic distinctions, verifiable on the basis of archival or archaeological data, between one early medieval speech community and its abutting neighbors, these researchers see virtue in characterizing the north-Mediterranean language map of the tenth century as monolingual in the sense that its language(s)—neither singular nor plural—had yet to be subjected to effective partitioning into this or that territorialized, supra-local repertoire, approximating the modern designation of "a language."

Ladurie's classic account of the thirteenth-century Occitan village of Montaillou (1978: 286) provides an even later illustration of this principle: namely, that most non-elite medium-distance travelers had neither a conceptual map nor a pertinent reason for identifying a neighboring region's speech as structurally foreign from their own. Difficulties in understanding would tend to strike the traveler as features of acoustic or social friction in the flow of communication, rather than as results of any discrete language barrier. A modern structuralist's potential rebuttal—that this happy traveler just doesn't understand the fundamentals of linguistics yet—misses the emic, practical point about situated knowledge in pre-modernity, while also indicating a more general disinterest in, or discomfort with, vernacular modes of language use beyond the reach of systemic or philological models.

For their part, elite medieval and early modern reading publics had been reasonably expected to navigate among a common set of erudite textual languages. The post-Enlightenment norm of writing and reading in one supra-local language, to the exclusion of others, grew first out of mass literacy initiatives and the invention of folkloristics, as standard national vernaculars eclipsed Latin in the university and French in the diplomatic sphere (Leonhardt 2013). In the learned and literary spheres of Enlightenment, theorists of nationhood from Herder to Grégoire and W. v. Humboldt thus inspired a new meta-formal constraint upon fictional representations in the modern age: the procedural unity of monolingualism, which succeeded earlier Averoean unities of place, time, and action. Prior to this eighteenth-century literary episteme of monolingual mastery, textual culture (both oral and written) had been trafficked by and for jacks-of-many-languages—whether clerics, scholars, royals, or scribes. Given a pre-modern Europe where orthography and grammatology were primarily scholastic practices, and not yet strategies of nationalization and naturalization, it would be less than tenable to speak of pre-seventeenth-century languages as having *de jure* "native speakers" in contradistinction to "non-native speakers" (Bonfiglio 2010).

It is thus a great deal more than theoreticist revisionism to claim that monolingualism was one of the pivotal innovations of the early modern and Enlightenment period. Alongside Foucault's account of the rise of sexuality as a regime of scientific knowledge, a similarly broad incitement to discourse about "national" languages became compulsory for elites and non-elites alike between 1730 and 1810, amid the brisk circulation of intercontinental travelogues, ethnographies, trade narratives, and pilgrimage testimonies (Foucault 1978). This new, historicist discourse about linguistic difference versus ipseity—buttressed as it was by a swelling traffic of documentary evidence about Europe's linguistic Others—provided a groundwork for perfecting hegemonic vernaculars at home. This resulted, for the first time, in a European middling class broadly predisposed to envision a global isomorphy of national monolingualisms, a world federation of discretely territorialized languages.

In the sixteenth and seventeenth centuries, the desirous and quixotic dream of the binding regularization, panfunctionalization, flexibilization, and assignability of speech into a roster of discrete "well-designed" languages (Chomsky 2009: 75) is what I consider the earliest form of monolingualism. While scholars of language *standardization* are primarily concerned with processes through which internal consistency in usage are imagined, managed, and controlled (though often by way of external pressures), a history of monolingualization must account for the metalinguistic rituals by which discrete, "well-designed" languages are inaugurated, upon a translingual leverage-system of mutual formal recognition. My modernist's perspective leads me to think of the "interdialectal" sociolinguistic landscape of medieval Europe, of which Wright, Trudgill, and others speak, not as (empirically) monolingual but rather as (structurally) alingual. This is not to say that early medieval speakers and writers *lacked* anything in their language, which needed fixing or filling by learned grammarians, but that they rarely had logistical grounds to dependably assign a string of talk to a specific, politically conceived language unity beyond their immediate context of utterance. The English literary critic George Puttenham put a point on this latter-day performance ritual early on, writing in 1589 that "After a speech is fully fashioned to the common understanding, & accepted by consent of a whole country & nation, it is called a language" (cited in Mugglestone 1995: 9). Once such early modern "languages" were able to achieve diplomatic recognition as such, they had accordingly to further refine themselves through calibrated translational relationships with their peer monolanguages across newly regularized language barriers—a process I call translational monolingualization.

Paradigm, ideology, doxa, or mechanism?

Clever and agile as it is, monolingualism is indeed to be praised for having thrived so deep into its own obsolescence, all the while forging new and robust technological afterlives in the twenty-first century. Even critical Francophone theorists like Lyotard and Glissant, even Foucault and Bourdieu, left us with our monolingualisms of method and theory more or less intact—more than two hundred years after Henri Grégoire went before the *Convention nationale* to garner political favor for the then improbable abstraction we today call "speaking French" (Bell 1995). As of yet, the humanities and social sciences have no working definition of monolingualism, and there is little agreement about what we researchers would do if we had a shared definition. Despite and perhaps because of Derrida, "monolingualism" remains an "othered" epithet without much of an actionable analytic discourse. Consider for instance why it might be that, at the time of this writing, the search term "multiculturalism" on the online research clearinghouse academia.edu has attracted 18,600 research followers, "multilingualism" 4,000 followers, and "bilingualism" 5,300 followers, while "monolingualism" rings in with only two (apparently wayward) inquirers.

Sidestepping the totalizing explanatory reach of empire and nation-state might allow us to explore another account of monolingualism, namely, how the *scientific* discovery of monolingualism preceded and laid the groundwork for subsequent (imperial, national, civic, and disciplinary) technologies of governance, ultimately making a global federation of isomorphic language-states plausible and thinkable. A logic of semantic exogamy and transposability between coequal languages, hard won over Europe's early modern centuries, created (and continues to create) monolingualism—as a modest but compulsory structure, one that until the early sixteenth century had lain well beyond the horizon of political fancy and civic plausibility. It is a logic that both structuralism and post-structuralism inherited whole and could not simply shake off amid the throes of critical theory and deconstruction, despite Jacques Derrida's emphatic summation: "If I had to risk a single definition of deconstruction, one as brief, elliptical, and economical as a password, I would say simply and without overstatement: *plus d'une langue*—more than one language, no more of one language" (Derrida 1986: 14–15).

Not initially prone toward domination or purification, the monolingual imagination in the seventeenth century did little more or less violent than to perceive a global grid of discrete, namable, rationally extensive languages, and a corresponding aspirational hypothesis of ultimate functional transposability among them. It taught each speech tradition that sought recognition as "a language" how and why to play nice with the others, to have an orderly social life in the incipient linguacene. Monolingualism's underlying principle has never quite been that other languages are bad or inferior, but that they are contextually unnecessary. Monolingualism *manages* other languages; it does not oppose them. This book will thus forego the temptation to rely on the countless and captivating historical accounts of how any one self-appointed language came to dominate or efface any other language (which is, I will claim, something very different from monolingualism). Rather, the chapters that follow offer a composite account of the underlying mythic logic by which a given speech collectivity can be made enumerable, as "one language among many peer languages"—how it becomes recognizable by, transposable into, and symbolically substitutable for, any other such collectivity.

Much of this monolingualization process has indeed occurred hand-in-hand with colonial evangelization and missionization endeavors, as the linguistic anthropologists William Hanks (2010) and Bambi Schieffelin (2007) demonstrate in the sixteenth-century Yucatec context and in contemporary Papua New Guinea, respectively. Hanks labels the complex process of linguistic refunctionalization in the missionary context "commensuration," which he describes as follows:

> The heart of the process lies in redescribing in grammatically correct Maya the objects or concepts stood for by the corresponding Spanish. The result is a generalized medium of semantic exchange in which the conceptual backing of the Spanish is paired with existing or newly formed signifiers in the Maya. In both cases, the resulting sign is a neologism.[10]

10. For a summative introduction to commensuration and other linguistic resources for translation in the missionary context, see Hanks, "The Space of Translation" (2014): 30.

In contrast to prevailing reductive images of linguistic imperialism—as the bellicose imposition of the colonizer's language and an abrupt, simultaneous moment of epistemicide in an indigenous language— Hanks describes the longue-durée micro-processes by which individual missonaries, lexicographers, indigenous deputies, and townspeople collaborated in the production of newly tempered local languages that ensured an efficient traffic in meaning between Spanish catechism and a commensurated Maya vernacular.[11]

Viewing this sort of commenusration process as indeed a global strategy of colonization, the applied linguists Makoni and Pennycook throw their critical weight behind what they describe as the "enumerative modality" of linguistic invention, which:

> [u]nlike other modalities, is based on the idea that African languages can be converted into countable forms, are describable, and can thus be prescribed. In short, the enumerative modality is predicated on the belief that languages in general, but African speech forms in particular, can be contained and controlled. In order for the counting to take place, the languages are labeled, even though "naming languages is a type of consciousness, an artifact embedded in the consciousness of Western formal education" in a continent in which a majority are not formally literate in a Western sense of the term. (2006: 66)[12]

But before this process of naming, misnaming, consolidation, marketing, and reproduction was to arise, one needed to induce a system of transposable and equivalent integers that makes a global cartography of languages thinkable. That is, in order to have enumerability as a stable resource for thought about languages, language(s) needed to be worth counting at one go and then recounting in the same manner in other contexts: a protocol of happy, inter-rater reliable exchangeability.

From this perspective, it would be an act of methodological monolingualization to take early medieval writings as representative artifacts of any modern "monolanguage" or another. Rather, they are moments in a viscous social ecology amid, say, Occitan, French, and Catalan "ways of speaking" [*parladura*]. Naturally, this intractable non-identity of pre-modern language(s) causes messy logistical problems for today's

---

11. On the concept of epistemicide, see for instance Joshua Price (2014).

12. The embedded quotation is from Sinfree Makoni, Geneva Smitherman, Arnetha F. Ball, and Arthur K. Spears, "Toward Black Linguistics" (2003): 3.

national literary studies associations, journals, archives, and scholarly departments, who are justified in wishing to know, for instance, whether the English scholars ought to be responsible for a text written in what looks like French in fourteenth-century London, or whether that "belongs" to the French Department instead. As Susan Buck-Morss reminds us, "disciplinary boundaries allow counterevidence to belong to someone else's story" (2000: 822).

Perhaps pre-modern speech subjectivity is best understood in terms of linguistic repertoires rather than linguistic systems, as mixing and matching among them carried less of the rigid structural symbolism of allegiance or dissidence as they would in the age of nation-states. Speakers made meaning from an inherited chest of conventional expressive possibilities, rather than from an imagined coordinate grid of rational infinity named French or English, as became the conceit of post-Cartesian linguistics. Writing on that threshold between what Wright considers the sociolinguistic monolingualism of the Romance Middle Ages and what will become rationalist multilingual early modern Europe, the late twelfth-century Catalan Raimon Vidal de Besalú touted his own unencumbered habits around language choice as follows:

> French speech [*la parladura franscesca*] is better and more attractive for composing romances and pastourelles, but the one of the Limousin is better for composing vers, cansos, and sirventes. And throughout the lands of our language [*notre lengatge*], the songs of the Limousin tongue have greater authority [*autoritat*] than any other language. (cited in Léglu 2010: 9, translation modified)

Vidal is more than happy, in his turn-of-the-thirteenth-century landscape, to select from French, Catalan, and Occitan *parladura*, or ways of speaking, in order to outfit his compositions with attractive and authoritative words. For this troubador, the selection process entails none of the modern political consequences often presumed of code-switching or code-meshing; his "translingual" practice is much more akin to what moderns consider to be the mere basic intuitions of stylistic agility. Unencumbered of the monolingualist notion that each language can and should do everything on its own, such practices of mixing and matching were a common sense way to be worldly, rather than a bid for multilingual or intercultural competence.

Tempering language

Literary and social monolingualism after the seventeenth century will, however, make of such free movements a diplomatic scandal, triggering analytical arbitration or sheer admonishment on the part of pedagogues, publishers, and bureaucrats. As Mikhail Bakhtin stresses, "The Renaissance is the only period in the history of European literature that marked the end of a dual [vernacular and ecclesiastical] language and a linguistic transformation. Much of what was possible at that exceptional time later became impossible." In gradually losing what Bakhtin called an "intense interorientation, interaction, and mutual clarification" between church and folk languages (1994: 465), the trade-off for modern monolinguals was the new promise of rational extensivity in one language— making the troubador Vidal's intuitive trilingual practices *excessive*, to cite a key vice of seventeenth-century linguistics. In this sense, monolingualism, according to its early modern proponents like Sprat and Arnauld, lobbied for the suppression of translingual combinatory agility, on the basis that such a constraint ultimately expands language's world-making, propositional capacity.[13] Other/ more language(s) weren't quite bad—just inessential, in the emerging economy of civic personhood.

This retrospective claim that monolingualism is a modern order, with no precedent in human history, may tempt us to misconceive medieval Europe as a panlingual utopia, free of the violent language hierarchies characteristic of the sixteenth century onward in colonial, provincial, and cosmopolitan contexts alike. It is certain that politicized, group-level speech practices begat violent responses long prior to the modern rise of monolingualism, at least since the Ephraimites tried to cross the Jordan River around 1200 BCE (Judges 12:5-6; see McNamara 2005). Disliking the way others speak and finding ways to draw social advantage from that judgment is, I believe, no modern innovation. The challenge in coming to grips with the mechanism of modern monolingualism, however, begins with imagining the symbolic livelihood of a premodern speaker who knew no such structuring abstraction as monolingualism, and who thus had little day-to-day need for a) political-linguistic nativism, b) personal

---

13. On monolingual "constraint," see for instance Till Dembeck and Georg Mein, "Philology's Jargon: How Can We Write Post-Monolingually?" in Minnaard and Dembeck (eds) (2014): 53–70.

assignability to a certain "lingual" unity, c) capacity to distinguish between what moderns routinely call languages, d) consistency in her own grammar, orthography, and usage, or e) an abstract, rational, "well-designed" grid of exhaustive propositional potential, housed within one language.

Such practical presuppositions and personal capacities became, however, mainstays of the idiom of colonization, amid the rise of the monolingual hypothesis in the late sixteenth century, as indigenous speakers in the Americas were gradually de-competenced by their European interlocutors through a multilingual process of monolingualization. Drawing on the indigenous sociolinguistic landscape of early colonial Peru, Mary Louise Pratt (2012), for instance, joins other recent scholarly attempts to provincialize Ferdinand de Saussure's epoch-making 1915 tableau of the *circuit de la parole* (the normative image of speech between two equally enfranchised, bodyless, Liberal speakers of a single language).[14] Pratt contrasts Saussure's model with the seventeenth-century bilingual Quechua political operative Felipe Guaman Poma's drawings of linguistic encounter between missionary priests and Andean women. It is worth quoting Pratt's analysis at length:

> From the standpoint of liberalism, Guaman Poma's drawing depicts everything Saussure's seeks to dispel. We see "two individuals" joined in multi-faceted relations of radical hierarchy, inequality, passion, and violence. They differ by gender, race, age, status, education, livelihood, and emotional state. The drawing marks all of these differences on their bodies. An institutional setting is present. The point of commonality that brings them together here is Catholicism, which is also the arbiter of their differences. The speech act involved, confession, is predicated on an asymmetry of power: one has the power to give or withhold absolution. The other has the power to ask or beg for it. There is no reciprocity or reversibility here. There is despair, rage, lust, rape, mala fe—and multilingualism. The two are native speakers of different, wholly unrelated languages. The acoustic signals passing between them will not be identical. They will be marked by their social and historical differences. Three languages are in play, likely distributed as follows: the priest is a native speaker of Spanish and is literate in it as well as in Latin. He may have sufficient

14. In addition, see Saba Mahmood's critique of "Protestant semiotics" in "Religious Reason and Secular Affect" (2009).

mastery of Quechua to preach and receive confession, as the Spanish church encouraged. The woman is a native speaker of Quechua who may know some Spanish or none, and she is not literate. Her access to the doctrines that bind her body and soul runs through the priest, who does not administer them in her interest. But she also inhabits an Andean history, cosmology, and social world to which he has little access. Both probably understand a good deal more of the other's language than they speak. (2002: 20)

Amid the disparity Pratt opens up between these two scenarios— Saussure's dehistoricized, statutorily equal, genderless, power-agnostic, rights-bearing citizen-communicators and Guaman Poma's embodied, hierarchically multilingual colonizers and supplicants—the figures depicted in Guaman Poma's drawings can be seen as exerting an illocutionary force across colonial time, toward Saussure's high-modern normative image of human speech. They ask for an ethical and historical response—what Bakhtin describes as "answerability" (1990 [1919]). That is, Saussure's heuristic vision of equality and communication in language practice may indeed be a latter-day monolingualized technocratic fable, purchased upon the colonial experience of adverse multilingualism that the seventeenth-century Guaman Poma documented.

Together, the composite figural story emerging among these two juxtaposed models (Saussure and Guaman Poma) is a story of the making of monolanguages—discrete, isomorphic, panfunctional, indivisible languages.[15] Though scholars of "hard science linguistics" (Yngve 2004) hold that such monolanguages are impossible in the empirical and logical world, monolanguages are nonetheless effective and practical myths, desired and cultivated by historical actors with certain investments and epistemes at their backs.

Thus far, we have briefly surveyed ways in which medievalists, literary critics, historians of education, applied linguists, and philosophers have found use for the word monolingualism, and we will expand on this review of disciplinary and social usage over the course of Chapter 1. In the end, I find each of these contrapuntal usages of "monolingualism"—from the liberatory to the agonic, from

15. Chapter 1 of Beata Staworska's 2015 monograph on *Undoing the Doctrine of the Course in General Linguistics* has helped me to understand how the "Saussurian" model, as expressed in the *Cours*, is in fact an aggressive reformulation, as ghostwritten by Saussure's two students Charles Bally and Albert Sechehaye, with assistance from Albert Reidlinger.

the premodern to the postmodern—to be tenable in its context of argumentation. This book will hold each to be true, useful, and relevant in its often contradictory relations with neighboring definitions. Itself a rather recent addition to the popular lexicon on identity and positionality, "monolingualism" is indeed still something of a free radical on the scene of political ascriptions, bouncing from usage to usage among vernacular and expert users alike, each of whom has good reason for "letting [it] drop, or modifying it, or deflecting it or betraying it, or adding to it, or appropriating it" (Latour 1986: 267). Drawing on Urciuoli (2010: 56), Robert Moore characterizes such words as diversity, multiculturalism, and multilingualism as "strategically deployable shifters" (2015: 20), slogans opportunistically invoked in top-down, performative, and programmatic ways to achieve ever-new technocratic goals. Given the growing range of usages in evidence in the case of "monolingualism," it is clear that this word is likely to become another such potent and strategic "shifter". Yet it appears to be one that—unlike diversity, multiculturalism, or *multi-lingualism*—has as yet no articulated political or scholarly discourse to steer it, for better or for worse.[16]

What most scholarship on the topic shares is a sense that monolingualism has come at great gain to some and unspecifiable cost to others. The essence of that cost is, I suspect, monolingualism's overwhelming and yet unostentatious structural constraint upon social meaning. The realms of social meaning constrained by monolingualism include, of course, the literary, political, ecological, historiographic, clandestine, artistic, theological, intercultural, methodological, stylistic, metalinguistic, and indeed also the scientific—as Michael Gordin shows with his magisterial book about "how science was done before and after global English" (2015). In all of these realms, monolingualism effects "a kind of *arrest*, in the physical and legal sense of the term," as Barthes writes of myth's basic signifying structure: "[A]t the moment of reaching me, it suspends itself, turns away, and assumes the look of a generality: it stiffens, it makes itself look neutral and innocent" (2012: 235).

In the main, scholarly approaches have confronted monolingualism under the aegis of language ideology, which Michael Silverstein defines as "any set of beliefs about language articulated by users as

16. This, despite the sustained efforts at "unmarking" monolingualism among scholars like Elizabeth Ellis, Adrian Blackledge, Ingrid Gogolin, Yasemin Yildiz, and Brian Lennon.

a rationalization or justification of perceived language structure and use" (1979: 193; see also Kroskrity 2004; Gal and Woodward 1995). While Silverstein's definition of language ideology facilitates a range of analyses about specific languages and their use, most of the underlying features of monolingualism reproduce themselves, I contend, far beneath the threshold of individual belief and articulation, and even beneath the kind of terrain easily recognized as ideological. Monolingualism's "ideology" is precisely to become transparent and plain, unworthy of comment or critique, and thus impervious to the ascriptions of racism, nationalism, purism, and elitism often leveraged at "beliefs about language." If, as Adorno has it, "all reification is a forgetting" (Adorno and Benjamin 1999 [1940]: 321), monolingualism is primarily invested in erasing its own history of production—a history that Franz Kafka, for one, cannot refrain from tampering with throughout his early career (see Chapter 2).

Structure of this book

With the exception of computational engineering, machine translation, and logistics,[17] most theoretical and applied disciplines continue to treat monolingualism as a conceptual orphan—spurned, disowned, and afforded only the most sidelong of critical glances. For all this disfavor, monolingualism's structuring presence in these disciplines is no less ubiquitous, and there is no good reason to presume that its methodological, epistemic, and aesthetic impact is now on the wane, after a high-modern period of predominance. In light of the perennial unwantedness of monolingualism, this book seeks to track its object of inquiry through a constellation of disciplines and fields that ought, by rights, to have as much to say about monolingualism as they do about multilingualism, translation, and transnationalism. This book is thus conceived in dialogue with four scholarly fields in which a detailed account of monolingualism seems always—almost—on the tip of the collective tongue: applied linguistics, literary studies, comparative world literature, and citizenship studies.

17. On the multilingualism of logistics, see for instance Barbara Ellen Smith, Marcela Mendoza, and David H. Ciscel's analysis of FedEx and Amazon logistics at a Memphis, TN, distribution park, in their "The World on Time: Flexible Labor, New Immigrants, and Global Logistics" (2005): 23–36.

The four main chapters are devoted to specific, interrelated, problem-based arguments in these four fields, and to allowing more general implications among them to emerge and cross-inquire. The chapters animate for critical purposes four primary inventions that monolingualism has been able to shepherd forth since the seventeenth century: the monolingual individual, monolingual literary text, monolingual world literature canon, and monolingual pan-ethnic citizenship models. Each of these inventions lay well beyond the threshold of fantasy and practicability until the early modern period, and each of them is today experiencing a kind of renaissance, amid the discursive crosscurrents between civic "superdiversity" (Vertovec 2007) and the globalized translational monetization of content, intellectual property, data, and meaning (Pym 2004).

Chapter 1, "Monolingualism: A User's Guide," opens with two vernacular preludes: one at an Idaho science fair, and one on a Turkish social networking site. These preludes pursue two distinct angles for initial hypotheses on the social and scholarly use of the word monolingualism. What do people get from using the word monolingual—about themselves, about others? How has monolingualism become, of late and somewhat suddenly, a *useful* word for commerce and politics alike? Chapter 1 explores how the garish and clinical morphology of the word itself has generated a spectrum of usage over the late twentieth century that is pejorative, positivistic, and impervious to vernacular sense. No one in her right mind wants to be associated with *mo-no-ling-ual-is-m*. The second prelude—on Turkish Facebook, sometimes transliterated in jest as Feysbuk—suggests however that digital platforms like Google Translate have rendered "monolingualism" itself a complex site of participation and resistance, particularly among non-English-dominant speakers. "Monolingualism: A User's Guide" thus queries not *what* monolingualism means abstractly, nor *whether* it should be a meaningful word at all, but rather what its current *meaninglessness means*—in civic discourse, popular culture, and in scholarship. While this Introduction has focused on scholarly approaches to monolingualism, Chapter 1 turns to its various debuts in social and political life, primarily outside the academic realm.

Chapter 2, "Kafka's Well-Tempered Piano," backs away from the troubling terminological status of "monolingualism" today, and explores two telling moments roughly book-ending the scientific diffusion of monolingual doxa into European civic modernity: the initial publication of J. S. Bach's *The Well-Tempered Clavier* in 1722 and the composition of Franz Kafka's first unfinished novel *The Missing Person* (1910–14).

This juxtaposition—of Bach's early-Enlightenment technical primer of "preludes and fugues through all the tones and semitones" (2006: 4) and, 200 years later, a high-modern German-language novel about becoming a monolingual Anglophone American—allows us to trace the technical advent of literary monolingualism, abreast with that of equal temperament in music. Both monolingualism and equal temperament have been disliked by aesthetes and elites in their respective moments of public debatability, and have become subject to damning pronouncements about the "end of music" and the "death of languages" respectively. Yet equal temperament quietly outlasted its critics and became a hegemonic, indispensible means of production for Western musical culture after 1850, such that moderns and postmoderns can hardly register what an untempered musical composition sounds like.[18] It is the wager of this book that monolingualism—though utterly condemnable at the current moment—is precisely the kind of promising innovation (in the technical transposability of meaning and data across languages) that is likely to experience an overwhelming long-term success as (equal) temperament once did.

Temperament is the mathematically complex craft required for tuning a keyboard instrument in such a way that one can play melodies and harmonies in multiple keys (A major, D# major, Gb minor, for instance), sequentially or in combination, without needing to re-tune the instrument at every key-change.[19] Tempering a piano or clavichord required the invention of highly complicated proportional formulas, called "commas," that are then applied in the form of regulated tension upon brass or carbon steel strings. Like various forms of language ideology, temperament is thus an endeavor to marry systematic

18. For those curious to hear what alternate temperament systems sound like, Isacoff and Duffin both provide examples of contemporary orchestral conductors who work in systems other than equal or well-temperament. Easley Blackwood's "Microtonal Etudes" offer listeners a jarring introduction to what untempered tonality sounds like when deliberately exploited as such. The Arabic *maqam* system operates, of course, well beyond the Western temperament orthodoxy altogether. See, for an introduction, David Muallem's *The Maqam Book: A Doorway to Arab Scales and Modes* (2010).

19. For a general overview on temperament prior to Johann Sebastian Bach, see Martin Jira, *Musikalische Temperaturen in der Klaviermusik des 17. und frühen 18. Jahrhunderts* (1997), as well as Hartmut Schütz, *"Nothwendiger Unterricht in der musikalischen Temperature"—Ein Abriss der Stimmungsarten vom 15. bis zum 18. Jahrhundert* (1988).

supra-local abstraction with everyday artisanal materials and practical capacities. *Equal* temperament, in turn, is the mathematical pinnacle of temperament standardization culminating around 1915, a step even beyond Bach's revolutionary invention of well-temperament in the 1720s.[20] Whereas well-temperament allowed for some internal tonal shading in keys, such that the interval of a fifth might be slightly "wider" in one key and "narrower" in another, equal temperament—considered global industry standard by World War I—rendered the proportions among acoustic intervals from one key to the next identical in their (quite audible) imprecision.[21]

The problem of temperament stems from a natural gap in harmony that confounds mathematically pure ratios of pitch. This gap is called the Pythagorean Comma and is equal to twelve pure fifths, less seven octaves, or 531441/524288 cents, so roughly a quarter of a semitone. Imagining the space between *mi* and *fa* on a major scale, the comma is about one fourth of that tonal distance.[22] A "cycle" of twelve fifths spanning 49 whole tones on a piano keyboard—fifths being, say, the interval between C and G or A and E—must be shortened by exactly one Pythagorean Comma in order for its octaves to remain pure. Failure to remove one PC when tuning the clavier will render an irritating, unpleasant listening experience. Early modern tuners prior to well temperament thus needed to exploit various provisionally "unusable" spots on the keyboard to hide this interval, so that the rest of the notes would be reconciled to their expected tone. From 1650 to 1722, the search was on for a compromise, such that the discrepancy might be distributed over all twelve half-tones of the scale (Lehman 2005: 5).

The ideal of well-temperament tuning was to distribute these fractions of correspondence over all twelve half-tones in such a way that their tonal imprecision is hidden, so that all of the notes can be played without fear of audibly foul tuning. The pay-off was that, suddenly, no

20. On *The Well-Tempered Clavier* from the point of view of technical innovation, see Martin Jira, *Musikalische Temperaturen und Musikalischer Satz bei J. S. Bach* (2000): 186–92.

21. On the development of the discourse of musical intervals in early modernity, see Rolf Klein, *Die Intervallehre in der deutschen Musiktheorie des 16. Jahrhunderts* (1989): 164–70. For a contemporaneous treatment of pitch in the late seventeenth century, see Bruce Haynes, *A History of Performing Pitch: The Story of "A"* (2002): 115–58.

22. For a general introduction to Pythagorean tunings, see J. Murray Barbour (2004 [1951]): 1–13.

notes would be off-limits to the player or composer; one could play an
A minor chord one second after playing an E flat major. Yet it would
be inaccurate to say that composers and musicians had been searching
frustratedly over the centuries for ways to solve this problem; they had
not. It was first with the rise of symphonic forms—musical genres that
moved by definition from key to key, sometimes within individual
movements, sometimes only switching keys at the brief pause between
movements—that the ideal of a well-tempered keyboard instrument
became perceivable and desirable.

Under what conditions did musicians begin to think it was a good
idea to pursue the liberal use of accidentals (sharps and flats), of
intra-piece key changes—to *code-switch*? This question takes us back
out of musical aesthetics and into the episteme of global transposability. The moment, and then the episteme of well-temperament
came at a cost: a progressive desublimation and disimplication of key
and mode, a radical reorientation toward etic, exogamous valuation
in harmony and melody. Musical tones no longer *signified* primarily
within the relational micro-ecology of their own key (whether D
minor, A major, or what have you); their primary intension strained
outward toward all theoretical others. A given pitch was now
valuable not because of its ecological essence within one key, but
because of its presumed future anterior of translatedness into all
potential others.

But why, in the course of a critique of literary monolingualism,
should we range into music in this way? Is this an allegorical sally,
designed to model parallel developments in language use and musical
theory? Kafka's *The Missing Person*—often referred to as his "America"
novel—draws on the history of keyboard tuning systems in order to
critique literary monolingualism as its own kind of "temperament
system," designed to mitigate the unruly multilingual world through
certain technical constraints upon textual composition. A speaker of
multiple languages himself, Kafka stages his struggle with monolingualism not first in the agonistic alleys of his last novel *The Castle*, nor
in the bureaucratic maze of *The Trial*, but in what he imagines to be
the fast-and-furious, open-road dreamland of early twentieth-century
Rooseveltian *Amerika*—where the Austrian immigrant Karl Rossmann
finds his way into the newly consolidating discourse of American civic
monolingualism. Karl's tempered piano, gifted to him by his rich uncle,
becomes the critical riddle through which the young ingénue comes to
grips, and blows, with the monolingual constraints of the very novel in
which he appears.

Kafka's novel prompts us to de-compartmentalize music and language from one another, in keeping with the pre- and early modern comparative perspectives into which we have become invested thus far. Early modern arguments for and against tempering keyboard instruments were not carried out primarily in terms of "music" alone, in the modern, secular sense, but in terms of sound's relation to and reflection of God, meaning, truth, precision, health, order, temporality, systematicity, and the nature of the senses. To temper a musical instrument was, for early modernizers, a crucial step in guiding a slowly secularizing, tentatively empirical civilization in its pursuit of complex beauty, social truth, and orderly meaning.[23] For detractors, however, temperament systems were a violation of eternal consmological values and of God's own law. (Descartes, for one, found himself on both sides of the temperament debate at different moments in his career.) Thus, in turning to musical tuning as not only a heuristic but also a co-constitutive domain of modern meaning-making, Kafka seeks to shift focus not away from language, but toward a composite understanding of both realms as increasingly subject to technocracies of translated and translatable meaning, as they gained conjuncture over the course of modernity.

Subsequent to Bach and his contemporaries, semiotic transposability also formed the relational principle behind the comparative language projects of Herder and Hamann, though they argued bitterly about how these transpositions were to take place, and what they would yield. For them both, discovering the nature of the human condition was a process of comparative semiotic deciphering among the world's recently enumerable, countable languages. Languages were newly imagined as always already essentially *in dialogue* with the other languages of the world. They were made epistemologically exogamous; languages meant to the extent that they liaised productively with other world languages. This vision of transposability is the ecstatic achievement, in all senses of the word ecstatic, of Bach's well-temperament—and of modern civic monolingualism. Indeed the wager of monolingualism was also Bach's wager: that the sacrifices one makes in achieving transposability, say from the key of E to the key of A flat on a "well-tuned" clavier, were negligible when compared to the

23. See for instance Chapter 12 of Stuart Isacoff, *Temperament: How Music Became a Battleground for the Great Minds of Western Civilization* (2001). See also Wolfram Steude, "Zur Rolle der Musik in der Fruchtbringenden Gesellschaft unter Fürst Ludwig von Anhalt-Köthen" (2001): 155–70, particularly 160–3.

pragmatic benefits of exchangeability across keys. Musical keys that, throughout medieval music, had been mistrustful neighbors to one another, now had become mercantile counterparts, ready traders in one another's goods.

Chapter 3, "The Passing of World Literaricity," extends the arguments proposed in Chapter 2: namely, that a progressive, "well-tempered" relationship between literature and monolingualism has been enacted in European modernity, one from which neither party can abscond at will—even and especially through contemporary (inter)disciplinary constructs like world literature or translingual writing. Surveying (world-)literary works from Orhan Pamuk, Junot Díaz, Terézia Mora, James Kellman, Murathan Mungan, Horacio Castellanos Moya, and Peter Waterhouse, Chapter 3 argues that world-literary authors in the twenty-first century are often wholly aware of this historically inextricable relationship between world literature and translational monolingualism, and are cultivating the constrained textures of this relationship as one of their primary aesthetic, political, narrative, and (anti-)translative resources.

This is a very different, indeed opposing stance than to maintain that world literature is an aesthetic haven for multilingual creativity and critique, or that world-literary canons offer a rare, safe space for multilingual authors to just be themselves in a world otherwise lost to monolingualism. As Kafka had done in his debut novel in 1914, writers of prospective world literature today are nourishing a kind of modest critical *passing* in global literary monolingualism—a disposition that is aware of the attenuating formal constraints on multilingual appearance in the public and symbolic order.[24] These constraints are, I argue, the products not of language systems as such but of the sanctioned circulation of certain kinds of translatedness at the expense of others, a phenomenon Yaseen Noorani, in his explorations of mid-twentieth-century Arab nationalist poetry, has termed "soft multilingualism"

---

24. The notion of literary *passing* offers an alternative account, for instance, to that advanced in Fredric Jameson's "Third World Literature in the Era of Multinational Capitalism," as critiqued in Lydia Liu, *Translingual Practice: Literature, National Culture, and Translated Modernity: China 1900–1937* (1995): 185–7. For a brief summary on "The Politics of Passing," see Elaine K. Ginsberg's introductory essay in *Passing and the Fictions of Identity* (1996): 1–18, as well as Martha Cutter's essay on Nella Larsen's classic novel *Passing*, "Sliding Significations: Passing as a Narrative and Textual Strategy in Nella Larsen's Fiction," in Ginsberg (1996): 75–100, particularly 84–5.

(2013). With Kafka's early-career "multilingualism of the other" as their aesthetic touchstone (Kramsch 2011), twenty-first-century novelists design ways to undermine the contemporary monolingualization of world literature, even as that very monolingualization process often serves as their ticket of entry into world literaricity—through advance translation and distribution contracts, literary promotional awards, and internationally curated book fairs.[25] *Passing* amid this traffic in "soft multilingualism" has thus become an artisanal competence that authors cultivate in the hopes of critiquing and decamping world literature in the age of compulsory (monolingual) translatability.

Chapter 4, "A Right of Languages," expands this literary-aesthetic argument into a civic-political one, proposing that a new model of citizenship is afoot in the age of postmultilingual statecraft, a model that conceives of prospective citizens no longer through their supposed blood-rights to citizenship (*ius sanguinus*) or territorial rights (*ius soli*), but through their demonstrated language competences (*ius linguarum*). Drawing on scholarly work on modes of citizenship in contemporary Germany, the United Kingdom, Belgium, France, the Netherlands, Canada, Senegal, Singapore, Turkey, and the U.S.A., the chapter explores how the "right" to speak the post-ethnic nation-state's superdiverse lingua franca is marketed to immigrants and post-immigrants, often as a symbolic promissory note to redress their systematic precarization since the mid-twentieth century, particularly in European immigration countries. In good neoliberal fashion, forms of multilingual upskilling are promoted as models for global success and competitiveness for immigrants, always through the functional aperture of the nation-state and its primary symbolic language. Deployed in this ideologically coercive way, boot-strapping discourses of language competence and self-assessment are helping to "thicken" the citizenship apparatus of the postmultilingual, pedagogical state (Smith 1998).

While as recently as 1999, nation-states like Germany were fundamentally uninterested in governing the use of language among their domestic migrant and postmigrant population, the last fifteen years have seen a thickening of citizenship around language competence and use, a process that co-extends with the ostensive de-ethnicization of citizenship in the same contexts. At the same time, an irony inheres in the fact that citizenship thickened around language use is a complex form of translational monolingualism, in that it places primary value on a citizen's ability to be transparent and translatable for commercial and

25. See for instance Kong (2004) and Thompson (2010).

securitarian purposes. The fatigue around multiculturalism in Europe and the search for a more formally satisfying rhetoric of belonging can be heard in Jürgen Habermas's public remarks in March of 2007:

> The constitutional state can only guarantee citizens religious freedom under the requirement that they no longer barricade [*verschanzen*] themselves in the integral lifeworlds of their religious communities and partition themselves off in opposition to it. The subcultures must release their individual members from their clutches [*Umklammerung*], so that they can recognize each other in civil society as citizens of the state, that is, as bearers and members of the same political commonwealth. (2011: 334–6, my translation)

Here, the politics of recognition towards multilingual, transnational persons come with a lien attached: namely, a set of prescribed, stable, demonstrable modes of civic emergence for recently immigrated "members of society" to perform in the public language of the state.

Efforts to institutionalize a pan-ethnic lingua franca had come onto the German federal legislative docket between 1998 and 2004, when a major shift in the state's concept of immigration ushered forth a progressivist naturalization discourse with linguistically retrogressive consequences, in keeping with its postmultilingual, postmulticultural moment. Throughout the decades of mass labor migration to West Germany (1955–73) and East Germany (1960–89), immigrants were permanent aliens under law, with recourse to naturalization only in a handful of situations. Heritage language preservation was thus preferred as a means to facilitate eventual "readiness to return" to the ancestral country (Kohl 1982). Germany's 1999 Citizenship Law and its 2005 Immigration Law, however, brought the republic closer to a French or U.S.-style *ius soli*, or citizenship by territorial birthright. This apparently post-ethnic logic for naturalization in Germany replaced the country's Imperial Citizenship Law of 1913, which had envisioned civic belonging as conferred by ethnic inheritance alone.

As ethnic models of citizenship cede to superdiversity as the organizing heuristic for the twenty-first-century state (Vertovec 2007, 2010; Blommaert and Rampton 2011), "language competence" increasingly has swept in as the symbolic guarantor of social cohesion (Gramling 2009, Cameron 2013). From 1913 to 2000, "being German" had overwhelmingly meant demonstrating German blood quantum, regardless of the (single or multiple) languages one might speak (Göktürk et al. 2007). Such was the principle, for instance, for many hundred thousand ethnic

"Russia Germans" in the 1980s, who were entitled to nearly automatic repatriation from various Soviet republics according to Paragraph 116 of the German constitution, with little regard for what they knew or felt about German democracy, governance, social custom, history, or indeed language. This legal principle of (linguistically and ideologically indifferent) ethnonational citizenship has, since 2000, undergone a progressive monolingual retrofit, such that the ostensive path to becoming a German today is to demonstrably speak like one—by displaying discursive and communicative competence in German, but also by reiterating constitutional values and rehearsing ideals of integration and social cohesion. Chapter 4 is thus concerned with demonstrating how and why a new myth of cosmopolitan monolingualism is informing citizenship law, policy, and practice in many "superdiverse" societies, giving rise to a thickened *ius linguarum* ideal of civic personhood.

Deborah Cameron has tracked the development of English-language initiatives in post-9/11 Great Britain, a country where preference for English had never before been a serious topic of political contestation, either on the right or the left:

> Its sudden emergence as a recurring motif in political discourse was not prompted by any evidence of real-world resistance to learning English on the part of minority speakers. Arguably it was prompted more by the political need to find compelling symbolic correlates for the dry and abstract term "cohesion"—and also for the much-debated idea of "Britishness," attempts to define which often became bogged down in an unsatisfactory mixture of general principles with no distinctively British content (e.g. belief in democracy and the rule of law) and trivial minutiae (e.g. talking about the weather and forming orderly queues). Language offered a solution to this coding problem: monolingualism and multilingualism were pressed into service as the metaphorical correlates, respectively, of social cohesion and social fragmentation, while speaking English became one of the marks of Britishness. (2013: 62)

Cameron further notes that conservative Britons often reject monolingualism on the basis that it violates the privacy rights cherished by the English as far back as the Magna Carta.

An Afterword, entitled "Into the Linguacene," revisits from a methodological perspective the conceptions developed in the previous four chapters: 1) monolingualism's excitable and expanding spectrum of use in commerce and policy; 2) postmultilingual temperament and transposability in modernist literary and performance aesthetics; 3) monolingualism's structuring power in world literature and scholarship, as well as vernacular critiques of that power; and 4) postmultilingual, post-ethnic *ius linguarum* citizenship models in Germany and elsewhere. The afterword proposes a conception of the "linguacene" as a period of geological time in which algorithmic multilingualism is exerting primary control over human manipulations of the natural world.

On the monolingualism of this book

Though this book will, after all that, hold that monolingualism is indeed a recent historical invention—one that has no more claim on reasonableness or even efficiency than do the many other alternate ways of organizing or not organizing language—the title *The Invention of Monolingualism* parts gently with a venerable tradition of scholarship on "inventions": from Mudimbe on Africa (1988) and Hobsbawm and Ranger on Tradition (1992) to Katz on Heterosexuality (1997) and even Hunt on *The Invention of Everything Else* (2009). Its arguments will account less for the eras, logics, conditions, and people who went to great lengths to invent monolingualism than for the eras, logics, conditions, and people that monolingualism itself has since been uniquely equipped to invent—including, of course, this book. Its title thus works more like *The Inventions of Grace Murray Hopper* than, say, *The Invention of America*. As a linguistic-technological zero-hour for global civic and literary modernity, monolingualism soon became the flexible, renewable resource for imagining certain kinds of states, nations, ethnicities, industries, normative conceptions of personhood, and a totalizing planetary order. Along the way, monolingualism has also partaken in inventing systems of universal schooling, industrial standardization, the possibility of a middle class, and a gamut of aesthetic and generic lineages many of us cannot imagine living without. Monolingualism is also axiologically responsible for instituting certain forms of labor, for regulating how language is studied and defined today, and perhaps even for evolving conceptions of exchange value itself on planetary markets.

The Invention of Monolingualism thus betrays a complicitous, somewhat acquiescent relationship to its object of inquiry—an object from which the book itself issues by virtue of its own relations of production. For a research monograph published in the early twenty-first-century scholarly landscape, striving to be something other than monolingual would be disingenuous. Like most books published since 1800, this study has had to find some provisional delight in rehearsing monolingualism, reiterating it, and performing it, in hopes of rendering its implications audible, legible, and sensible. Whereas a history of an invention—or even a genealogy of an invention—must first imagine the world without the invented device, term, system, or element, this book cannot sustain such a leap, precisely because of its own acutely monolingual form and format. It can only endeavor to *play* the invention of monolingualism, as if it were a complex and improbable keyboard instrument, full of inexhaustible plentitude and inaudible constraint—and, in the process, to take it into hand for critique. That said, this book will not eulogize monolingualism any more than it has done thus far. It will rather offer a sustained alternative account in hopes of displacing the positivistic pedestal upon which the word "monolingual" currently rests: derided and derivative, yet left relatively undisturbed in theory, policy, and practice.

Let us consider for instance an early exemplar of this optimistic spirit of monolingualism, J. S. Bach's own little book of *Inventions* from 1723, in which Bach presents to the world:

[an] honest method, by which the amateurs of the keyboard— especially, however, those desirous of learning—are shown a clear way not only (1) to learn to play cleanly in two parts, but also, after further progress, (2) to handle three obligate parts correctly and well; and along with this not only to obtain good inventions (ideas) but to develop the same well; above all, however, to achieve a cantabile style in playing and at the same time acquire a strong foretaste of composition. (1964 [1723]: 176)

The technocratic design of Bach's early Enlightenment *Inventions*— much like the postnational Common European Reference for Languages three centuries later—sought to model a communicative, translingual, tutelary, and democratic approach to praxis. As a compendium for musical citizens, particularly for his son Wilhelm Friedemann, Bach's *Inventions* were a guidebook for musical travel, a therapeutic and enabling grid upon a semiodiverse and expanding world, an invitation to practice that was both disciplining and competencing in nature. The *Inventions* embodied the gestating Enlightenment imperatives of empirical rigor, bourgeois mobility, logistical pragmatism, epistemological sovereignty, and the mastery of complex systems. Over the course of the 1720s, Bach sought to systematize an audible, playable universe that extended in all directions, free of hindrances in creation or reception.

Particularly striking all the while, in the German original, is Bach's comfort and ease with what moderns call "code-switching"—with using Romance words like *inventiones, Clavires, progreßen, cantabile, Composition*—words that were not yet, nor needed to be, unequivocally "German" for anyone's taxonomic or political purposes. Like the troubador Vidal five centuries prior, Bach selected words translingually at will without the compulsion to italicize or gloss them, comfortable as he was in the belief that German needn't provide wall-to-wall meaning in order to be an adequately "designed" language, in Chomsky's sense. There is irony in this: while designing what is the epitome of a monolingual system of semiotic transposability, Bach nonetheless continued to move freely amid the "alingual" habits typical of the seventeenth century and prior. Like other paradigm-founding monolingualists in the eighteenth century, Herder among them, Bach's own linguistic habitus was multilingual through and through.[26]

As Bach further extended the democratic, tutelary impulse of his *Inventions* into the more comprehensive *Well-Tempered Clavier* (1722–42), he offered this compendium of twenty-four "preludes" and twenty-four "fugues" explicitly "for the profit and use of musical youth desirous of learning, and especially for the pastime of those already skilled in this study" (Bach in Jones 1997 [1722]: 114). Not unlike the recalibrated, twenty-four-language system of the twenty-first-century European Union, *The Well-Tempered Clavier* represented a truly multiplicative paradigm leap for composition and practice, one that brought with it not only a portable universe of aesthetic and communicative discourse, but also a corresponding technical apparatus of equal girth and claim. In the idiom of Innovation Studies, well-tempered monolingualism is the innovation that follows from the invention of semiotic transposability.[27]

26. I thank Ann Marie Rasmussen and James Parente for helping me come to understand Herder's own multilingual subjectivity.

27. In his 1974 book *The Economics of Industrial Innovation*, Chris Freeman clarifies this distinction: "An invention is an idea, a sketch or a model for a new or improved device, product, process or system [...] An innovation in the economic sense is accomplished only with the first commercial transaction" (1974: 22).

Though pious, Bach was also what we might today call a logistics wonk: he was interested not just in theological order and divine meaning but also in the worldly protocols by which these are most ideally manifested, organized, and accessed. By "well-tempered," Bach did not mean temperance, moderation, or mastery. Tempering the clavier rather meant achieving acoustic *transposability*—a triumph in the early modern effort to make melodies easily movable from one key to another. Though such transposition is an affordance that electronic keyboards and synchronizers have been able deliver instantaneously since the mid-1970s, it was a laborious affair on an eighteenth-century clavichord to accommodate the transposition of a melody from the key of E major to A major. Doing so entailed not only a lengthy and labor-intensive pause between performances, but also the social lapse and logistical regrouping that such a break in the music brought about.

Bach's technocratic innovation in the face of these problems of untranslatability opened the floodgates for a new kind of musical multilingualism, or glossodiversity: suddenly everyone who could get their clavichord tuned in something approaching well-temperament could play in all the keys whenever she wanted, without fear of "cross-cultural pragmatic failure" (Thomas 1983), "cultural cringe" (Lawson 1972 [1894]: 108–9), or "untranslatability" (Apter 2013). Obviously, I am daring here to mix the analytical metaphors of early Enlightenment aesthetic technocracy with those of applied linguistics and postcolonial cultural studies, and somewhat wantonly so. I do so however not only for heuristic purposes, but to suggest how our own age's optimistic investment in the technocratic ordering of the world-language system along lines of mutual compliance descends indeed from the spirit of predecessor technocracies around meaning-making in times of planetary political change.

A critique of multilingual reason

One pair of concepts circulating today in applied linguistics has been particularly helpful in tracking the rise of technocratic multilingualism and translational monolingualism. M. A. K. Halliday (2002) introduced a distinction between glossodiversity (a diversity of linguistic codes) and semiodiversity (a diversity of meanings conveyed). With this binary heuristic, Halliday hoped to show how glossodiversity—a diversity of codes in service of common meaning-making—is only one archetype of multilingualism, and that it is (historically speaking) an outlier model, with no peer or precedent as visionary as the European Union's current twenty-four-point constellation of politically exogamous languages. The paradigm of glossodiversity empowers speakers to say the same thing in many languages, to disseminate intellectual property translingually with heightened efficiency and reduced incidence of accidental content.[28] In previous work I have sought to illustrate glossodiversity as the "fast lane" of contemporary commercial multilingualism, drawing on the work of Malena Samaniego Salinas and Mary Louise Pratt to do so (Gramling 2014; Pratt 2002; Samaniego, forthcoming). Yildiz's cogent analysis of Karin Sander's Wordsearch artwork also offers an extended case study in the conceit of glossodiversity, though Yildiz does not invoke Halliday's terms (Yildiz 2011, 2012: 21–5).

With the counterpoint term semiodiversity, Halliday drew attention to another, often neglected plane of language diversity: that of meanings and referents, rather than strictly that of codes and words. On the semiodiverse plane, scholarly critique and creative praxis concern themselves less with how many different ways world languages have to say "I'm lovin' it," but rather with how many divergent, untranslatable, and often mutually irreconcilable meanings the semantic field *love* intends in languages from Igbo and English to Frankish, Yucatec, Icelandic, and Old Church Slavonic.[29] Semiodiversity is not, however, reducible to how various recognized languages can house divergent meanings for an ostensible cognate concept, but also attends to how such meanings become stretched and unmoored amid historical and ecological constellations among those languages. The Jordanian word *zgurt*, for instance—meaning strong, dependable, and masculinely so—bears an "untranslatable" meaning precisely because the word is in constant translingual tension with Jordan's history under the British Mandate, during which the Anglophone predicate adjective "is good" was truncated into the Jordanian lexicon as *zgurt* amid contact-linguistic processes.[30]

In his essay on "English as a Language always in Translation,"

28. On accidental content, see Cronin 2013: 37.

29. Barbara Cassin and her team's *Vocabulaire européen des philosophies: Dictionnaire des intraduisibles* (2004) offers an extended experiment around semiodiversity in comparative intellectual history—though, as with Yildiz, the concept is not itself invoked.

30. I thank Jamilah Shubeilat for pointing me toward the translingual provenance of the word *zgurt*. On Arabic users of global English more broadly, see Ahmad Al-Issa and Laila S. Dahan (eds), *Global English and Arabic: Issues of*

Alastair Pennycook asks why such an engagement with semiodiversity has not been forthcoming in the "massive global enterprise of English language teaching" (2008: 34). Pennycook writes:

> Current thinking about the global spread of English has also fallen into the trap of becoming over-obsessed with English as a language unto itself, rather than focusing on the ways in which English is always a language in translation. [...] If defence against English is to be carried out through a new nationalism (the defence of diversity is the defence of national languages and cultures), we are left only with a model of diversity guaranteed by language fortification. (37–8)

While prevailing civic models like the Common European Framework of Reference for Languages (CEFR) increasingly see multilingualism as a *glossodiverse competence* or acquired instrumental status, i.e. a personal ability to translate one's "own" perspective and IP (intellectual property) for emergent commercial and social purposes, Halliday seeks to make methodological room for multilingualisms that may be best conceived of as a semiodiverse situatedness—i.e. how speakers become subject to compulsory, inconvenient, and opaque meanings in others' languages, regardless of the competence they have acquired or continue to lack. Often, these other forms of personal multilingualism are laden with an emotional, political, and institutional precarity that overshadows whatever hybrid delights and flexible competences may be assumed of jet-setting linguistic cosmopolitanism.[31] Consider the Somali refugee to Southern Arizona with very little training in the language(s) of that locality: her situation there, regardless of proficiency, will be anything but monolingual; the linguistic landscapes in which she now traffics *require* her to shepherd meanings of mutually incomprehensible linguistic provenances, whether or not she can pass an English/immigration test.[32] In coming to terms with monolingualism, this book is therefore far less interested in ideal demonstrable *competences* than in the experience of emergent *situations*. I have found Hamers and Blanc's broad and inclusive definition of bilinguality useful

Language, Culture, and Identity (2011), particularly the contributions by Fatma Faisal Saad Said and Anissa Daoudi.

31. Throughout the book, I use "bilingual" and "multilingual" somewhat interchangeably, following Aneta Pavlenko's (2005) approach.

32. On "English you need to know" as a requisite for residency, see Griswold (2011).

in suggesting that being bilingual is a circumstance of social access, and not just an internal trove of abilities:

> Bilinguality is the psychological state of an individual who has access to more than one linguistic code as a means of social communication: the degree of access will vary along a number of dimensions which are psychological, cognitive, psycholinguistic, social-psychological, social, sociological, sociolinguistic, sociocultural and linguistic. (2000: 6)

While neurological rationales for the virtue of acquiring more languages have become a popular orthodoxy,[33] it is unclear that such acquisition is the primary solution to the putative problem called monolingualism, any more than turning off the tap while brushing teeth impacts a liberal market economy that treats water as a disposable abstraction and capital as the moral steward of civil justice (see Liddicoat 2002; Lambert 1999). Nor is it clear that acquiring languages, or fractions of them, is tantamount to divestiture from monolingualism as a civic structure. Indeed speakers of multiple languages can and do use language in ways that are more monolingual, or monological, than those who "only" speak one language. The approximately 1,000 lawyer-translators who work full-time for the Luxembourg-based European Court of Justice must for instance constrain their multilingual work to the ideal of shared translingual meanings, lest rogue translations result in expensive accidental content and jurisprudential mishap. These multilingual lawyers from all twenty-eight E.U. member states translate 1,000,000 pages each year for the court. Each of these pages costs $200 to write (given the legal and case-law competences required), and each costs upwards of $1,200 if the page is translated into all twenty-four of the E.U.'s working languages. Such centripetally multilingual products are under ceaseless manufacture, as multilingual documentation is necessary for overseeing everything on the continent—from the training of plumbers and the energy efficiency of lightbulbs, to air-traffic control regulations and university credit-transfer protocols (Mendick 2014).

Naturally, there are ideas about how to drive down translation costs, and one of the major cost-cutting measures is an institutional commitment to *plain language,* or, in a Hallidayan spirit, semiosuppressive glossodiversity. Companies like globalenglish.com offer their

---

33. See, for instance, the broad media uptake of Ellen Biyalistok's important work in Fox (2011).

consulting services to bodies like the European Court of Justice in a bid to help with "promoting and refining the use of English as a tool for global communication. Native speakers of English need to become more responsible about the global role of our language. This means speaking and writing English more clearly so that it can be understood throughout the world."[34] As European multilingualism aged from a halcyon vision in 1995 to a workaday institutional contingency in 2010, glossodiverse pressures upon meaning have compelled service sector workers to attenuate their language use to those repertoires that do not portend "accidental content."

Amid the boom in studies that look to the explanatory power of "superdiversity" (Vertovec 2007) for answers regarding social and civic phenomena in Europe, I have wondered why Halliday's conception of "semiodiversity" has had relatively modest impact on the way multilingualism is planned, assessed, researched, and operationalized, both in applied linguistics and public policy. I can only speculate that, while superdiversity-based research rises forthrightly to the policy challenges of a new era, semiodiversity does not lend itself operationally to any one burning social issue that interior ministers are eager to resolve through innovative programming. Indeed, the disorderly phenomena of semiodiversity themselves appear poised to slow compliance efforts between institutions and communities, because they highlight the kind of "hard multilingualism" (Noorani 2013) that makes systematic, immediate translation of values, standards, terms, and even apparent cognates more unwieldy than at first glance. Indeed, when lived, everyday semiodiversity becomes part of the picture, multilingual immigrants become harder to "integrate," and "end-users" in allolingual markets become harder to "target." A spirit of dialogue culture and mutual goodwill cannot mitigate the underlying social fact that the abutting ecologies of meaning constituting urban multilingualism in Paris, Brussels, or Berlin do not easily resolve into a consonant tonic, as the European Union hymn would have us hope. Nor is "getting to shared meanings" the design or disposition of semiodiverse multilingualism—which, in the end, is viscous, slow, and in no particular hurry. For a compliance subcontractor for the Bologna Process or an interpreter at the European Court of Justice, semiodiversity is a logistical nightmare;

---

34. For an extended analysis of globalenglish.com's role in the pursuit of "controlled languages," see Michael Cronin's study *Translation in the Digital Age* (2013): 38.

for an anthropological philologist (Hymes 1981), semiodiversity is all there is.

While glossodiversity appeals to the ideal of an exogamous world-language system, one geared towards the efficient trafficking of common meanings across language barriers and politicized contact zones, semiodiversity is ultimately less friendly to systematic coordination and approximation. Meanings on a semiodiverse field are less exogamous than they are *ecological, endogamous, semi-sovereign, opaque,* and *anaphoric.* Like pre-modern musical scales, language ecologies are understood from a semiodiverse perspective as tending to refer internally rather than externally for verification and correspondence. This being the case, such ecologies have no particular political rationale for suppressing traffic with neighboring languages or for policing their borders in any conscientious or coordinated way. Like Bach's introduction to his *Inventions,* semiodiverse repertoires are more than happy to incorporate new-found foreign phrases in their broad margins, without much concern for whether these should be italicized, cited, glossed, or footnoted. In contrast, glossodiverse systems must fastidiously monitor their borders, precisely so as to ensure efficient, documented, and centrally sanctioned crossings.

Programs and initiatives conceived by way of glossodiverse frameworks, focused as these are on the orderly enumeration of cognate concepts from one language to the next for the purpose of intercultural understanding and translating, have no logistical room for semiodiversity. As we have noted, in the European Union's translation infrastructure, semiodiverse meanings are referred to as "accidental content," i.e. the expensive, bulky excess of language that emerges when there appears to be simply too many different ways to say passably similar things in multiple European languages. This excess overloads the information pipeline, makes everyday documents drastically more expensive to translate, and in some cases threatens to undermine everything from political clarity to occupational safety. One wonders what it would mean for Europe to institute a Commissioner for European Semiodiversity, and whether the prospective brief of that office might include redesigning and reinvigorating new protocols for mutual inquiry between the Balkans and Brussels, between Berlin and Westminster, and between Barcelona and Copenhagen—not to mention between Ankara and Versailles, or between Glasgow and Whitehall.

Meaning in the postmultilingual order

I have used the word linguacene above, as derived from the more common term anthropocene, to suggest that it is not only human industrial *activity* that has become the defining geological feature of the planet's last three centuries, but that industrial *discourse*—via the glosso-diverse coordination of meanings or "soft multilingualisms" (Noorani 2013) among world languages—has had an equally defining geological and environmental effect. Translational monolingualism, like styrofoam, has become a hyperobject and a by-product of global industrial deregulation—capacitating and then incapacitating the human species' ability to experience freedom, mobility, well-being, and longevity. Like its archetype, coal, it is everywhere and nowhere at once (Morton 2013).

This is not merely to claim that, since all industry requires coordinated, language-intensive communication between at least two people, *lingua-* ought to replace *anthropo-* in the designation of the current age of geological time. Rather, I want to suggest that the glossodiverse management of common meanings across languages in industrial design—whether medical, chemical, humanitarian, metallurgic, geographic, petro-extractive, or digital—has resulted in a coordinated translingual idiom of industry that profoundly changes the planet, regardless of which surface-language those industries are being deployed through. The *linguacene* is in this sense that latter stage of the anthropocene, in which multilingualism becomes sufficiently organized among global industrial actors such that alternative vernacular meanings are effectively decommissioned amid the pursuit of coordinated transnational oil production, geostationary orbit policy, counter-insurgency, data storage, and the like.

The linguacene indeed requires that semiodiversity be kept minimal in matters affecting industrial and geopolitical coordination, and that glossodiversity become an efficient, fast-lane, "well-tempered" network of near simultaneous exchanges. Whereas the anthropocene is often dated to the 1712 invention of the Newcomen atmospheric engine, the linguacene may be said to have begun when, in the 1990s, rule-based machine translation was overtaken by the promise of the corpus-driven cross-lingual algorithm. Accordingly this book intends to take a long and indeed reverent look at the confluence of glossodiverse ideologies around multilingual civic and commercial prospecting, and the digital translation technologies that love them. How is this convergence effecting what people tend to say in their languages, when a certain regime of translatability favors some meanings as travel-ready and discredits others as "accidental"?

Now that most insistence about the *clarity* of French, the *organic complexity* of German, or the *practical sturdiness* of English has been put to rest, there is less and less comparative debate about the imagined merits of one language versus another in accomplishing whichever task may arise in the conduct of global commerce. This is delightful news for the Globalization, Internationalization, Localization, and Translation industry, in that GILT can now transpose all the intellectual property that bears capital into every possible discrete language that has speakers with an appreciable amount of capital to spend. Of course, this logic of maximizing glossodiverse transposability rests on two fallacious tenets: 1) that the ideal end-user is monolingual and prefers to traffic in his or her "own" language; and 2) that state-sanctioned languages actually correspond to the quotidian linguistic practices of the end-user, for whom—for instance in Nigeria—Naija English would often be the preferred code for commercial narrowcasting. Few local-izers in Sunnyvale or elsewhere would be willing or able, however, to produce copyrighted tradaptations in "9ja".

Nonetheless, the GILT industry is now one of the avant-gardes of what at first appears to be *multilingualism,* carrying the mantle for what the Microsoft Corporation calls "World-Readiness." Microsoft's online "Go Global Development Center" describes the virtue of "World-Readiness" as follows:

So, what is this "ideal" situation? It is a software product that is a single "World-Ready" binary that runs on every localized version of a specific OS [Operating System] and presents its data and User Interface according to local standards without any custom modification needing to be performed to its source code before the software is introduced into new foreign markets. Before Windows 2000, creating "World-Ready" software had hardly been achievable because no platform provided enough universal support to create a convenient functional international development platform. And since "World-Readiness" was not part of the basic design, creating guidelines to test these functions where next too [sic] impossible. In the past, such QA [Quality Assurance] guidelines for the "ideal" situation were basically only good for academic discussions. (2010)

Understanding that this prose is of a pragmatic nature, geared toward the needs of working software developers in the field, it is nonetheless striking how many of its terms and conceptions originate from Enlightenment philosophies of cosmopolitanism. Still, the putative effeteness of "academic discussions" about multilingualism (now that World-Readiness has come along) must also be unnerving for those of us who have long participated in them. We must be honest, however, about the extent to which the boom in multilingualism scholarship over the past twenty years has been an epiphenomenon of transnational business logistics, and not necessarily a critique of it. In order for literary studies, applied linguistics, or any other field to get ahold of contemporary monolingualism, we must take the internal semiotics of international business as seriously as we once did the *Cours de linguistique générale.*

Despite occasional optimization errors, World-Readiness as an operational rhetoric puts multilingualism to extraordinarily efficient use. WR promises a controlled set of functional signifieds, such that they may be transposed automatically, regardless of end-locality and without need for "custom modification." The basic constitutional features of an "end-locality" are not necessarily political difference, but size and purchasing power (Pym 2004: 3). At the core of WR's form of multilingual localization is thus rather a glossodiverse monolingualism—an apparatus for delivering proprietary meanings in multiply flexiblized world languages. Language studies and language industries are therefore in a tense practical and procedural battle over the definition of multilingualism, and industries are winning—both in the prerogative to define language and the ability to operationalize this definition (see Chapter 1).

Because of its focus on technocracies of meaning, *The Invention of Monolingualism* will not be concerned as much with the discrete processes by which any one particular language has become hegemonic—whether World English(es), diplomatic French, National Socialist German, colonial Castilian, or Republican "pure" Turkish. Existing scholarship has robustly attended to these processes. Nor will this book try to account for any one language's consolidated supremacy over any other in a given historical moment or social circumstance. These, I hold, are features of linguistic *purism, imperialism, colonialism, nationalism,* and *apartheid,* which emerged in very different social timescales than monolingualism has done.[35] Indeed, to get to the heart

35. On linguistic purism from a historical perspective, see for instance William Jervis Jones (ed.), *Sprachhelden und Sprachverderber: Dokumente zur Erforschung des Fremdwortpurismus im Deutschen (1478–1750)* (1995). For a theoretical perspective, see Crépon (2015). Robert Phillipson's classic, *Linguistic Imperialism* (1992), remains a standard-bearer. On linguistic empire, see Jürgen Leonhardt's *Latin: Story of a World Language* (2013). See also

of monolingualism, we should perhaps entirely forego the temptation to intuit it under any specific (nationally or imperially conceived) political tradition or conceit. In making this claim, I realize that I am asking for a departure from much of the commonsense political usage attending the word. I do so based on the wager that these usages—motivated by a hunger for social justice or cosmopolitan worldliness—often distort, unduly polemicize, and ultimately minimize the underlying structure of monolingualism in modernity. Monolingualism—as a discourse—isn't merely linguistic mean-spiritedness plus securitarian fear-of-the-unknown. Nor is monolingualism, as a putative character trait, a mixture of self-satisfaction, civic diffidence, and lack of access to language education. If we indeed dwell long enough on Mary Louise Pratt's directive that "Monolingualism is a handicap. No child should be left behind" (2003: 118), we may find that the metaphors in this equation will need creative reformulation for the new postmultilingual age I am calling the linguacene.

Data, discipline, method

By the time I began writing this book, I had become convinced that any sustained study of the relationship between multilingualism and monolingualism must engage with methods beyond those emerging from any one discipline alone, whether that be comparative philology, literary theory, political science, or applied linguistics. This book is thus not meant "for" a particular discipline, as much as it is meant for readers, speakers, and critics who, in the course of their routine inquiries about language(s), find themselves at play in the conceptual folds between literary text and political appearance, between poetics and pragmatics, between language learning and language use, and between conventional genres and unruly linguistic landscapes. The arguments throughout this book are accordingly pursued through a kind of philology-once-removed, an approach that is unable to stake a claim on one core analytic from which other, neighboring resonances can then be ascertained. Studying monolingualism requires a vigorous itinerancy, not just because there is no discipline eager to house such an inquiry, but because disciplines go to great lengths to maintain plausible deniability about our own monolingualist forms and formats.

Louis-Jean Calvet's *Linguistique et colonialisme: petit traité de glottophagie* (1974). On linguistic apartheid, see Combs et al. (2014).

I am reminded here of a painstaking and heroic attempt in a recent Call for Papers to reach beyond monolingualism, in which philologists of German were invited to contribute to a colloquium. Unwilling to restrict the event to "German literature" or "German language" topics, the Call gently suggested that: "Desirable, but not mandatory, is some reference to contemporary literature that is in some way related to that which we habitually call 'German language.'" This kind of postironic disciplinary acrobatics, which most of us in the twenty-first-century academy routinely undertake in some fashion, is indeed proof positive of what Yildiz calls an unsettling "postmonolingual condition" in scholarship. But monolingualism, as a historically durable and modulating structure, is well equipped to outflank such a sally. The Call ultimately cannot mitigate the underlying suspicion that a "core" or "well-designed" stable language is worthy of pursuit, "a language" around which related linguistic phenomena may have occasion to cluster and clamor.

Because monolingualisms, nationalized literature(s), and state schooling systems have rushed to each other's succor at various crucial moments throughout modernity, and because worldly multilingualism often operates at acute cross-purposes with traditions of high culture and educational excellence (Grosjean 2010; Valdés 2005; Canagarajah 2007; Seidlhofer 2007; Shohamy 2006), the tools at large today in literary studies are often among the least well-equipped for shoring up literature's own monolingualism. While traditional literary texts play a prominent role in the chapters that follow, they offer us but one kind of picture. After fifteen years of active literary productivity, Franz Kafka for instance saw fit in 1917 to summarize that "Literature—to express it in reproachful terms—is such a drastic curtailment of language [...] The noise-trumpets of nothingness."[36] I find it heartening that such an unabashed lover of literary figuration as Franz Kafka was nonetheless able to square his shoulders to the inherent formal constraints of (modern) literary monolingualism, and to do so in a much more forthright fashion than contemporary discussions are often willing to do. Taking a cue from Kafka's methodological admonition, if not quite from his despair, a book like *The Invention of Monolingualism* must be equally concerned with those aspects of literary practice that are for one reason or another barred from publishability and translatability, due to the vague and yet non-negotiable linguistic criteria conditioning literary-political emergence. I will stress again in Chapter 3 that literary

36. Kafka (1990): 818. "Literatur, als Vorwurf ausgesprochen, ist eine so starke Sprachverkürzung [...] Die Lärmtrompeten des Nichts."

publication ought to be regarded primarily as a category of *political* emergence, one that is for the time being generally coterminous with the compliance mandates of translational monolingualism.

A philology of monolingualism thus often requires alternate routes: through insights and data gained from such ostensibly non-literary events as legislative committee sessions, personal testimonies, public happenings, language memoirs, promotional campaigns, translation protocols, online threads, fuzzy algorithms, student testimonies, paratextual features, and experiences of formal and informal language learning, all of which exert pressure on how we come to define multilingualism and monolingualism today. These arenas of production are alive with a kind of emergent multilingual literaricity (Dobstadt and Riedner 2013; Warner and Chen, forthcoming) that requires new conceptions of authorship, civic personhood, pedagogy and semio-diverse research methods. In this, we may be guided by Dell Hymes and his *In Vain I Tried to Tell You* (1981: 5–10), a highly philological, data-rich survey of native North Pacific Coast oral literatures in the United States. In a preparatory article from 1965, Hymes lays out the predicament of an anthropological philology, a predicament tantamount to that of a critical philology of monolingualism:

> There is no continuing tradition of philology in most of the languages in which the poems of [Navaho, Zuni, Nahuatl, Papago, Nootka, Keresan, Takelma, Tewa] exist. Appreciators, including anthologists, are willy-nilly forced to rely upon and rationalize the uncritical use of whatever English the ethnologists have provided [...] On the one hand, some of those who concern themselves with the materials of verbal art assert or assume the irrelevance of linguistic control and analysis to their interpretive interest. Contrary to the experience and standards of scholarship in other fields, the style, content, structure, and functioning of texts seem to be declared "translated" (in the theological sense of the metaphor as well as the linguistic) bodily from their original verbal integument, and available for interpretation without it. [...] In many branches of anthropology today there is an intensified concern with quality of workmanship, partly focused on the use of new tools. The tools of philology are in kind among the oldest the student of human culture knows, but so long as there are texts worth knowing they are indispensable. (334, 336–7)

The title of the next chapter, "Monolingualism: A User's Guide," is offered only partially in jest. More often than not, monolingualism indeed guides users of language; individual speakers have little power to guide the use of monolingualism. In the end, I am not presuming to guess how monolingualism ought best to be used, whether it has good uses at all, or whether it can indeed be claimed to have an ontology, beyond its effective mythic structure (see Chapter 4). The chapter subtitle "A User's Guide" is nonetheless meant to provoke discussion about how, when, and why we *use* monolingualism, regardless of whether or not we are speakers or writers of multiple languages. For whom and for what processes is monolingualism effective and why? How has the word been used historically, and what can we learn from those usages, if we allow the word to be meaningful beyond its positivistic, commonsense exterior? How is the word and the structure of monolingualism becoming more effective in a twenty-first-century context that requires the minute management of global data, capital, intellectual property, and meaning—most often independently of the speakers who create them? What means and positionalities have writers found for critiquing monolingualism from within its contemporary constraints?

Chapter 1

MONOLINGUALISM: A USER'S GUIDE

In the mid-1990s, an unattributed report made rounds on the young internet under the title "Dihydrogen Monoxide: Unrecognized Killer." According to this text, the substance DHMO proves so caustic when consumed that it "accelerates the corrosion and rusting of many metals, [...] is a major component of acid rain, [and] has been found in excised tumors of terminal cancer patients." Symptoms of exposure include "excessive sweating," and "for those who have developed a dependency on DHMO, complete withdrawal means certain death" (Glassman 1997). Controversialized in this way, dihydrogen monoxide was something no conscientious citizen would want to be exposed to, let alone consume on a regular basis. Inevitably, a fourteen-year-old science enthusiast in Idaho Springs, Idaho, decided to survey fifty of his classmates to see whether the substance should be banned by law, given its clinically proven hazardous properties. A vigorous 86 percent of the junior high school population queried—many of whom were ambitious, ecologically minded science students—voted for the ban, while the other 14 percent harbored unspecified reservations about doing so. When the young experimenter Nathan Zohner presented his findings at the local science fair, he revealed—or rather pointed out— that dihydrogen monoxide was another word for *water*.

The bulky and authoritative term *dihydrogen monoxide*—hyper-accurate in nomenclature, cloying in timbre, and utterly alien to vernacular charisma—had been packaged up as a stand-in term for a common, everyday thing we all avail ourselves of; that we combine with other substances; that we cook, bathe, and wash with; harvest, hoard, waste, and design conservation plans around; fight over rights to; bottle, market, and manipulate for profit; and develop geopolitical strategies about. Word of this Kantian stunt quickly spread coastward, where David Murray, research director of the Washington, DC-based Statistical Assessment Service, responded to the teen's findings as follows: "The likelihood is high that I could replicate these results with a survey of members of Congress" (Glassman 1997).

Zohner's meta-science project in an Idaho classroom, inevitably called "How Gullible Are We?", made his peers feel ashamed, and then incensed, at what seemed to be untowardly aggressive, scientistic snobbery. Thinking he had made a useful contribution to the advancement of knowledge, the young man instead found that he was presumed guilty of a mild but unforgiveable civic misdemeanor—that of testing, and then making a big poster about, his own peer group's credulity toward crypto-authoritative language. Structurally, it mimicked the social opportunism of the *snitch*. As in many such cases of community-based research, respondents were disappointed to discover that his project was about *mere* language, rather than about the advancement of, say, health sciences or technological innovation. Suspecting entrapment, people were particularly upset at what seemed to be this precocious Enlightener-of-the-moment's practical joke on them, this seditious bait-and-switch in something so mundane as "semantics." Whether to blame the message or the messenger was a secondary concern, in this moment of collective social face-threat.

After decades of debate on cultural hybridity and transnationalism in the humanities and social sciences, a threshold situation of distemper with the word *monolingualism* has been lately afoot, similar to the messy public showdown *dihydrogen monoxide* incited in an Idaho town circa 1997. Monolingualism—no longer a clinical, ethnological, or demographic term alone—has gone *social*. It has taken up a performative role in the broader micro-political economies of what Deborah Cameron (1995, 2013) has called "verbal hygiene," finding diverse and meaningful functions in a variety of discourse genres. This newly explicit and flexible role for monolingualism—as we will explore in this chapter—is not entirely an unprecedented innovation in public life, but the word's spectrum of social usage and political utility has expanded significantly in recent decades.[1]

While the words "monolingualism" and "monolingual" continue to bear little to no specific discourse that might make them meaningful in a scholarly context, the words themselves are rapidly becoming an effective and pejorative force in twenty-first-century political and commercial contexts. Companies like Inglés sin Fronteras and

---

1. Though the accuracy of NGram statistics are debated (Zhang 2015), the word's adjectival and nominalized forms grew from near non-circulation in the 1920s to a steady rise in the 1970s, with peaks in the early 1980s and early 2000s (in English, German, Spanish, and French).

Education First increasingly present Spanish-language consumers with ultimatums like "If you are monolingual, the limits of the world are more clearly defined. But in an era of borderless communications and global travels, it seems almost archaic to be limited to one language alone."[2] Buttressed with scientific-sounding claims about the bilingual mind, Education First's advertisements conclude their pitch with the clickable buttons "Prepara tu Gap Year [Prepare for your Gap Year]" and "Hazte bilinguë con nosotros [Make yourself bilingual with us]." For its part, Inglés sin Fronteras is currently being investigated on allegations of defrauding and blackmailing consumers who are living undocumented in the United States. Having purchased the Inglés sin Fronteras CD-bundle as a ticket out of monolingualism, in the hopes of gaining the kind of "English you need to know" for a chance at legal residence, they reportedly find themselves under extortionary threats of deportation from the same company that had promised them an escape from "their" monolingualism.[3] This new-found commercial and culture-political utility of the word indicates that, if monolingualism was indeed once a clinical, universitarian abstraction, the experiment has long since left the laboratory and is now at large in all manner of social discourses about what it means to be a good, effective, and intelligent world citizen.

A proto-historical snapshot

Despite its recently expanding usage, "monolingual" isn't quite a neologism. In the pages of the London-based political magazine *The Spectator* from the late nineteenth century, we find the (admittedly rare) indication of what the word "monolingual" used to leverage in eras past. In a review of *The Intellectual Status of the Aborigines of Victoria* (1878), an anonymous reviewer for *The Spectator* paraphrases

2. "Si eres monolingüe, el mundo tiene unos límites más definidos. No obstante, en una época de comunicaciones sin fronteras y viajes globales, parece casi arcaico estar limitado a un solo idioma" (Alvarado 2015).

3. On *Inglés sin Fronteras*, see Alvarado (2015). See also Griswold (2011) on language ideology in U.S. naturalization classrooms. That the ascription of personal monolingualism is now more effectively being used to de-competence and intimidate prospective citizens multiplies the implications of Bourdieu's contention that misrecognition of the arbitrary legitimacy of dominant language reproduces existing power relations (1977: 30).

Robert Brough Smyth's findings about the Koori people of southern Australia:

> They have good memories, but it is in the way children have,—memories, for instance, for words, and for stories, and for the customs of the house, but not for anything requiring separate and original mental exertion, nor, it may be suspected, for things that are long past. They learn English, for example, very readily, and sometimes very perfectly, just as children in India will learn two or three languages apparently without any mental effort, and certainly without any draft upon the intelligence, which remains as undeveloped in the trilingual child—such, for example, as the well-to-do child in Pondicherry often is, and the English children in Calcutta always are—as in the monolingual one. (1879)

This unnamed reviewer's summary of Brough Smyth's findings on the Koori are—as the stacked prepositions in this sentence indicate—composed at great remove from the linguistic experience of actual living, speaking persons. Drawing as it does on ambient imperial truisms about how young people in Puducherry and Calcutta spoke and thought, the review expands its summary findings into a general claim about language and intellect, obscuring whether the prospective "monolingual" person is still to be understood specifically as a colonial subject or, as a potentially normative case of British home citizenship. Amid all this leisurely obfuscation, a few other things happen: 1) language and language learning are cast as not necessarily helpful in the development of intelligence, particularly for indigenous learners of English as a Second Language; 2) the monolingual child is by default characterized as the most likely candidate for achieving "separate and original mental exertion"; and 3) the colony is staged as the proper symbolic locale for "lingualism" of any sort. The colony has languages, whereas the metropole has intellect. Perhaps regrettably, *The Spectator*'s hypotheses about monolingualism found their way through syndication to Eliakim Littell's popular American review *The Living Age*, where it debuted for U.S. readers in the same year.

Though users of the word "monolingual" in 2016 are less Lamarckian in their bid to better the lot of individual speakers, shades of the minute narratives about language emanating from *The Spectator*'s imperial gloss above do continue to inhere in the ways the word is deployed today. In one sense, the label "monolingual" has returned over the course of the twentieth century from the colony to the home territory.

That is, the ascription "monolingual," as presumptively applicable to persons, has mutated from a reductionist descriptor bolstering colonial discourses about the intellect of indigenous speakers abroad, to what it has become today: a reductionist descriptor bolstering moral discourses about intercultural world-readiness among citizens "at home." What has changed, then, is the complex social mode of othering that accompanies the ascription, and the scales upon which it is found to be applicable.[4]

The innovation and industrialization of a concept

The title of this chapter, "Monolingualism: A User's Guide," is meant to openly acknowledge how little defining has been done around this bulky, inelegant, six-syllable, Latinate term. It is also meant to conjure up the "metaphors we live by" in professional discussions on language subjectivity. Is monolingualism, for instance, something one is susceptible to? Something one suffers from or under? Or is it something that one owns and instrumentalizes? Is it on loan from a regulatory body— like the electrical meter outside one's house? Or is monolingualism a home-fashioned artesian well, cobbled privately and without external doctrine from the resources at hand in one's own family kitchen or vernacular landscape? Does monolingualism come from the land, from God, from school, from the internet, from global capital, or from vernacular reactions to global capital?

Where *The Spectator*'s reviewer is thrice removed from an observed speech situation, in which the Koori are endeavoring to communicate translingually with the Anglo-Australians eager to research them, the discourse of monolingualism in the twenty-first century has set up camp in many of our most intimate social discussions: about civic responsibility, educational achievement, parenting and child development, military and counter-insurgency strategy, citizenship and migration, and the presumptive characteristics of the modern person. It has also moved into our technical lives as users of social media, electronic devices, and service interfaces. On our computers, we can download a program called Monolingual, which will remove all of the extraneous "other-language" user-interface data designed for us according to Microsoft World-Readiness protocols, so that our ever-expanding hard-drive space can remain reserved for language we really need or desire. Copyrighted by Igmar Stein and J. Schrier in 2001, the program

4. On sociolinguistic scales, see Blommaert (2007).

Monolingual is represented by an on-screen program icon depicting the German, French, and U.S. flags being stuffed into a trash-bin.

The social debut of "monolingualism" is thus not merely a termino-logical development, but an infrastructural one. Newly laid translation and distribution pathways in the global film and fiction markets, the rise of the corporate content-management industry GILT (Globalization, Internationalization, Localization, and Translation), discontentment with L2-only or nativist approaches to teaching English as an Additional Language, as well as War-on-Terror language panics in national security and intelligence-gathering discourse have conspired to bring this awkwardly named mountain of monolingualism to the Mohammed of public discussion. This is in itself a remarkable turn, offering a unique moment of reflection for thinkers, teachers, and activists working toward what Philippe van Parijs calls *Linguistic Justice for Europe and the World* (2011). Though *The Spectator*'s usage in 1879 bodes ill for those inter-ested in a critical reframing of monolingualism for scholarly or political purposes, the fact that the review was able to posit such a phenomenon as monolingualism, even in a register of effacement and oppression, is a feat of some note. In its various forms throughout modernity (Gogolin 1994; Bonfiglio 2010; Yildiz 2012), monolingualism has been able to naturalize itself, render itself unremarkable, and pre-empt its own historical contextualization, such that, as the Romance comparatists Jan Walsh Hokenson and Marcella Munson have it, "Bilinguality seems to be the one category of language user that high modernist thought did not, indeed perhaps even refused to, consider" (2007: 148).

The Australian applied linguist Elisabeth Ellis's essay from 2006, "Monolingualism: The Unmarked Case," was a watershed moment, followed by Yasemin Yildiz's pathbreaking discussion of the "postmono-lingual condition" (2012). Both of these works helped raise critical consciousness about the problematic conceptual underspecification of monolingualism in scholarship, creative work, and civic policy. As it turns out, however, there are more than a few ways to "mark" a previously unmarked category of human experience or structural privilege. As I will claim in Chapter 4, "marking the unmarked" can easily become less of a critical process than a pejorative maneuver. A phenomenon as historically and structurally complex as monolin-gualism requires something beyond being merely marked—it must be, in Roland Barthes's (1957) sense, de-mythologized.

Since 2000, however, efforts—scholarly and otherwise—to open a public conversation about the conceptual and experiential substance of *monolingualism* have tended to run a similar course as *dihydrogen monoxide* once did in 1990s Idaho. The word has taken on the social tenor of a scold—especially in academic scholarship, where the register of moral condemnation is otherwise traditionally reserved for undebatable grand values like "academic freedom." While scholarship in most spheres of the social sciences and humanities has long been circumspect about moralizing on the positionalities of others, there has indeed been, in the young twenty-first century, an odd sense that it is open season for pronouncements about so-called "monolinguals" and "their" monolingualism. Though memoirists like Richard Rodriguez, writing amid the U.S. bilingualism debates of the 1970s and 1980s, acutely illustrated what it feels like to be called a linguistic *pocho* by one's own family (2004 [1982]: 29), being called "monolingual" has become in the intervening thirty years a politically generic speech act, with a majoritizing mode of address. While the young Rodriguez in 1950s Sacramento had been singled out for his bad monolingualism on the presumption that he "of all people" ought to have been otherwise, the word monolingualism now portends that *most everyone* is or has been on the verge of some form of bad linguistic behavior, regardless of their particular circumstances. We might, finally, decide this is a good thing: linguistic diversity provincializing cultural purism. In the meantime, whatever good ends we researchers or teachers hope to achieve by talking about monolingualism usually ends up leaving half the room feeling detained for critique and remediation, the other half feeling vaguely spared.

This is the case in part because the loose bundle of phenomena that trade under a term like "monolingualism" still remains shapeless and undefined, though most of us feel entitled to hold strong opinions about its relative vice or virtue. Twenty-first-century scholarship and public policy alike—from North America to Europe to Australia and Africa—struggle to coordinate with one another in identifying when and how monolingualism may be considered contextually present, effective, binding, or detrimental.[5] The social psychologist Michael Billig, reflecting on the routinely dry press coverage on language allegiances in multilingual Belgium, has suggested that so-called "analytical" treatments of monolingual phenomena often suffer from the same disinterested glossing that convinces readers that there must be, in the end, no particular *there* there. After all, "Social scientists often assume," continues Billig, "that it is natural that speakers of the same

5. In the Germanophone context, Ingrid Gogolin was the first to offer a clear guide on these questions in *Der monolinguale Habitus der multilingualen Schule* (1994).

language should seek their own political identity"—and, conversely, that political communities should pursue a common language (1994: 13; see also Gal 1993).

Researchers are often hampered in our incipient inquiries about monolingualism by our suspicions that the concept may ultimately be too easily debunked, too retrograde, or too flash-in-the-pan false-ideological to do any substantive intellectual, literary, or historical work around. Bakhtinian visions of the carnivalesque, the dialogic, and the heteroglossic seem further to furnish us with scenarios of complexity that make the notion of "being monolingual" an ever-shrinkingly implausible category for social life and scholarly analysis. Maybe we have never been monolingual, after all? How else could such a thing as monolingualism have been allowed to have the run of the place for so long—over the course of structuralism and post-structuralism—while whiteness, maleness, empire, the nation, and all manner of other hegemonic structures were being called to answer to critique, one after the other, or in combination? How did monolingualism so effectively give us the slip? The linguist Jason Rothman puts a fine point on this stammering, incredulous stance in scholarship, when he writes: "What is monolingualism, then? What is monolingualism, *really*?" (2008: 442).

De-competencing speakers

Left out of the critical furor for so long, monolingualism now seems to have arrived unwelcome and belated, amid ongoing discussions about disciplinary reconstitution, cultural politics, naturalization, education, language learning, and literary production. Like a sudden and inscrutable diagnosis, the imputed ascription of *personal* monolingualism—the ability of an individual speaker to communicate in one language alone—comes onto the globalized neoliberal civic scene clamoring for an urgent and expensive pharmacopeia, which can be monetized in any number of untested, purportedly remedial forms.[6] Just going about their business, many previously healthy

6. These include, for instance, GoEnglish courses in Hermosillo, Mexico, which promise to offer "algo muy novedoso" (something very novel): that is, courses taught by instructors with "inglés limpio y sin accento" (clean English without accent) by "maestros extranjeros" (foreign teachers), as opposed to local multilinguals. See GoEnglish (2011). I thank Migdalia Rodríguez for this reference.

language-users are surprised to discover that, in a certain scholarly or cosmopolitan light, their own home-grown speech and writing practices do not add up to even an entry-level position in latter-day global citizenship. Their most intimate acts of communicating now having been downgraded into *monolingualism*, and their messy, vibrant variations on language having been folded into this newly problematized packaging by an expert discourse, individual speakers predictably bristle at the word "monolingual"—or perhaps they ought to. Though they have committed no common-law offense, speakers—of various generations, classes, genders, ethnicities, speech communities, vocations, socialities, and/or citizenships—may feel that this designation "monolingual" is just one more opportunistic, inhumane prank played on them and their friends, one more disingenuous gerrymander of metropolitan power. In terms of the sociolinguistics of globalization, we might choose to understand this feeling as an (increasingly common) experience in the "scalar de-competencing" of vernacular subjectivity, a procedure that "resides in the ways in which unique instances of communication can be captured (indexically) as 'framed' understandable communication, pointing towards social and cultural norms, genres, traditions, expectations—phenomena of a higher scale level" (Blommaert 2007: 4).[7]

Deborah Cameron's *Verbal Hygiene* (1995) and *Good to Talk: Living and Working in a Communication Culture* (2000) have offered dramatic evidence of the augmented role afforded to linguistic prescriptivism in contemporary social life. According to Cameron, "linguistic bigotry is among the last publicly expressible prejudices left to members of the western intelligentsia. Intellectuals who would find it unthinkable to sneer at a beggar [...] will sneer without compunction at linguistic 'solecisms'" (1995: 12). While Cameron's early work in the mid-1990s focused on how elites and language preservationists used (implicitly monolingual) linguistic prescriptivism as a way to perpetuate social exclusion, the subsequent rise of multilingualism as the "politically correct" way to be a global citizen has multiplied the potency of verbal hygiene discourse, such that monolingualism itself has become a kind of solecism.[8]

7. On "scalar de-competencing," see Chantelle Warner (2015).

8. For a more recent complement to her early interventions on linguistic bigotry, see Deborah Cameron, "The One, the Many and the Other: Representing multi- and mono-lingualism in post-9/11 verbal hygiene" (2013). On multilingualism and political correctness, see Gohard-Radenkovic (2012).

Following Cameron's metaphorics of "verbal hygiene," monolingualism appears to belong less to the behavioral realm of bad hygiene or disorderliness than to a second-order realm of metalinguistic infrastructure, namely, the ways that languages are understood as zoned and organized in relation to one another in social life. Being monolingual is thus a metalinguistic and metapragmatic predicament, a way of being compromised in the interstices of the world language system in various moments of time-space compression. While the kind of class-/gender-based and ethnicized "verbal hygiene" Cameron theorizes may be understood as an attempt to keep a certain customary space linguistically clean in the face of superdiversity, monolingualism meanwhile is implicated in threats to the dimensions, borders, load-bearing integrity, safety plan, and external compliance protocols for the linguistic space in question. Initiatives toward verbal hygiene in society can indeed call on the discursive orthodoxies of monolingualism, and vice versa, but they traffic in different registers of virtue and vice.

Aside from its affront to individuals and their ways of living, the historical stakes in the word "monolingual" are a great deal more acute than just hurt feelings. Though the epithet "monolingual" carries little of the sheer historical pain that any repeatedly experienced ethnic, racial, classed, or gendered slurs tend to bear, this is so in part because the structure of monolingualism has always already been inscribed into other, apparently non-linguistic, epithets—whether indigenous, ethnicized, racialized, medicalized, or gendered ones. Postcolonial and critical race studies thinkers have been working toward an implicit conceptualization of monolingualism since 1900 at the latest, long before an explicit discourse on *multi*lingualism would emerge in the era of post-structuralism. Toni Morrison was in part pointing out the pre-history of such experiences, when she famously wrote:

> Black women had to deal with "post-modern" problems in the nineteenth century and earlier. These things had to be addressed by black people a long time ago: certain kinds of dissolution, the loss of and need to reconstruct certain kinds of stability. Certain kinds of madness, deliberately going mad [...] in order not to lose your mind. These strategies of survival made the truly modern person. (Cited in Gilroy 1995: 220)

This time-lag Morrison describes between, for example, the West European cultivation of monolingual civic ideals in the seventeenth through nineteenth centuries and their thematization in current public discourse corresponds to what Pierre Bourdieu, in a Nietzschean sense, called "genesis amnesia" (Bourdieu and Passeron 1970: 59). The ethnically coded use of the term "monolingual" has, however, taken on a newly explicit role in geopolitical securitarian and anti-insurgent discourse since the 1990s. As Abraham Acosta notes, reflecting on the Zapatista uprisings of 1994, the Chiapan government's first communiqué announcing the insurgency warned (non-indigenous) Chiapanec@s about the danger of a communication-averse indigenous mob approaching them: "Various groups of Chiapan peasants, numbering close to 200 individuals and consisting mostly of *monolinguals*, have carried out violent, provocational, attacks in four districts within the state, including San Cristóbal de las Casas, Ocosingo, Altamirano, and Las Margaritas" (my emphasis).[9]

This Chiapas state directive saw fit to use "monolingual" appositionally, depicting an undifferentiated mass of combatants—"other" people—whose diverse linguistic indigeneity and meaning-making practice are condensed here into a single threat-body. And yet, as Carlos Montemayor points out, the label "monolingual" ought in this case to stick less to indigenous Chiapanec@ citizens of Mexico—who, "in addition to speaking their language, often have knowledge of another, neighboring, indigenous language as well as Spanish"[10]—than it ought to apply to the non-indigenous Mexican who may speak only the state language of Spanish. Acosta goes further:

'Monolinguals' in this report is thus used to communicate that, because they only speak one language and that language is not a language, the combatants are incapable of speech, and therefore may obtain no right to political representation. As such, nameless and deprived of *logos*, anything these indigenous peasants express will

9. Díaz Arciniega and López Téllez (1997): 106. "Diversos grupos de campesinos chiapanecos que ascienden a un total de cerca de 200 individuos, en su mayoría monolingües, han realizado actos de provocación y violencia en cuatro localidades del estado que son San Cristóbal de las Casas, Ocosingo, Altamirano y las Margaritas."

10. Montemayor (1997): 38. "En nuestro continente los monolingües suelen no ser los indios: es monolingüe el mexicano promedio, que sólo habla español, como el norteamericano promedio, que sólo habla inglés. Los indios mexicanos además de hablar su idioma suelen conocer otra lengua indígena vecina y también el español."

carry no meaning other than noise; they do not speak at all, they are simply of no account. (2013: 30)

In accordance with the logic of scalar de-competencing in globalization, monolingualism becomes less-lingualism, or what a recent Dutch minister of education referred to as zero-lingualism (*zerotaligheid*).[11]

How, we may ask, has the object called "language" moved historically—in uneven surges from the thirteenth century onward—from being something uncountable to something countable in this way? From an ecolinguistic standpoint, M. A. K. Halliday highlights why countability matters as a symbolic means of production and reproduction:

> [English] makes a categorical distinction between two kinds of entity: those that occur in units, and are countable in the grammar, and those that occur in the mass and are uncountable [...] Our grammar (though not the grammar of human language as such) construes air and water and soil, and also coal and iron and oil, as "unbounded." That is, as existing without limit. In the horizons of the first farmers, and the first miners, they did. We know that such resources are finite. But the grammar presents them as if the only source of restriction was the way we ourselves quantify them: a barrel of oil, a seam of coal, a reservoir of water and so on—as if they in themselves were inexhaustible. (2001: 194)

11. On "*zerotaligheid*" see Jaspers (2005). On "less-languagedness" see Phipps (2013a) and Gramling (2013). The German semantic framework around language plurality, for instance, encourages not just the logical binary between multi- and monolingualism (*Mehr-* versus *Einsprachigkeit*) as in English usage, but also one between *more-languagedness* versus *less-languagedness* (*Mehr-* versus *Wenigersprachigkeit*). In contrast to "multi" in English, this "Mehr" in *Mehrsprachigkeit* associates easily in German with civic and commercial virtues like *Mehrwert* (surplus value). It confers a sense of advantage, achievement, and desirability, which "multi" does not quite offer in English. Where *mehrsprachig* emphasizes an abstract, non-countable comparative advantage, *multilingual* conveys a mathematically additive array of instruments and options. (German also, it should be noted, uses the Anglo-Latinate loan word *Multilingualismus* somewhat interchangeably with *Mehrsprachigkeit*.) A series of panels on this topic of *Wenigersprachigkeit* was organized by Till Dembeck, David Martyn, and Georg Mein at the German Studies Association convention in Denver 2013.

The effective countability of languages, as it shapes institutions and speakers' experiences of language, is what some Germanophone researchers call *Sprachigkeit*, or "lingualism" (Dorostkar 2014).

The Chiapas communiqué and its rhetorical aridity may remind us of Franz Kafka's 1919 fable "An Old Document," in which a cobbler in the provincial capital square has become begrudgingly resigned to the presence of northern nomads crowding the entrances to the alleys around the imperial castle, posing quality-of-life issues for the fatherland:

> One cannot speak with the nomads. They don't know our language, they don't even seem to have one of their own. Among their own kind, they communicate with each other like jackdaws. Over and over one hears that cry of the jackdaws. (1994: 264)

As the Czech Slavist Marek Nekula (2003: 18) notes, the Czech word for the German "jackdaw" (*Dohle*) is "kafka," and the emblem over the door of Franz's father Hermann Kafka's store in Prague featured a jackdaw, perched on a German oak branch (Bruce 2007). In "An Old Document," the cobbler sees these *monolingual Kafkas* then—nomads from beyond the polyglot imperial city—as undermining the equanimity of the fatherland with their screams in the town square.

Barely possessing a language that could properly be called their own, the nomadic Kafkas are so incommensurable in relation to the institutions and customs of the state that "You can dislocate your jaw and pull your hands out of their joints, they still haven't understood you and never will" (1994: 265). In this resigned observation, the cobbler describes the futility even of rudimentary gestural language; the dislocated jaw and the hands wrested out of their joints epitomize a dismantling of communicative potential at its embodied inception. A Chiapas communiqué about the urban migration of Franz Kafka's grandparents, this text is one of the most outwardly political figurations of linguistic otherness in Kafka's fictional works, where the encrypted language repertoire of the writer's own family signifies from the horizon of the page.

Ill-fitting labels

The epithet *monolingual* is thus indeed a form of "excitable speech" in Butler's sense, one that draws on ages of activism and entrenchment on ritualized linguistic frontiers (1997). But calling someone monolingual is a diffuse and anti-vernacular act unlike other injurious or invective speech. On the one hand, the experience of being called a "monolingual" corresponds to what politeness researchers like Penelope Brown and Stephen Levinson might call 'a bald, on-record, positive face-threatening act, without redressive action' (1987). That is, calling someone monolingual does in a certain register of discourse, impinge on that individual's ability to be viewed favorably by other participants (what Goffman calls "positive face"), and there is little room for redemptive interpretation. In a culture aspiring to favor interculturality and global communication, "monolingual" is meant to stick to a person like a scarlet letter, until she reforms or skulks away.

But unlike other such face-threatening epithets, the label "monolingual" routinely fails to stick to its social targets, as the word itself carries little of the essentializing vernacularity that other epithetical speech-acts do. Were there a lay term for monolingualism or monolingual—an Anglo-Saxon one, say *onespeech/onespeaker*—it would have none of the preposterous timbre *monolingualism* carries now. But there is no lay term, and there will be none. Because the phenomena this technical term describes are at such mortal cross-purposes with the sovereignty claims of each transposable, enumerable, nationalized language, that the word monoligulalism will continue indefinitely to look like an unwelcome interloper, an inhumane implantation in the charismatic vernaculars of any national community. Anne Pitkänen-Huhta and Marja Hujo's 2012 study about elderly Europeans' language practices amid the multilingual boom in European policy making highlights an interview with a ninety-year-old Finnish couple who had been asked to share their feelings about their own Finnish (Suomi) monolingualism. When asked whether they felt remorse, exclusion, or affront amid the E.U.'s ascending multilingual civic self-redefinition, they replied—somewhat perplexedly—that their only regret about being so-called monolinguals was that they were unable to effectively warn foreign tourists about a ditch a quarter-kilometer up the village road (Pitkänen-Huhta and Hujo 2012: 275). Even in such an earnest, qualitative research interview, designed to elicit respondents' feelings about language identity and practice, the ascription "monolingual" failed to garner much in the way of internalized subjective rumination among these elderly Finns, whether positive or negative.

More often, the imputed ascription "monolingual" prompts a kind of post-ironic stance on the part of those about whom it is used[12]—a combination of clinical alienation and ginger, rueful appropriation

12. On post-irony, see Konstantinou (2009).

reminiscent of some of the more troubling, catch-all diagnoses from the latest *Diagnostic and Statistical Manual of Mental Disorders*. A kind of monolingual drag, the performative gesture "I'm a monolingual," when delivered in mixed company, reanimates the mood of a 1993 rock single by the Canadian alt-rock band the Odds, gleefully entitled "Heterosexual Man":

> Do you know what's the matter with me?
> I'm a heterosexual man, just a heterosexual man [...]
> It's just a problem with my glands.

The Odds' self-celebrating, self-deprecating, prophylactically incantatory repetition of the auto-epithet *heterosexual* portends how the term *monolingual* might limp its way into sociality in the twenty-first century. Like monolingualism, heterosexuality is a bulky Latin-based erstwhile neologism that itself had been in mostly clinical and juridical circulation for almost a hundred years before its vernacular debut through this song, nurturing over the decades an impossibly strained relationship to everyday speech. Less a source for reactionary umbrage, it often finds uptake as a defensive mirror-shield against the hygienic, expropriative advances of expert discourses. Consider how the vice-president of Bolivia Álvaro García Linera framed his own monolingualism in 2014, during an address to a teachers' organization in Warisata, La Paz:

> Never make a child feel embarrassed about what he is; if he doesn't command Castilian (Spanish) don't make him ashamed, make him feel proud of his indigenous language and help him to learn another [...] in which he is already bilingual. Unlike me: I'm monolingual. I'm ignorant. A bilingual is more capable.[13]

The vice-president's remarks made waves in the Bolivian press, not because he was sticking up for the self-esteem and well-being of indigenous youth, but because he thereby outed himself as violating a 2012 law (the General Law of Linguistic Rights and Policies) requiring all

---

13. El Diario (April 12, 2014). "Nunca hagan sentir a un niño avergonzado de lo que es, si no domina el castellano no lo hagan avergonzar, háganle sentir orgulloso de su idioma indígena y ayúdenle a que aprenda otro [...] de que ya es bilingüe, no como yo soy monolingüe, ignorante soy yo, un bilingüe es más capaz."

civil servants to learn a second Bolivian (i.e. indigenous) language within three years of the law's passing. García, in a sense, uses the indigenous schoolchildren of La Paz as an emotional beard with which to shield himself from public criticism as monolingual, then dramatically performing a threat to his own positive face by declaring himself ignorant and incapable. This disingenous ceremonial maneuver is what Bourdieu describes as a "strategy of condescension" (1989: 16). With a morphology so bulky, shrill, and antibacterial as *mo-no-ling-ual,* only such an ironized (dis)identarian strategy could ever make the word palatable in public.[14]

A lingering impugnity

As Acosta's and Montemayor's analyses of the 1994 Chiapas communiqué show, the word monolingual remains at its most politically effective when it is allowed to be exempt from conceptual scrutiny altogether. Indeed, given the pejorative, disfigurative inflection the word carries, and the kind of indiscriminate, misanthropic erasures that the Chiapas communiqué puts on display, it is little wonder that the project of recuperating (or historicizing) monolingualism for analytical purposes has been less than an attractive proposition over the scholarly decades. Perhaps even just calling attention to "the dilemma of monolingualism" today threatens to introduce a new permutation of a very old form of social domination—that of transurban, transcoastal elites over autochthonous people, who traffic meaning in a vast array of registers and idiolects (Milroy and Milroy 1985: 101; Agha 2003), but have never been prompted by the circumstances of their upbringing to undertake formal "second language studies," or to clamor for the recognition of their own linguistic diversities. Indeed, perhaps scholarship is at its best and most helpful when it focuses on *multilingualism*—in literature, social life, and governance.

This book, however, suggests an alternate course: one that acknowledges the broad interdisciplinary conjuncture of scholarship on multilingualism in recent decades, but nonetheless heads straight for the evacuated symbolic positions that monolingualism "covers" in academic and social debate. Consider the searing positivistic erasure

14. For another illuminating example of self-stylization as "monolingual," see Robin Dale Jacobson's *The New Nativism* (2008): 32.

that underlies the commonly traded joke about the United States as a *"cementerio de lenguas"* (Pratt 2002):

> What do you call a person who speaks three languages?
> A trilingual.
> What do you call a person who speaks two languages?
> A bilingual.
> What do you call a person who speaks one language?
> An American.

In the main, the telling of this joke expects a rueful, knowing response from its listeners, and is keyed toward a particular political fable as to who, and whose languages, may be said to genuinely occupy the label "American." This is equally the case whether one assumes as a backstory Werner Sollors's account of an ideologically monolingualist United States society that first became monolingual in the xenophobic advent of World War I (Sollors 1998), or whether one opts for the version in which U.S. English was always already "good enough for Jesus" (Pratt 2012). Presuming either of these narratives, one might imagine the awkward discomfiture this joke regularly elicits in mixed company, depending on whether those within earshot of it have ever been excluded from Americanness on the basis on their, or their forebears' multilingual practices. How is this umbrage compounded when one has, thanks to the adaptive efforts of a person's immigrant parents or elementary school teachers, also become somehow monolingual too? One may further imagine the vague indignation nursed by so-called monolinguals (often masters of multiple dialects, registers, and specialized languages) who are very well accustomed to indulging the bi-coastal fantasy that the rural North American interior is not only monolingual, but monological.

Bonfiglio, for instance, notes how, amid the robust revisionist fantasy that tours under the aegis of United States civic monolingualism, "The speakers who have appropriated authority—those of the industrial cities of the north—are often unaware of 1) the nonstandard elements in their own speech patterns, 2) the nonstandard nature of the Americanisms that they frequently employ, 3) the fact that the standard language is a written construct, and 4) the fact that written competence does not correlate with geographical location" (2010: 3–4). Nonetheless, the ritual power of the joke above is most often able to erase all counter-evidence, leaving in its stead "the monolingual American" as a palliative communal anti-mascot, at once cherished and risible.

Monolingualism, of course, isn't just a the punchline of a joke however; it is a logic embedded in the conceptual fiber of a structural linguistics that presumes abstract systematicity and contiguity for any speech community audacious enough to consider itself the beneficiary of "a language." Despite ample data in dialectology and variationist sociolinguistics disqualifying monolingualism as a stable category for social science analysis (see for instance Jane Hill's work on "white linguistic disorder" [2008]), the descriptor "monolingual" is nonetheless poised to proliferate, as policy initiatives in Europe begin to embrace certain state-sanctioned forms of multilingual practice as opposed to others—an emergence I call a *ius linguarum* (see Chapter 4).

The rise of state multilingualism

The abstract binary opposition between multi- and monolingual identity—statutorily irrelevant throughout most of the twentieth century for anyone but diplomats, computer engineers, literary polyglots, interpreters, and border agents—has, over the past twenty years, grown into a normative distinction for citizenship in a policy era inclined toward solving the problems of societal superdiversity and populist insurgency by way of language. In accordance with "community cohesion" campaigns (Cameron 2013), Europeans and candidate Europeans are asked to become multilingual *in a certain way* and not others, in concert with the Common European Framework of Reference for Languages (CEFR) and other technocratic regimes of "language in late capitalism" (Duchêne and Heller 2012). Increasingly, social and immigration policy in the European Union is thus constructed negatively around suppressing certain mythic forms of monolingual being, while educational programming seeks to redistribute social prestige and symbolic virtue toward ideal forms of *de jure* multilingual citizenship (see Piller 2001; Eades et al. 2003). Indeed, the European Union's adoption of the CEFR means that the status "multilingual" is conferred now by state-certified language assessors and private subcontractors (see Chapter 4).

European language policy envisions for the Union a future body politic of so-called "1+2 speakers" who command their own native language in addition to two other statutorily European languages. A properly European multilingualism, for instance, for a Danish-born citizen in 2000, according to the CEFR, would prompt her to demonstrate normative standard forms of her native Danish, as well as advanced English (C2 proficiency) and advanced-intermediate Italian

(B2 proficiency). The mission of the CEFR has evolved into the issuance of "linguistic passports" that, though playful and promotional in their current forms, model new visions of civic formation in twenty-first-century Europe. Indeed, policy makers and educational consultants are currently seeking to develop a Common European Framework of Reference for Culture, as well (Oonk et al. 2011).

Despite these painstaking efforts toward state multilingualism among cosmopolitan policy elites and street-level bureaucrats alike, not to mention millions of dedicated classroom language learners and teachers, the language permutations and "multiethnolects" most commonly used among pupils in Dutch and German schools today are rather dissimilar to the orderly trilingual predicates of the E.U.'s twenty-four-member-language civic palette. German-born secondary school students in 2000 are, for instance, more likely to be competent trilingual speakers of Turkish, African American Vernacular English, and working-class Berlinish dialect than they are of standard classroom Italian, English, and German. Yet the lived multilingualism of this multiethnolectal first class of speakers is eclipsed in policy initiatives by the idealized, projected multilingualism of the latter class, prompting—on a continental scale—the kind of relation Lauren Berlant (2011) describes as a "cruel optimism" around linguistic subjectivity in the European language system. Inevitably, the transnational class of postmigrant European multilinguals presents an irritant to the orderly civic multilingualization of Europe's future, and it is this generation of wayward multilinguals and their families that becomes the perennial social target of state campaigns against immigrant *mono*lingualism or linguistically coded "parallel societies."[15]

The concept of reification helps identify some of the potential consequences of the rapid orthotic consolidation of language policy in Europe since 1995. The CEFR is encouraging speakers to assume a detached, "neutrally observing mode of behavior" (Honneth 2008: 26) about languages, and to engage with it through a "praxis that is structurally false" (ibid.)—false because natural, ubiquitous phenomena like interlanguage transfer (de Angelis and Selinker 2001) and dynamic multilingualism (Herdina and Jessner 2002) play little role in the behavioral model underlying the CEFR. The Luxembourg-based theorist of education and plurilingualism Adelheid Hu recalls how philologists,

---

15. On the monolingual coding of the notion of "parallel societies," see (then) German interior minister Wolfgang Schäuble's remarks in Carstens and Wehner (2006).

pedagogues, and philosophers of multilingualism in contemporary Europe, faced in the early years of the CEFR—with its "dominant metaphors of quality, competence, modularization, autonomy, evaluation, standardization, efficiency, knowledge management and so on"—found themselves struggling against a positivistic mood of compliance and coordination around languages that, claims Hu, "scarcely anyone can resist. The underlying concept of language was considered to be one-sidedly instrumental-functional; the aesthetic, affective, creative, moral and cultural dimensions of language and language learning seemed underdeveloped." Amid the celebratory collective endeavor toward a multilingual Europe, dissenting voices found themselves cast as those of "a denier, a refuser, a troublemaker, an antediluvian, or a ditherer" (Hu 2012: 68, 72).

The technocratic design of the Framework explicitly stages the individual speaker as the sole integer for competent language consumption and production, while language-ecological insights from Vygotsky to Steffensen have long envisioned a mode of intersubjective meaning-making whose positionalities range beyond discrete pragmatic transactions between rational actors.[16] A rigorously critical, and historical, account of monolingualism can however be pursued not at the expense of those *individuals* rightly or wrongly conceived of as monolingual speakers. Of course, it is a question of some magnitude whether there has ever been a human speaker for whom "monolingual" is a fitting descriptor. The pre-eminent Bakhtin translator and comparatist Michael Holquist is convinced that the idea of monolingual being is itself a fallacy (2014). And yet various public and scholarly debates today continue to find the term "monolingual"—monistic and debunked as it may be—not only methodologically unproblematic, but also often a cornerstone concept for pre-assessing political programs, cultural production, educational policy, and individual positionality. We are left then with the question whether, in the end, ontology matters in a discursive context that finds "monolingual" to be an increasingly useful way of characterizing speakers in the age of global data and capital exchange.

---

16. On the 4E hypothesis of language use—as Embedded, Enacted, Extended, and Ecological—as opposed to Internal, Instrumental, and Individual (or so-called "3I-linguistics"), see Steffensen (2015) and Cowley (2011).

The posthistory of reducción

News came, for instance, in early 2014 that Emily Dickerson of Ada, Oklahoma, had died at home at age ninety-three. The reason Ms. Dickerson's death became news for more than her friends, family, and fellow Chickasaw nation members was not the fact that she was one of only sixty-five surviving fluent speakers of Chickasaw, but that she was the last *monolingual* speaker of it. Bi-coastal news organizations like National Public Radio schematized the moment as follows: "What happens when a language's last monolingual speaker dies?" The NPR story contextualized its ponderings about Dickerson's life in language as follows:

> She didn't need English. She was from a traditional community, Kali-Homma', and didn't work in a wage economy. Though the Chickasaw language is very different from English, it shares features with other Native languages. Chickasaw is a spoken language, replete with long, intricate words that have the same amount of information as a sentence or sometimes two sentences in English. Take the word *Ilooibaa-áyya'shahminattook*. This means something like "We (including you, the person I am speaking to) were there together, habitually, a long time (more than a year) ago." (K. Chow 2014)

The national newsworthiness of Dickerson's passing rested both on a particular set of assumptions about languageness and about the almost metaphysical facticity of monolingual being, just as the Chiapas communiqué had done in early 1994. The idea behind the NPR report is that something specific and discrete must *happen* when lived monolingualism passes from the world, or from a speech community. Yet to designate a ninety-three-year-old Chickasaw nation citizen "a monolingual," particularly after that nation's four-century-long struggle against displacement, genocide, and compulsory compliance with Anglophone and Francophone institutions, is both a gesture of epistemic diminution and a reinvestment in the racialized linguistics of purity that had once constructed the indigenous speaker as an object of cultural taxonomy and assimilation. Can methodology in linguistics and language studies—including comparative literature, anthropology, and second language acquisition—ever claim reliable tools with which to designate a monolingual speaker, beyond "you know it when you hear it"? Would Dickerson's purported monolinguality stand up to what Yngve calls "hard-science linguistics" (2004)? Perhaps more importantly, what experiences of indigeneity are omitted from the discourses of language when we see fit to describe Dickerson with this term?

If Emily Dickerson is to be remembered even reverently as a monolingual, the multigenerational course of events by which her "one" language *became one* must be at the core of that line of scholarly thinking, as must be the markings of this monolingualization process upon the words she herself spoke. Such a research and policy commitment across space and time is what Sinfree Makoni and Alastair Pennycook call "disinventing and reconstituting languages," the title of their 2006 collection of applied linguistics essays. An exemplary study in this alternative line of thinking is the work of the linguistic anthropologist of Yucatec Maya William Hanks, who describes in patient detail the sixteenth-century project of *reducción* in occupied Yucatán, where Spanish missionaries gradually over two centuries guided the repurposing of Mayan language(s) into a functional monolanguage, commensurate with doctrinal needs (2010). Over centuries of colonial administration, Maya speakers' linguistic practices and repertoires were made to become systematically exogamous—able and predisposed to dock translationally with liturgical Spanish in everyday interaction. Through intricate and intensive longue-durée labor, Maya was "reduced" (to use the terms the missionaries themselves used) to a monolanguage: a *Maya reducido* able to perform the institutional and symbolic functions that Catholic Castilian Spanish required of it. Hanks describes this long-term process as the result of minute, quotidian "commensurations" in the documentation, use, and usage of Maya under European colonization. In the Maya context, then, monolingualism—the fashioning of a functionally exogamous and *tempered* language—is an arduous historical process. Monolingualism's "ism" announces as much: a sedimented, practical ideology with stark consequences for individuals and communities, whose entrance into the modern often continues to be purchased by way of violent linguistic hygiene (Cameron 1995).

In Chapter 4 I will argue that what Hanks calls linguistic *reducción*—the vernacular technocratic term used by ground-level colonizers in Yucatán—is as present and formative in today's world-language system as it was during early colonization campaigns. The civic technologization of translatability—a structural shift in the early twenty-first century from state monolingualization to state multilingualization (in the European case)—results in a particular kind of sanctioned and "reduced" exogamy among languages. Consider the fatigue with which the European Commission—in its official document outlining the "rewarding challenge" of linguistic multiplicity—describes its technocratic endeavor:

> Language diversity entails constraints; it weighs on the running of European Institutions and has its cost in terms of money and time. This cost could even become prohibitive if we wanted to give dozens of languages the rightful place which their speakers could legitimately wish for. (European Commission 2008: 4)

Whereas multilingualism in the early days of the Common European Framework of Reference for Languages (1995–2000) registered as an uplifting, collaborative ideal, capable of healing rifts and emboldening world citizenship, the Framework has since necessarily aged into what I consider its *implementational turn*. This process has resulted in forms and expressions of what Robert Moore (2015) calls "reactionary multilingualism," of which the European Commission's "first come, first served" attitude to linguistic rights above is an unsurprising, though nonetheless disheartening, example. This shift toward reactionary multilingualism incurs major consequences for human rights and citizenship discourses, reconceiving as it does the relationship of speakers to states and markets—whether those speakers are citizens, denizens, or stateless persons. If, as the legal historian Samuel Moyn contends, "[t]he central event in human rights history is the recasting of rights as entitlements that might contradict the sovereign nation-state from above and outside rather than serve as its foundation" (2012: 13), then the recent selective incorporation of certain kinds of multilingual subjects in European naturalization policy discourse—as opposed to others who register as multi- or monolingual in the wrong ways—constitutes a latter-day complication in the potency of human rights discourse as a critical corrective to state power.[17]

Two responses to crisis

We have thus far explored a spectrum of ways public discourse diffusely invokes the term *monolingualism*, and how these contextual invocations most often presuppose a self-evidentiary meaning for the term. We have

17. On the translational landscape for human rights discourse, see for instance Kellman, "Omnilingual Aspirations" (2016).

speculated what the consequences of this terminological positivism may be for broader conceptions of personal, literary, and political life-in-language. Drawing on Elizabeth Ellis's work, we have also tried to come to terms with how uninterested scholarship throughout the twentieth century appears to have been toward a phenomenon such as monolingualism. It is perhaps a tribute to the recalcitrant power of monolingualism that Pierre Bourdieu—throughout his half-century of prolific scholarship on linguistic practice—never explicitly oriented his model of habitus/field to the question of mutually incomprehensible languages. (Nor, for that matter have Bakhtin, Barthes, Derrida, Kristeva, Adorno, Latour, Gramsci, Goffman, Althusser, or Foucault elaborated conceptually on mono-/multilingualism—except in the form of personal memoir, in the case of Bourdieu, Derrida, Adorno, and Kristeva.) Throughout structuralism, post-structuralism, and cultural studies, the dilemma of translational adequacy and the specific historical nature of monolingualism remained methodologically *under*-complicated and procedural issues—labors of post-production, but not quite candidates for rigorous theorization themselves.

And yet, the language crises—indeed terrors—that gave this century's first decade its mood of parochial exposure and retrenchment in the United States have led to *ad hoc* moral pronouncements about monolingualism, ranging from the acrimonious to the ruefully sober. Shortly after 9/11, leaders in North American higher education foreign language studies delivered occasional addresses that sought to identify some enduring misconceptions about the societal role of second language learning, and how these abetted monolingual thinking in both research and public life. Mary Louise Pratt's "Building a New Public Idea about Language," for one, stressed that "monolingualism should be shown to be a handicap" (Pratt 2002). A Modern Language Association committee was constituted in 2006, which reported back on the need for "translingual competence" in the humanities (MLA 2007). These timely interventions from the Modern Language Association struck some, however, as procedural directives without thorough conceptual elaboration—fruits of an exhortative discourse, characteristic of the somber crisis mood of the early War-on-Terror era. With next to no exception, monolingualism in the early 2000s remained a specter to be warned against, the Hyde to cosmopolitanism's Jekyll—but not yet a critical concept with an articulated history or form.

Over the course of monolingualism's social emergence in the 1990s and 2000s, the preconceptual force of the term remained located at the default position of the individual speaker (Djité 1994; Mughan 1999;

Crozet et al. 1999; Kirkpatrick 2000; Peel 2001). As Pratt's equation of monolingualism with handicap reveals, monolingualism was still preferentially understood as a negative possession of the individual person, an embodied disposition or naturalized predicament that requires arduous, aggressive, even moral intervention. Monolingualism *happens to someone*, and its symptoms present in the language, presence, competence, and habitus of that person. The most vivid metaphorics on this point come from Tove Skutnabb-Kangas, with her assertion that "Like cholera or leprosy, monolingualism is an illness which should be eradicated as soon as possible" (2000: 185). Others, including Oller (1997: 469) and Peel (2001), likewise take recourse to the rhetoric of blindness and disability to raise the alarm about monolingualism.

Those of us who negotiate the world with some form of actual disability or chronic illness—whether or not we dialogue with that world in one or more languages—often find these kinds of symbolic conflations disheartening. Oller has seen fit, for instance, to push even further on the clinical garishness of the word monolingualism, blending it with an "-osis" suffix, such that it is just one syllable shy of "mononucleosis": "Monoglottosis is a special blindness towards the general dependence of all sign-users on such conventions in some particular language/dialect" (1997: 469). Other scholars, such as Florian Coulmas, have taken recourse to the rhetoric of (non) awareness, helplessness, mercy, difficulty, and oblivion in characterizing the experience of monolinguals:

> Monolinguals are much more at the mercy of their language than those of us who have more than one at our command. Also, monolinguals are seldom aware of the limitations of their vocabulary whereas we remark on a daily basis that a certain word doesn't match the concept we want to express or that a lexical differentiation in one language has no direct counterpart in another. (2007: 6)

As the War on Terror aged, the exhortative campaign against monolingualism split into two directions. One camp continued to sloganize against monolingualism in hopes of agitating for bolstered political and fiscal support for traditional language-learning curricula and multilingual social services. Another camp, however, began to reconceive the challenge of multilingualism as one that pertains not at the level of the individual citizen/language learner, but rather in the ways firms, networks, markets, divisions of labor, and supply chains are designed in linguistic terms.

The first, traditional position in the later War-on-Terror era of language ideology—which we may consider a rhetoric of "multilingualism as enlightenment"—was given voice at the 2013 Asia Society Chinese Language Conference, where Gregg Roberts, world languages and dual immersion specialist, Utah State Office of Education, announced that "Monolingualism is the illiteracy of the 21st century." Programmatic, visionary, and corrective *interventions* about the apparently overt social fact of monolingualism continued to abound, filling the rhetorical gap where explicit conceptual exploration had been slow to emerge in the methodological discussions of various disciplines, from political theory, to literature, to anthropology, or even applied linguistics. The good news coming from this traditional camp continued to be that individuals and populations, perhaps even whole societies, can be relieved of the symptoms of monolingualism by engaging in intensive and guided language study—preferably at an early age, but any age will do. Health benefits will abound. Heritage learners need to be encouraged and invited to draw on their multilingual subjectivity in public and higher education, before their experiences of their other languages, as Julia Kristeva describes in *Strangers to Ourselves*, dissipate "like a secret vault—or a handicapped child—cherished and useless—that language of the past that withers without ever leaving you" (1990: 15).

At the same time, a second trend took hold in how (and whether) commercial "stakeholders" approached monolingualism as a problem. In January 2012, former Harvard president and treasury secretary Lawrence Summers sparked unified, stunned consternation among U.S. foreign language teachers. In a *New York Times* editorial blithely titled "What you (really) need to know," Summers assured *Times* readers that:

> English's emergence as the global language, along with the rapid progress in machine translation and the fragmentation of languages spoken around the world, make it less clear that the substantial investment necessary to speak a foreign tongue is universally worthwhile. While there is no gainsaying the insights that come from mastering a language, it will over time become less essential in doing business in Asia, treating patients in Africa or helping resolve conflicts in the Middle East. (2012)

This set of claims met with immediate shock from academics, certain as we tend to be of the essential value of being more-than-monolingual. But it did not generate much thought on why Summers's cosmopolitan monolingualism had become an intuitive option in the early twenty-first century we have come to understand, with Yildiz (2012), as "postmonolingual." Summers's argument relies on the twofold gesture of diagnosing "fragmentation" among the world's spoken languages and then reinvesting in a kind of structural-functionalist global metalanguage map—comprising business-in-Asia, conflict-in-the-Middle-East, and illness-in-Africa. These pragmatic arenas of "knowledge transfer" are, for Summers, the global "languages" of the twenty-first century, which will be managed through the translational media of global business English, Mandarin, pidgin subsidiaries, and translation technologies, while traditional, so-called peripheral languages have become too fragmentary to do so reliably. Summers's functionalist vision for the twenty-first-century global map of metalanguages recalled Holy Roman Emperor Charles V's self-reported multilingualism, i.e. worship-in-Spanish, heterosociality-in-Italian, homosociality-in-French, and equestrianism-in-German. The difference is that Summers's vision foregoes any need for multilingual competence altogether among young Anglophone entre-preneurs preparing for global power.

It is worth thinking through Summers's approach to see both its method and its madness, and what both may have to do with the workings of monolingualism. It is clear through the hedging in the latter part of his first sentence that Summers has in mind a strategic monolingualism, usable in all manner of global negotiation, one which heralds as progressive the offshoring of languages to those non-Americans who, history shows, are simply better at languages than those sedentary Anglophones who might be tempted to struggle their way into functional multilingualism. Since the global student and creative-commercial class abroad have been successfully "skilling themselves up" linguistically through English-medium universities and apparently multilingual mnemotechnologies like Google Translate, the Anglophone metropole (here embodied in Secretary Summers) has factored this offshore upskilling into their balance sheet—namely, with a corresponding prescriptive downskilling of the U.S.-based workforce toward a focus on technical and business acumen rather than language learning. From a "Varieties of Capitalism" standpoint, this managerial strategy reflects the objectively declining asset value for language learning in LMEs (liberal market economies), given the unflexible asset-specificity of individual languages (Hancké 2009: 3). That is, learning Tigrinya or Dutch has a much lower market value in 2016 than it did in 1976, because a) more speakers in those languages can work in English, b) fewer transnational corporations operate in a one- or two-language market alone, and c) translational technologies have reshaped languages in such a way that the surplus value of personal fluency has become a boutique "intangible" x-factor, rather than a sine qua non for complex commercial relationships. What scholars in Second Language Studies call "symbolic competence" (Kramsch 2006) is simply too expensive and "unswitchable" (to use the idiom of Varieties of Capitalism) to sustain on a sequentially bilateral basis through the upskilling of personnel. Speculatively, we may understand Summers's metalinguistic model of global preparedness as a latter-day analogue to the commensuration process Hanks observes in seventeenth-century colonial Yucatán. In both cases, languages are envisioned, reformed, and reduced so as to dock with the functional requirements of a set of globalizing metalanguages keyed to particular commercial or doctrinal arenas.

So what Secretary Summers proposes "you (really) need to know" was ultimately something rather different from a cosmopolitan monolingualism based on general forms of intercultural knowledge for building global bridges of understanding. Despite his former ministerial post in the federal government, Summers envisions something less politically visionary, and more technically exacting, than the constitutional, coordinated-market multilingualism expected of citizens in "pedagogical states" like Germany. Summers is not so much betting against individual language learning—as it is promoted by the Modern Language Association and other academic spokespersons noted above—as much as he is betting on a new technocratic model of global information management that demotes the market value of advanced foreign language proficiency.

Warm fuzzy monolingualism

It would be tempting to regard Summers's essay as quite an avant-garde sally indeed—one as brash, inconsiderate, and baseless as its title suggests. But it is not. While humanities scholars spent the 2000s promoting multilingualism and symbolically de-competencing monolingualism, computer engineers were engaged just as sanguinely in an attempt to harness the multilingual world in ways that would place it in closer grasp for those muddling their way through what Peel (2001) called "the monotony of the monoglots." Summers was well aware that, in the twenty-first century, the "monolingualism of the other" was not apt to be the colonial language of French, as it had been for Derrida in his twentieth century, but rather the language of Base 2.

Even the title of Fusa Katada's short 2002 paper "The Linguistic Divide, Autolinguals, and Education-for-All," published a full ten years ahead of Summers's controversial *Times* editorial, encapsulates the optimistic horizon that computer engineers had set for themselves in the late 1990s. It clarifies why Summers is no avant-garde in his investment in postmultilingualism, but rather a retrospective observer. Writing from her post at Waseda University in Japan, Katada claims in 2002 that English language learning in "English-nonnative" countries like her own will never be adequate for the task of global information and education management, always leaving a "linguistic disparity" that reproduces injustice and inequality of access. Here is her subtly astonishing historical reasoning:

> Despite such zeal and efforts for mastering English, it is unrealistic to expect that the nonnative-English world achieves a level of competence similar to that of the native-English world; hence the "linguistic disparity." If English is taught early enough, powerful bilingualism may be achieved, and we may expect it to be a possible solution. However, this expectation may even be questionable as we see in California Spanish–English bilingual education which, everyone seems to agree, did not work very well (ABC *World News Tonight* 6/1/98), even in the English speaking world. (2002, n.p.)

Katada continues with a cost-benefit analysis of English language learning in Japan and suggests that the United States' historical experiment in bilingualism in educational contexts (as glossed by *World News Tonight*) bodes less well than do other technical solutions, such as the proposed "Autolingual." This device, under development at the Nikkei University, would use a Universal Networking Language, such that "It would no longer be a dream that papers written in French are directly read in Swahili on the Internet" (Katada 2002).

My purpose in sharing Katada's visionary gesture from 2002 is precisely not to find fault with a colleague in another discipline, nor to cast doubt on her historical reasoning about the persistence of linguistic disparity in nonnative English settings. To the contrary, I wish to suggest that Katada's rhetorical stance—of seeking durable solutions for the good of the majority of the developing and non-Anglophone speech communities of the world—is not only quite mainstream in the computational sciences, but is also unimpeachably progressive in its own idiom and context. Indeed, the engineers of postmultilingualism since 2000 have effused with an eagerness to help allay intransigent imbalances in access to precious (linguistically mediated) commodities, and have done their due diligence, in the sense that they use their training and the tools available to them to do precisely that. Consider this opening salvo about the problem of multilingualism from the Maryland-based computer scientist Douglas Oard, in his 2006 essay "Transcending the Tower of Babel: Supporting Access to Multilingual Information with Cross-Language Information Retrieval". Writing from amid the heated and urgent early days of the U.S. War on Terror, Oard begins by reflecting back on the last decade of progress:

> We have come a long way toward seamless access to the information needed for commerce, security, and society. Language, however, has the potential to balkanize the information space. (2006: 299)

It is difficult to disregard the mirthful spirit of this assessment, which epitomizes the lion's share of the literature in computational engineering around mono-/multilingualism. In computer science departments, often housed only a short walk away from modern language buildings, monolingualism is a workaday, load-bearing concept—free of suspicion, disfavor, or rancor. It is problematic only to the extent that it presents engineering difficulties. It ought to be no surprise, then, that a Web search for "multilingual" and "monolingual" deliver page after page of research in computational engineering, rather than, say, on Chican@ poetry or Bengali language learners.

Perhaps a brief retrospective glance will help contextualize Oard's triumphalism, as well as the accompanying burst in postmultilingual engineering around the U.S. Department of Defense's vigorous discovery of critical languages in the early War-on-Terror period.[18] Machine translating, up until the 1990s, had been rule-based, predicated on finding grammatical constants within individual languages like Dutch or Mandarin, according to which an obedient, rule-following machine could make a dependable, readable, passable translation. Most businesses and institutions involved in global information retrieval, then as now, have no real and consistent need for anything far beyond this level of translational passability for prose texts that primarily

---

18. For an introduction see Karmani "TESOL in a Time of Terror" (2005). See also Emily Apter's short essay "Translation after 9/11" (2005).

interact with human readers. The switch from this prescriptive mode of mechanical translating, based on correctness, to a descriptive mode based on corpus data from human-generated documents, foregrounded appropriateness of use, rather than correctness of usage. With increasingly massive corpora of prose at its disposal, mechanical translation was now wise to how humans actually speak and write, rather than how they perhaps should speak and write according to grammar books. Increasingly sophisticated algorithms over the course of the 2000s mined these corpora in search of a more and more dependable basis upon which to ground what came to be called "cross-linguistic fuzzy ontologies" (Cross and Voss 2000).

A "fuzzy ontology" meant a relatively accurate predictive algorithm about what it is that most people appropriately say in Tagalog for a potential corresponding phenomenon in Yoruba, based on massive amounts of corpus data. For major language pairs like English–French or Spanish–Russian, such equivalents had already been available from prior human-identified translingual synonymies. What wasn't available yet in 2000 was immediate cross-lingual data retrieval access to documents in less commonly paired languages like, say, Japanese and Estonian. For this, one could turn to an intermediary pivot language, like English. But most programmers sought a better solution: developing what they called fuzzy cross-linguistic algorithm queries or fuzzy cross-language ontologies. Here was one definition that two researchers, Valerie Cross at the University of North Carolina, Charlotte, and Clare Voss of the Army Research Laboratory at Adelphi, Maryland, offered early on:

> A *cross-language ontology* is an ontology whose concepts are *lexicalized* in more than one language. That is, each core node in the ontology represents an abstract concept and has associated with it a "label" (a word or phrase) that identifies it in a natural language, given that concepts must be expressed in the vocabulary of some natural language. (Cross and Voss 2000: 642)

By establishing a "fuzzy" associative realm around one concept in Japanese and a workably equivalent fuzzy realm in Estonian, automated retrieval could hone in on targeted cross-linguistic data exchanges between them.

Let's be CLIR

Since 2000, Cross-Linguistic Information Retrieval (CLIR) engineers like Cross, Voss, and Oard have been engaged in this endeavor to establish a reliable grid of "synsets" and "cross-language ontologies" between pair lexicalizations in heretofore unacquainted languages, such that data management can occur not through translation as traditionally conceived, but through *synonymy*, a word in frequent use in CLIR literature. What is being generated, then, is a new (and hegemonic) translingual axis of signification, in which—corresponding to the Saussurian model—a signified in one language is tied to a signifier in another. Under this regime of technocratic multilingualism, the general relationship of signification has necessarily shifted ninety degrees, from the traditional intralingual dyad to a translingual routing system of sign to meaning. Under such a regime, languages are to become effectively exogamous, producing a traffic in meaning that, in its bid to flatten the semiodiverse inherencies in each language, is monolingual.

Consider the following assessment, now ten years old, on the state of the art of CLIR:

> When well integrated, it is possible to exceed 100% of a credible monolingual baseline system's mean average precision using these techniques [of Cross-Linguistic Information Retrieval]. It may seem surprising at first that any cross-language technique could exceed a monolingual baseline, but this merely points up a limitation of comparative evaluation; it is difficult to introduce synonyms in monolingual systems in a manner that is comparable to the synonyms that are naturally introduced as a byproduct of translation, so (relatively weak) monolingual baselines that lack synonym expansion are often reported. (Oard 2006: 305)

This is a fascinating claim: namely that multilingual information retrieval delivers comparably more reliable results than monolingual information retrieval does, because monolingual data sets (say in English) have no strongly normative expert system of internal synonyms that can enable a fuzzy algorithm to capture the searcher's desired information. While CLIR has already developed a dependable infrastructure through the process of establishing and standardizing synsets (cross-linguistic ontologies), languages themselves meanwhile remain internally mushy, unpredictable, and impervious to organization.

One way to understand what is occurring with mechanical translating in the context of CLIR is that a kind of interlanguage highway system is being established through synsets, which makes data travel from language to language easier, while travel within a given language is still awkward, round-about, and often counter-intuitive. We can see this process at work in how algorithmic synsets and cross-linguistic ontologies are pursued and in how subsequent documents are produced multilingually through a combination of fuzzy algorithms, corpus-based mechanical translation procedures, human editors, and quality control personnel. In this centripetal large-scale system of human and algorithmic practices of translation, which I call the linguacene, monolingualism and multilingualism cease to mean what they may have only twenty years ago. Let us now shift focus away from the engineering back-end of the linguacene, and toward an example of the kind of users and user interfaces they produce.

Language hacks

In December 2010, an anonymous internet personality named Komedi Kral (Turkish for Comedy King) put out a call-to-action on Facebook, to which over 500 users had already responded, and which 1,500 people had "liked"—all of them Turkish speakers. The prompt read, in Turkish: "Go to Google Translate, choose English-to-Turkish, enter the word 'eğitime' ["education," dative case] and let's see what comes out." This prompt had been forwarded to me by a former student living in Ankara, along with a note saying "David hocam bir bakar mısınız?" ("Teacher David, would you look at this?").[19] I wondered what could be so compelling as to incite more than a thousand users of Facebook to flash-mob the Turkish word for *education*. I typed in *eğitime* and, at the right of my screen, I got my results in Turkish: "*ihtiyacımız yok*" (= "*We don't need no*").

In the emerging translational infrastructure of postmultilingualism, this was something that simply wasn't supposed to be able to happen. Google Translate provides equivalents on the paradigmatic axis, not predicates on the syntagmatic one. The clean, well-lighted space of Google Translate—hard-won after seventy-five years of humbling folly in mechanical translation (Lennon 2012)—was a ceremonial space where only certain transformations were permitted. "We don't need no = Education" broke the doxa of translingual

19. I thank Nurulhude Baykal for sharing Komedi Kral with me.

equation; it revealed another possible world, in which technologies of translation aren't measured on their efficiency and accuracy but on their performative, citational grandeur. This "monolingual" code-unswitching non-translation "We don't need no education" *re-minded* us, repoliticizing and recollectivizing a space of public practice about which classical political theory as yet had little to say.

Most of the initial respondents on Facebook did indeed get the joke; some indicated so by dragging out their aghast response *yok!* ("no") into *yoooooook xD!*, expressing not only their bliss in the translingual counter-syntax emerging before their eyes across the forbidden interstices of the technology, but also their own critical eagerness to obfuscate the global hubris of Google Translate. Only one of the ten initial, almost instantaneous commentators really didn't know what was going on, and indicated as much by typing in "*Ne çıkıyo ya*"—an expression of smug impatience, along the lines of "Well, so, what was it then?"

Commenter 17 of 457 first took the step of articulating the whole "sentence" as a piece— *We don't need no education*—to which the very next user responded: *Why not?* This user's guileless move met with a gaggle of cyber-laughter, after which the unfortunate straight-man commenter recovered, less than a minute later, with a congenial "Oh, ok, now I get it" ("*Ha tamam şimdi anladım*"). A minute (and fifty commenters) later, one technocratically minded user mused about the utterance at hand: "Even the internet knows [we don't need no education!]" ("*internet bile biliyo :P*"), and another, this time an epistemologist, added "Ah super, how does google know facts like this?" ("*ayy süper ya google nası da biliyo gerçekleri :D*"). At long last came the ethnonational interpretation, "Dude, what do you expect from our turks. I mean, look at this language!" ("*lan zaten bizim türklerden ne beklersn şu dile bakk*") (Komedi Kral 2010). Within thirty-five minutes, the conversation had taken its due course toward how amazing Pink Floyd is, while other contributors began to suggest their own "x" values for others to translingually solve for, by collectively "misusing" Google Translate.

It is doubtful that the curator of this hack, the anonymous Comedy King, had struck out from his or her IP address on Christmas Day 2010 to incite critical intervention about "translational monolingualism as a means of production in global cognitive capitalism." But the sensibility of the language hack did prompt a public gathering, an ephemeral online experiment in what Michel de Certeau called "*la perruque*" (the wig)—the "appropriate misuse" of authoritative materials:

La perruque is the worker's own work disguised as work for his employer. It differs from pilfering in that nothing of material value is stolen. It differs from absenteeism in that the worker is officially on the job. La perruque may be as simple a matter as a secretary's writing a love letter on "company time" or as complex as a cabinetmaker's "borrowing" a lathe to make a piece of furniture for his living room. Under different names in different countries this phenomenon is becoming more and more general, even if managers penalize it or "turn a blind eye" on it in order not to know about it. (de Certeau 2011 [1980]: 25)

Though de Certeau's tactical sensibility about "practices of everyday life" had been thought out in more classical relations of production—those of the factory and workshop—his conceptual bearing seems even more apt in an age when the workplace technology in question is not a lathe or a smelting iron, but a rainbow-colored search-engine page that promises few occupational hazards on first inspection. And yet Google Translate, unlike the lathe or the iron, is at least potentially interpellative in all moments along a user's work–labor–leisure–play life spectrum. Efforts to maintain behavioral boundaries between these realms are increasingly all but quaint in the age of flexible cybercommuting and just-in-time supply-chain management (Standing 2011: 117).

Google Translate as precarian workplace

The liberal market presumption—that these Turkish-language users of Translate can always and everywhere use this translational mnemo-technology—only increases the corresponding normative demands on their memory, time, literacy, and symbolic productivity. Google Translate becomes an internal organ of the twenty-first-century World Englishes workforce in its negotiation with both the "monolingualism of the other" and the "multilingualism of the other," as online means of language production become a cognitive prosthetic that enhances all language users' *hypomnesic* access to translatedness, through a technical exteriorization of memory.[20] Hundreds of millions of students and knowledge workers globally avail themselves everyday of the

---

20. On the notion of "the multilingualism of the other," see Kramsch (2011). On hypomnesic technologies and the "industrial exteriorization of memory," see Stiegler (2010).

increasingly compulsory technologies of immediate translatedness. It is thus one of the goals animating this book to understand the monolingual claim (in both the propositional and political senses of the word "claim") that *We don't need no education, we don't need no thought control* makes. How is it that these young people, the diffuse global constituency of multilinguals in an age of cognitive capitalism, *use* monolingualism—as a critical rhetoric that does not simply end in linguistic nationalism?

Importantly, next to no English (nor any other language) was used throughout all 457 comments during this one emergent online event, except for a few incantatory uses of the single English word "education." What we might be tempted to call linguistic purism seems to have been the ideology underlying this utterance, seeing as all respondents spontaneously acceded to Turkish without prior agreement. Still, the whole congregation swirled around a magnetic catchphrase of English extraction, first popularized in 1979 on Pink Floyd's rock-opera album *Another Brick in the Wall*. Pink Floyd is uniquely beloved among generation after generation of young Turkish and Kurdish critics of empire, and the band often serves as a mnemonic device for the populist insurgencies of the era prior to Turkey's September 12, 1980 coup d'état.

We could indeed conclude that the surface-level monolingualism of the Facebook incident is but a threadbare cloak upon a deeper, ultimately multilingual hypotext (Genette 1997). In this line of thinking, *We don't need no education* performs a half-hearted post-ironic gesture toward the Erasmus Exchange infrastructure and the Cambridge English Language Assessment systems, which exert a profound impact on how, why, and when students in Turkey "get education" in certain forms of English. The slogan also potentially ironizes the omnipresent transcultural domestication of products emanating from the Anglophone metropole since customs reform in the 1980s, including anthems of political survival and insurgency shared among Turkish and British youth. But, resolving that surface monolingualism conceals truly existing multilingualism is itself a political claim that obscures, in this case, the means by which speakers "reconfigure the materiality of public space, and produce, or reproduce, the public character of that material environment" (Butler 2011). The 1,500 participants in this thread did, after all, eschew translingual conversationality altogether, opting for a kind of strategic monolingualism.[21] I view this moment, in Arendt's terms, as one of political appearance, in which a certain class of emergent

---

21. On "translingual conversationality," see Warner and Chen, forthcoming.

English-language laborers seize the *bios politikos* of corporate translation—a transnational, technocratic state without a traditional public sphere. Indeed, the fact that such online platforms as Facebook later played a crucial role in disseminating information among activists about police incursions during the Gezi Park uprisings of June 2013 strengthens the sense that online platforms like these are indeed constitutive of an active counter-public or political sphere.

The logic of postmultilingualism

If we do nonetheless view the outburst *We don't need no education* as crypto-multilingualism of some sort, it seems consequently to be an index of the emergence Yasemin Yildiz has recently described, in her compelling book *Beyond the Mother Tongue*, as a postmonolingual condition:

> This "post" [in postmonolingual] has, in the first place, a temporal dimension: it signifies the period *since* the emergence of monolingualism as dominant paradigm, which first occurred in late eighteenth-century Europe. Such a historicized understanding underscores the radical difference between multilingualism before and after the monolingual paradigm, a difference that previous studies have neglected [...] But besides this temporal dimension, the prefix "post" also has a critical function, where it refers to the opposition to the term that it qualifies and to a potential break with it, as in some notions of postmodernism. In this second sense, "postmonolingual" highlights the struggle *against* the monolingual paradigm. (2012: 4)

In the combined critical and temporal sense in which she uses the term, Yildiz envisions the postmonolingual condition as having begun to evanesce even as it was institutionalized in the late eighteenth century, generating resistance practices all along the way in literature, law, family, social relations, and in the very nature of language. Taking as our guide this composite critical-temporal notion of a "postness" in monolingualism, one that oscillates "between continuity and rupture" (Hirsch 2008: 106), we could view the *no education* performance as evoking several, ambiguous intensities:

- A domestic appropriation and retooling of the Anglophone world's own critiques of power (i.e. through Pink Floyd's anthem).

- A rejection of the hyperobject of English as a primary medium for knowledge by banishing it from the technology, while using it as a source language for a translated intervention that, in turn, rejects a translation culture predicated on U.S.-headquartered corporate capital.[22]
- A participation in, and citation of, modern histories of translingual practice and appropriation (a prevalent long-standing love of Pink Floyd among politicized Turkish youth), as opposed to partaking in "pure Turkish" cultural production sources alone.
- A reiterative valorization of the Turkish language as a mode of global "panoramic address" to the metropole (Saktanber 2002: 269).
- A provisional repossession and resocialization of the space of translation (Google Translate) for practices other than discrete, commercial, and functional decoding by individual users.

All of these things are arguably taking place in the laconic, reiterative slogan *Eğitime ihtiyacımız yok* [*We don't need no education*]. And yet, the collective enunciation on Facebook sought less to overcome *monolingualism* than to caricature a certain kind of *multilingualism*—delivered to users' doorsteps by Google Headquarters in Mountain View, California—in order to rehearse a kind of revivified monolingualism. The criticality of the utterance is squarely directed at the role of translation and translatability in global relations of production. There seems neither to be any temporal "post-" at work in this campaign, nor any vision of a world after monolingualism. In a dynamic system of global language-learning institutions and translation "tools," treasury secretary Lawrence Summers's Anglophone gesture *What you (really) need to know* finds itself in a complex global call-and-response relationship with the Turkophone rebuttal *We don't need no education / Eğitime ihtiyacımız yok.*

A twenty-year-old Turkish student named Necati describes (in English) the thinly veiled ambivalence among his own school classmates between multilingual orthodoxy and monolingual resistance:

> It was in "ortaokul" [middle school] that I was first introduced to the battlefield [of languages] and had to choose a side to fight for. I would either side with the Republic, English and other pervasive languages,

22. On "hyperobjects" see Morton (2013) and the Afterword to the current book.

or with the Rebel Army, Turkish. Since till that age we were brain-washed nonstop, I did as my class teacher bid and joined the ranks of rebellion [...] And (this is for all my previous teachers telling me that a paragraph can not start with "and"; apparently it can) that's when I saw the true face of the war, the two sides, the purpose, and decided on which army to side with: None! I neither support that Turkish should be the only one and that English must be purged from Turkey, nor I support a world where there is monolingualism with English and even more languages are now dead because of it.[23]

Here Necati stylizes his own linguistic sovereignty not by way of, but *against* membership in a rebel army, led by his rebel teacher, who advocated for the adversely positioned Turkish language in a field of institutional practices dominated by English competence acquisition and Kemalist étatism. For his rebel teacher, speaking Turkish was a collective resistance practice in a state-regulated schooling system that imagined the ideal educated individual as a multilingual whose languages of academic discourse were English, French, or perhaps in some situations German—but not Turkish. Indeed, Turkey's president Tayyip Erdoğan recently gave voice to this cultural politics of an elite "multilingualism of the other" (Kramsch 2011), when he claimed at a 2014 awards ceremony for the Scientific and Technological Research Council of Turkey (Tübitak) that "You can't do philolosphy in Turkish. You need to use Ottoman or English. These problems must be solved not by the state but by researchers."[24] Necati's teacher framed such elite multilingualisms (particularly those that include English) as a position of vulnerability toward state manipulation, whereas Turkish-only, or Turkish-Kurdish repertoires maintain a grass-roots, Anatolian populism that strives toward an organic historical coherence predating the Republic, and even predating the Ottoman Empire. Necati thus situates himself above a contentious field of populist rebel monolinguals-of-the-will and etatist hegemonic Anglophone multilinguals, and refuses (in English and in retrospect) to be claimed by either encampment.

23. This and other testimonies included in this book emerged from a study I conducted among university students at an English-medium institution in Turkey in Spring 2010. All names are anonymized, and I thank the student participants for sharing their insights. Bracketed notes are mine.

24. CNN Turk (2014). "Türkçe ile felsefe yapamazsınız. Ya Osmanlıca ya İngilizce kullanmanız lazım. Bu sorunlar devlet eliyle değil, bilim adamları eliyle çözülmeli."

The sensibility that Necati describes above among his middle-school classmates shows a profound ambivalence toward the critical, as well as the temporal, "postness" of the postmonolingual condition. What seems at work in Necati's account of his multilingual experience is rather a strategic monolingualism, or *postmultilingualism*, with an emergent criticality of its own. Though such stances are most often read as the unfortunate results of reactionary nationalist retrenchment, they are increasingly finding their way into the figurality of twenty-first-century world literature, where for example the protagonist of Nobel laureate Orhan Pamuk's 2002 novel *Snow*, just returned to Turkey after twelve years of political exile in Germany, tells his readers: "The thing that saved me was not learning German [...] My body rejected the language, and that was how I was able to preserve my purity and my soul" (Pamuk 2004 [2002]: 33). The novel's narrator then elaborates: "Because [Ka] could not understand the language, he felt as safe, as comfortable, as if he were sitting in his own house, and this was when he wrote his poems" (33).

Though Pamuk's Ka here describes his deliberate monolingualism in a rhetorical register untypical of discourses on cultural politics around language, his choice is clearly not tantamount to a commitment to Turkishness, nor a refutation of cosmopolitanism. Unlike the jingoistic harpings of an English-only lobbyist in the United States, Ka rather expresses a modest, defensive desire to safeguard the continued creative capacities of his own language as a poet. Nonetheless, such statements as Ka's are most often conflated with the xenophobic ideologies of Turkey's Nationalist Movement Party. Indeed, in a volume on *Intercultural Communication in Action*, Francis Jarman reads Ka's decision as one typical of "those who are frightened of losing their cultural *identity*, as a consequence of being in an alien cultural environment, [for whom] it is essential to maintain a psychological cocoon" (2012: 204). Such a psychologizing assessment, often openly ascribed to immigrants in Europe, participates in the conventional presumption that monolingualism is nothing more than an outcropping of reactionary ethnonationalism. Indeed, such sentiments linking language choice to religious political extremism are explicitly charted out in the European Commission's 2008 report "A Rewarding Challenge. How the Multiplicity of Languages Could Strengthen Europe," sometimes referenced as the Maalouf report. The committee's chair, Amin Maalouf, a Lebanese-born Christian residing in Paris since the 1970s, glosses such linguistic predicaments as Pamuk's Ka experiences in the following terms:

Excessive assertion of identity often stems from a feeling of guilt in relation to one's culture of origin, a guilt which is sometimes expressed by exacerbated religion-based reactions. To describe it differently, the immigrant or a person whose origins lie in immigration and is able to speak his mother tongue and would be able to teach it to his children, knowing that his language and culture of origin are respected in the host society, would have less need to assuage his thirst for identity in another way. (European Commission 2008: 20)

Pamuk's choice to have his protagonist Ka so explicitly reject the elite publishing language of German, and with it the European Commission's paternalistic psychologization of language choice, parallels the Facebook campaign in its structure and taciturnity. Just as the Turkish online commenters availed themselves of a global translational platform like Google Translate precisely in order to generate a "monolingual sentence,"[25] Pamuk used his only self-described "political novel"—a novel that would clinch for him not only the Nobel Prize but Germany's prestigious Peace Prize of the Frankfurt Book Fair—as a narrative staging for what Emily Apter imagines as a "right to untranslatability" (Apter 2013). These monolingualisms that Necati and Ka choose for themselves could thus be seen as *capacitating* monolingualisms, as they allow their users to do more densely creative work with their vernacular language than does the (monetized) translational multilingualism that interpellates them.

In contrast to this capacitating monolingualism that Pamuk's Ka and my student Necati claim for themselves, Summers's educational-resource-management model of language learning, which holds that some individuals in a global free market can and should rely on others' language competences in order to realize their own goals and bottom lines, would more accurately be called a *hypomnesic* monolingualism (Stiegler 2010: 37). In this model, elite and well-connected monolinguals can systemically store codes and meanings in others' minds and cultures, calling upon them when necessary for global business and diplomacy. As a feature of what Boutang Moulier calls cognitive capitalism (2011), offshore workers' multilingual labor helps business elites concentrate on what "really" matters for their respective

25. It may be noted that the apparently monolingual Turkish sentence "We don't need no education / Eğitime ihtiyacimiz yok" is obviously translingual to the extend that *ihtiyac* is also a loan word from Arabic.

daily enterprises. A recent Xerox commercial featuring the motorcycle concern Ducati Enterprises offers a diorama of global liberal-market multi-/monolingualism. In the advert, a middle-management office worker enters into a motorcycle test-drive chamber, where a helmeted rider is enduring a simulated high-speed ride against a stream of high-intensity wind, piped in for the purpose of the test. From the side of the test chamber, the office worker meekly approaches the unresponsive test rider and says: "Management just sent over these technical manuals. They need you to translate them into Portuguese. By tomorrow." At this point, the office worker loses his grip on the paperwork, and the pages scatter irrecoverably into the simulated wind, dramatizing the messiness and inefficiency of mixing multilingual translating with other kinds of R&D innovation. The moral of this story is spelled out in a voice-over as follows: "Ducati knows it's better for Xerox to manage their global publications, so they can focus on making amazing bikes. With Xerox, you're ready for real business."

The scattering of the staffer's papers, amid the wind of the test chamber, confirms Summers's prophylactic claims about the "fragmentation of the world's spoken languages"—clunky and unworkable local repertoires from which global business interactions need to be structurally insulated, through switchable-asset protocols like Cross-Linguistic Information Retrieval algorithms. This rechanneling of the global language system is to take place through a functionalist segregational discourse that creates a class of multilingual workers, corresponding roughly with the ancient Greek *banusoi* and *metics*, i.e. outsiders too busy laboring for the infrastructure of the *polis* to take part either in work or *phila* (civic friendship). Hypomnesic monolingualism outsources linguistic *labor* so that entrepreneurs can focus on thoughtful innovative *work*.

Given a global multilingual worker class held in technological relation with a managerial sphere of cosmopolitan monolingualists like Summers,[26] who do sometimes speak other languages, but not as their "real business," what exactly *was* the "appropriate misuse" of Google Translate that these young Turkish speakers found so worthy of sharing in 2010, and what should we call the epistemic paradigm they were hacking? Were these Facebook commenters borrowing from their employer of the moment (the global factory floor of mercantile plurilingualism) in order to make some phatic fun for domestic use (a.k.a.

---

26. For a literary dramatization of this relation, see Chetan Bhagat's novel *One Night @ the Call Center* (2005).

vernacular monolingualism) among friends? Given that many lower- and middle-class Turkish college students do English–Turkish and Turkish–English translations for their wealthier peers as informal labor alongside their studies, Google Translate is an essential component of the means of production for a growing professional creative class, rather than merely an occasionally useful "tool available to all." So what was the phenomenon that Comedy King's intervention called to account: multilingualism, monolingualism, translation, or something else altogether?

The social lives of language pairs

We could on the one hand say this was a rejection of a certain type of exchange value on the global free market in multilingualism. As Google Translate clears the path of linguistic commensurability for all and for a universal future-anterior of translatedness—substituting, in no less than triumphal fashion, one language with all of its various others at once—more than a thousand participant observers were inclined to envision an alternative. They used Google Translate not as a tool for *translational substitution* but as a staging area for *syntactical articulation* (Jakobson 1960). Where the tool they were asked to use assumed that functional equivalence was its only valuable purpose for them, the users produced rather an aesthetic syntagm: a grammatically correct phrase, a charismatic relation of subject and object. What had been implanted into their own linguistic ecologies as an expedient technology on the globalized paradigmatic axis of tempered languages was now rotated ninety degrees to become a kind of code-unswitching, amplified and reanimated through choral response.

This tradition of cultural politics around *not* code-switching is one that Till Dembeck describes as follows, in his study of Oscar Pastior's homophonic surface translations, or "intonations," of Charles Baudelaire's poems:

> The specific culture-political impact of homophonic translation [...] lies in the fact that it aims to highlight continuity where the "monolingual paradigm" presupposes rupture. It opens a semantic space between *langues* and makes them communicate in a way that seems to be systematically ruled out [...] Homophonic translation potentiates this effect in that it applies a constraint that de-naturalizes the commonplace relation between two *langues*, and

thereby not only the notion of *langue* as such, but also prevailing notions of multilingualism. (2015: 20)

Dembeck's insight here is that the kind of linguistic disinvention and reconstitution (Makoni and Pennycook 2006) that emerges in homophonic translation—of which the Facebook prank is, I claim, a meta-formal instance—is no mere language play, in the sense of a carnivalesque reconfiguration of otherwise mundane materials. Its cultural politics is one that shores up the structural underpinnings of "lingualism" (whether mono- or multi-), the ways these underpinnings are maintained by certain technologies of translation, and the constraints these exert on the political doxa of meaning-making in the most varied of contexts.

In the course of her work translating the French philosopher Gilles Tiberghien's monograph *Amitier*, the poet Cole Swensen helps to transfigure this doxa of paradigmatic substitution into a kind of social co-presence, alternatively imagining the relation of translingual syntax as one of awkward friendship:

> The fact that the etymologies of the English and the French words for this state [of "friendship"/"amité"] are not the same got me to thinking about etymology itself as a basis of friendships, and thus about which languages are friends with which others, or not—and which are relatives—and how close—which are siblings, which are cousins, and which are of such mixed parentage that there's bound to be conflict or at least a few really, really awkward moments at family gatherings— which, in our field, we call translations. (Swensen 2014: 149–50)

What Swensen is offering is the opportunity to resocialize languages in relation to one another, beyond their Mercatorian emplacement on a global map or market supply chain. Let us imagine this potential for vernacular rotation on Google Translate a bit further, bearing in mind that it is produced upon, and because of, a constellation of transnational mnemotechnologies that compel new kinds of social lives and linguistic capacities for those who use them. As mentioned, platforms like Google Translate are the very means of production for much academic writing in Turkey, where the educational hierarchy has long been predominated by English-medium institutions. That being the case, this monolingual utterance on Facebook pulses with a critical undercurrent about translation tools, a tenor unimaginable even at the end of the twentieth century.

It is unclear whether Komedi Kral's posting on Christmas Day in 2010 counts as an artifact of monolingualism, or multilingualism—and if the latter, what kind? What conceptions of language use were being trumpeted here, what notions of *translatability* were being pilloried—and why? What linguistic and technological relationship to the British/Anglophone/NATO/Special-Relationship metropole does it rehearse, with Pink Floyd as its guiding anthem? How was the utterance newly performative? Contemporary and fleeting as it was, this mechanically produced utterance is now already an obsolete artifact of translation archaeology (Pym 1998). Since this performance in 2010, Google Translate has learned to detect input languages while one types, such that the designative action triggering the translingual resistance anthem *We don't need no education / Eğitime ihtiyacımız yok* in 2010, namely inserting a Turkish word into the English field, is no longer technically possible. Thus the subversively translingual syntax hacked only six years ago can no longer be produced, and the record of its having been possible is as illegible now in the internet archive as a Gallic inscription.

Unmarking histories of monolingualisms

The Facebook thread is thus now a momentary flash in the unmarked history of diverse monolingualisms, whether nationalistic, cosmopolitan, performative, hypomnesic, or otherwise. While Alastair Pennycook has cautioned against the mere "pluralization of monolingualism" (Pennycook 2010: 12; see also Jessner 2003: 48 for a psycholinguistic corollary) in foreign language learning, we might also take a step back to think in a sustained way, and without naturalizing monolingualism itself, about a *plurality of monolingualisms* throughout history—that is, a complex account of the variously situated modes and contexts in which choosing "monolingual being" has made more than mere nationalistic or xenophobic sense. This line of thought is not intended as a lead-in for a revalorization of monolingualism or linguistic protectionism as such, but rather as a speculative attempt to allow more historical and contemporary forms of linguistic subjectivity to speak for themselves than is generally apropos in the age of celebratory multilingualism.

Let us suppose, for instance, that the collective performance *We don't need no education*—a picaresque monolingualization of a transnational translation platform—was in fact the opening volley in a dialogue between multilingual online Turkish speakers and another constituency, concerning the nature of language and translatedness in the twenty-first century. In both a Bakhtinian and an Arendtian spirit: who might that political interlocutor be, beyond the clean, blank walls of Google's Web presence? The Facebook campaign was an exercise in critical parody that shares features with drag performance, in which a subject adversely situated in the sex/gender system stylizes her-/himself by way of the historical repertoire of aesthetic conventions that constitute one normative pole in that system. In doing so, the subject not only provisionally obscures or disavows the normative position assigned to them, but also denaturalizes that inhabited pole through hyperstylization, often irritating or mesmerizing onlookers in the process. Likewise these students, multilinguals subject to lifelong assessment and selective inclusion by Anglophone institutions, stylize themselves monolingual (Turkish) so as to shore up the normative contours of that relation. The thread becomes their own mutual performance of monolingual drag, for which they are each other's audience.

In a similar vein, on August 2, 2012, Michigan congressmember John Conyers, a Democrat of African American descent, engaged in a similar activity of performative monolingualism. By performative, I mean *doing being monolingual,* in ways that denaturalize such "being monolingual" through embodied reiteration. During a congressional committee hearing in which federal legislators were to debate the annually reintroduced English-Only bill that had no chance of passing in that congressional session, Conyers read out the following text, in a Spanish he does not speak, a Spanish that wobbled with the ceremonious, deliberate diction of a papal bull:

> Bueno, estamos aquí otra vez, en este último día del período de sesiones antes de regresar a nuestros distritos para más de un mes, considerando legislación divisiva sobre un problema social que— afortunadamente—no tiene posibilidad de convertirse en ley. La legislación que estamos considerando hoy, la "Ley de la Unidad de Idioma Inglés del dos mil y once" es a la vez mal llamada y, yo creo, hará mucho daño a esta nación. (Conyers 2012)[27]

27. "OK, here we are again, in this last day of the session before returning to our districts for more than a month, considering divisive legislation about a social problem that—fortunately—has no possiblity of becoming law. The legislation that we are considering today, the 'Law of the Unity of the English Language of 2011,' is at once poorly named and, I believe, will do great damage to this nation." (My back-translation.)

Here, Conyers stages a somber practical joke, in which he ventrilo-quizes a "multilingualism of the other" (Kramsch 2011), to which he does not have practical access. With picaresque facial expression and posture, Conyers reads his statement in the sing-song, jocose, and expressionless voice of a fourteen-year-old pupil sitting in the back of his state-mandated foreign language class, reading his homework aloud at the teacher's desperate bidding, angling to impress his classmates with his dramatic detachment from the official focus of classroom attention. Mixing Church Latin pronunciation with French inflection and mock-Spanish phonetics (Hill 2008), Conyers's appearance displays more than just a disorderly mash-up of American arrested development around multilingualism. His reading indexed rather how monolin-gualism tends to "act out" in the presence of multilingual stimuli. Through mimicry, solicitous appeals for collective humor, embodied tactics of defamiliarization, and indulgence in dramatic repetition of difficult words, Conyers dilated into a composite sketch of what chauvinistic incompetence and dismissive disdain for other people's languages looks like (Conyers 2012).

Katrin Sieg's well-wrought conception of ethnic drag offers some inroads into a potential understanding of drag in the context of global translational monolingualism:

> As a figure of substitution, ethnic drag both exposes and disavows traumatic holes in the social fabric, and facilitates both historical denial and collective mourning. As a crossing of racial lines in performance, ethnic drag simultaneously erases and redraws boundaries posturing as ancient and immutable. As a pedagogy, it promises to reveal the dark inside of "Germanness" by taking up an outsider's perspective. As a technique of estrangement, drag denounces that which dominant ideology presents as natural, normal, and inescapable, without always offering another truth. As a ritual of inversion, it purports to master grave social contradic-tions, yet defers resolution through compulsive repetitions. As a symbolic contact zone between German bodies and other cultures, ethnic drag facilitates the exercise and exchange of power. And as a simulacrum of "race," it challenges the perceptions and privileges of those who would mistake appearances for essences. (2002: 2–3)

Conyers's *monolingual drag* tactically exacerbates the constructedness and intelligibility of his own and his interlocutors' linguistic proficiencies and deficiencies, as they are situated within a globalized metalinguistics of glossodiversity. The congressmember's dilatory behavior was not ruled out of order; rather, his performance compelled the committee chair into the position of accidental language-diversity advocate, asking Conyers to repeat his statement in Vietnamese, Yiddish, and French for the constituents of the other committee members' congressional districts. We might compare Conyers's and his fellow congressmembers' parliamentary drama around monolingualism to the banal procedural multilingualism of Canadian Parliamentarians, about whom Liberal MP Chrystia Freeland (Toronto Centre) says: "In our Parliament, Anglophone members speak terrible French every day. Our accents are so bad that sometimes our Francophone colleagues can't quite hide their winces."[28]

Unpacking the mechanism

Whereas the first section of this chapter focused on the excitable and positivistic status of the word "monolingualism," I have tried here to indicate various forms of monolingual performance and appearance in public space, concentrating on moments in which public figures and students have mobilized monolingualism in recent years as a way to deliver transnational critiques of globalization, translation technology, and linguistic purism movements. Without critical contextualization, "monolingual" will continue to be both an empty, and an effective, epithet used opportunistically to dis-figure individuals or communities under radically new geopolitical conditions.

In lieu of a conclusion, I will review some of the claims I have sought to advance in this chapter, offering them in axiomatic form:

- Monolingualism, as other previously unmarked terms like Whiteness, is not an embodied circumstance of the individual speaker. To the extent that it benefits individual speakers, monolingualism can be thought of as an unearned structural privilege.
- Beyond its advantages or disadvantages to individual speakers,

28. Eve Haque's pathbreaking book *Multiculturalism Within a Bilingual Framework* (2012) accounts for how normative conceptions of political multi-lingualism came to differ so vastly in the U.S. versus in Canada, particularly in the wake of Canada's Royal Comission on Biculturalism and Bilingualism (1963–9).

monolingualism is a technocratic infrastructure for regulated meaning-making, first broadly imagined in the seventeenth century. The basic term of the monolingual system is "a language."

- Monolingualism is not decreasing in potency or purchase in the age of the globalization of data, capital, and culture. Through technologies of translation and algorithmic cross-language data retrieval, monolingualism has become the procedural guarantor of economic globalization, pre-empting the "balkaniz[ation of] the information space" (Oard 2006: 299).
- If monolingualism is "ideological," it is so in the modest and far-reaching structural sense of a *doxa*, rather than in the provocative and politicizable sense of an orthodoxy.
- Monolingualism and multilingualism both derive historically from the pragmatic and rationalist axiom of "lingualism"—namely that the meaning-making world is organized by way of a countable roster of propositionally and functionally exhaustive entities called languages.
- Whether monolingualism "exists" is a less crucial question than whether, when, and under what auspices it is operative or effective.
- Divestment from monolingualism is as optional as divestment from any other form of global order. Learning additional languages does not necessarily displace monolingualism in personal or professional practice.
- Those called "monolingual" often make linguistic meaning in ways that are more diverse than those who are called "multilingual."
- Literary canons and scholarly disciplines are currently ill equipped to leverage a critique of monolingualism, as our formats of research, publishing, and communication are most often conceived and reproduced according to a monolingual contract.
- Monolingualism and multilingualism have become axes in a new form of verbal hygiene that arbitrates intercultural world-readiness according to certain polyglot forms of cosmopolitanism as opposed to others.
- Monolingualism has experienced an asymptotic spike in impact and innovation since the 1990s and has become the organizing fulcrum for a new era of human history, the linguacene.

Chapter 2

KAFKA'S WELL-TEMPERED PIANO

"You simply have to know the mechanism," Karl said to himself.
—Franz Kafka, *The Missing Person* (1910–14),
translated by Mark Harman

In 1907 a twenty-four-year-old, fresh from law school, was asked to fill out a personnel questionnaire for an Italian insurance company that was considering whether to hire him. The questionnaire posed to him the following questions: "Do you know other languages beyond your mother language? Which ones? How far does your knowledge reach? Can you merely understand these languages or also speak them, or can you also make use of them through written translations and compositions?" (Čermak 1994: 59). So prompted, the young man—not yet quite versed in the upbeat genre of the "personal statement"—wrote back sheepishly to the Imperial Regia Privilegiata Compagnia di Assicurazioni Generali Austro-Italiche in longhand: "Bohemian, and beyond that French and English, but I'm out of practice in the latter two languages." Less than a year later, and now more savvy in the diction of linguistic self-assessment, Dr. František Kafka responded to another such prompt with provident dispassion: "The applicant has mastery over the German and Bohemian language in oral and written form, and further commands the French, and partially the English language" (Čermak 1994: 59).

Leaving behind the confessional "I" of the preceding year's response, Franz Kafka now casts himself in the third-person guise of a regent who commands multiple languages as one might administer a vast revier. This emboldened applicant no longer betrays any hesitation about the extent of his multilingual talents, nor about the status of his "practice" (*Übung*) in them. Though he claims mastery over German and Bohemian, Kafka characterizes his relationship to French and English through a metaphorics of distance, of reach—rather than of weakness, rust, or disrepair. The intimate, apologetic tone from the previous year has dissolved beneath a spatial metaphor of sovereignty and proximity, in which some languages are "closer," some "farther" from the writer's command. The Assicurazioni Generali questionnaire item itself—"How *far* does your knowledge [of other languages] *reach*?"—was all but ready-made for the young author's emerging desire to "disinvent and reconstitute languages" (Makoni and Pennycook 2006).

A hundred years on, those of us foreign language teachers who have occasion to work with the Common European Framework of Reference for Languages may glimpse in Kafka's waffling multilingual self-assessment over the course of 1907–8 an inculcatory process of self-stylization similar to the CEFR's "I can" prompts in the twenty-first century. While scholars debate from a methodological perspective the merits and fallacies of the Framework's upbeat, empowering grid of self-assessment speech acts (see for instance Hu 2012: 72; and more generally Byram and Parmenter 2012), less attention is devoted specifically to the figural richness of these new "metaphors we live by" in linguistic self-assessment in the age of postmultilingualism (Lakoff and Johnson 1980). Consider for instance this I-can statement, from the English-language version of the A1 (i.e. Beginners) grid of CEFR competences: "[I] can manage very short, isolated, mainly pre-packaged utterances, with much pausing to search for expressions, to articulate less familiar words, and to repair communication" (Council of Europe 2014). Let us think of this ostensibly unremarkable barrage of metaphors from the point of view of Kafka's wily and suspicious literaricity a hundred years prior. We see management, isolation, packaging, pre-packaging, pause, search, familiarity, repair. Even the guiding metaphor of a "Framework" for language should prompt a fair measure of circumspection, as recent scholarship in language ecology suggests (Steffensen 2015; Cowley 2011; Goatly 1996). In this chapter, we will take the opportunity to follow a Kafkan line of thought about the performative rhetoric of multilingualism and monolingualism in the early twentieth century, as it animated Kafka's own literary production. For twenty-first-century practitioners in foreign language pedagogy and multilingual philology, this pursuit may ignite further inquiry into the underlying "mechanism" of today's emerging technocracies of multilingual meaning, and their consequences for subjects, mono- or multilingual alike.

By the time Kafka was hired on at the Assicurazioni Generali insurance agency in 1907, the notion that a singular, shared national language was and ought to be a constitutive prepossession of Western European subjectivity had become a generic expectation, as natural as Peter Schlemihl's shadow. Composed in the wake of the long nineteenth century of linguistic nationalization, Kafka's texts are poised to historicize the high-modern "mechanism" of monolingualism, of which they are a performative reiteration. Based in the multilingual provincial capital of a multinational empire, Kafka nevertheless committed himself and his readers to a monolingual contract—purified of calques, local references, social deixis, code-switching, and other ostentatious traces of Prague's multilingual context. While the poets of the George Circle were promoting a panlingual lyric expansionism,[1] Kafka's texts abstained from such play across languages, preferring instead to deepen what might be called monolingualism's *vow of poverty*.

Kafka's disappointing monolingualism

There is much conjecture about how and why Franz Kafka, the multiple-language speaker—the multilingual epistemologist, even— became renowned as one of literary modernism's archetypal stylists of monolingual German. Responding to Sander Gilman's somewhat severe take on this question, David Suchoff remarks that "If Kafka, like Josef K., does bear any fault, it is for having checked his Jewish languages at the door of his canonical German, which [...] tempted him with the lure of literary fame" (Suchoff 2003: 255). In sizing up Kafka's vested stake in the German-dominated literary-linguistic market, Suchoff and Gilman seem to suggest that the choice to be "bilingual in everything but his writing" (Gilman 1995: 40) was evidence of a sheer, if also reluctant, opportunism in Kafka. This view—that the author's choice of German as his exclusive language of composition is best understood sociologically—subjects multilingual writers to a greater burden of justifcation in language choice than so-called monolingual ones ever must answer for. Nonetheless, this view continues to hold an axial, if often rueful, status in Kafka studies, despite Deleuze and Guattari's hagiographic interventions now forty years ago.[2]

---

1. See for instance Giulia Radaelli's erudite study *Literarische Mehrsprachigkeit: Sprachwechsel bei Elias Canetti und Ingeborg Bachmann* (2011): particularly 243–79.

2. Deleuze and Guattari (1975). On the sociological bias towards multilingualism in literary studies generally, see also Georg Kremnitz, *Mehrsprachigkeit in der Literatur: Wie Autoren ihre Sprachen wählen* (2004): 8.

Instead of understanding literary monolingualism as a cultural politics of affiliation—as siding with a given speech community, audience, ethnic group, or political program—we may read single-language writing by multilinguals as a kind of ascetic authorial praxis, a "hunger art" that invites a new literary-critical response in the twenty-first century. It is this operative principle of aestheticized monolingual authoriality that distinguishes Kafka's texts from those of his other multilingually invested contemporaries, whether Karl Kraus, Kurt Tucholsky, or Fritz Mauthner. Yet most Kafka scholarship has been poised to see his inveterate wielding of monolingualism as a reticent devotion to German itself—to the *cultural* repertoire of the language, rather than as an experimental performance of the *formal* temperament of monolingualism.

There are a number of formidable reasons—literary-historical, literary-theoretical, and indeed language-ideological ones—why a critique of Kafkan monolingualism has generally remained arrested in its incipient stages. After the Third Reich fell in 1945, the Kafka of comparative literature accrued such oracular status on both sides of the North Atlantic that his corpus became a kind of prophylactic test palette for recuperating the modern German culture-language in its pre-Nazi form (Dowden 1995: 19). As a consequence of his canonization in the immediate post-war period as the prime, because unimpeachable, German modernist—thanks in no small part to the multilingual Muirs (Woods 2014)—the languages beyond German that Kafka "further commanded" were set aside as extra-textual, biographical matter. His Czech, Yiddish, Hebrew, English, Italian, and French garnered acknowledgment from mid-century critics only to the extent that personal multilingualism counted as a general indicator of an anti-totalitarian, cosmopolitan spirit, or the necessary accoutrement of a genial mind.[3] Consider Wagenbach's windy depiction from the 1964 biography:

> He was the only one [among Prague's German authors] to speak and write almost impeccable Czech, he was the only one to grow up right in the middle of the old town, on the edge of the ghetto district, which was then still an architectonic unity. Kafka never lost his intimate bond to the Czech people; he never forgot this milieu of his youth. (Wagenbach 1991: 17)

3. On an author's "conspicuous multilingualism" as a hagiographic element, see for instance Komska (2015).

Wagenbach treats Kafka's Czech–German bilingual competence as a mark of talent and personal exceptionalism, overlooking how utterly unexceptional bi- and trilingualism was in turn-of-the-century Prague, and thereby abetting an arbitrary distinction between Prague's polyglot intellectual elites and its "functionally" multilingual merchants and workers. Wagenbach's depiction of an additive polyglot Franz Kafka placed Czech, Yiddish, and other languages on a nostalgic pedestal, far removed from the concerns of close textual analysis and the experience of writerly subjectivity. Given a post-war New Critical ethos in which the manifest text was to be the only admissible artifact, Kafka's multilingualism was fated to remain crucial to the composite hagiographic sketch, yet tangential to any particular textual analysis. Even in Deleuze and Guattari's 1975 eulogy, other languages largely continued to serve this chiastic function. In portraying Kafka's Czech as a unique and improbable possession, Wagenbach not only trades on the aura of multilingual preciousness, but also glosses over Kafka's changing and difficult relationship to the languages he grew up with and continued to learn over the course of his life, including the ambitions, doubts, failures, and dissimulations that conditioned their use or disuse.

Ineffability reconsidered

A diary entry from one of Kafka's many "strenuous Sunday[s]" recalls such a moment of doubt, as the less-than-willing František is tasked with standing in as his father Hermann's surrogate negotiator at the family bookkeeper's home in Žižkov in 1911. It appears from the diary entry that this Czech-speaking bookkeeper wants to quit working for the Kafkas, on account of some divided workplace loyalties that have gotten out of Hermann's hands. The employee is thus not particularly eager for a Sunday home-visit from the boss's boy and his less-than-native Czech. Afterward, still smarting from the indignity of it all, Kafka reflects in the narrative present tense:

> The less success I have with my cajoling in Czech [....] the more cat-like [the bookkeeper's] face becomes. Toward the end of it, I try out a more easy-going feel for a bit. I look around the room, speechless, with a long face and narrowed eyes, as if I were following something hinted at into the unsayable. I'm not unhappy with this either, as I see that it has had little effect, and instead of being spoken to by him in a new tone, I must begin again to browbeat him [...]

I oblige him to come to Father in the afternoon. My argumentation
too abstract and formal. A mistake not to have asked for the woman
of the house. (Kafka 1992: 84, my translation)

Here Kafka tells of an intercultural and translingual errand gone sour,
riddled as it was from the outset with coercion and complex power
differentials of age, employ, language, territory, homosociality, hetero-
sociality, and an unconvincing ventriloquation of the boss. The father's
own competently multilingual authority, as embodied in the deputized
son's multiply inferior authoritativeness, devolves into a series of folly
for which Kafka has no available interpretive framework like Michael
Byram's five intercultural *savoirs*.[4] Despite the tensely overlapping
aspects of his own intersectionality in this moment, Kafka pins the
blame for the illocutionary infelicity of the exchange squarely on his
own (Czech) language, its register, and its inappropriate argumenta-
tional formality—and wishes he had had the presence of mind to call on
the employee's wife for social mediation and linguistic mitigation. (We
often find such urgent recourse to women as multilingual mediators
in Kafkan literary compositions, like Rosa in "A Country Doctor," the
women's section in "In Our Synagogue," and the inaudible voices in the
kitchen in "Returning Home.")

Of particular interest in this diary entry is Kafka's feigned gesture, his
face-saving tactic of following "something hinted at into the unsayable."
Such formulations of ineffability in Kafka generally tend to inspire
theological, psychoanalytic, or otherwise non-linguistic readings, in
which crises of meaning are assumed to transcend particular languages.[5]
This diary passage puts such language-universalist, theological readings
of the Kafkan "unsayable" on a questionable footing, prompting at least
a complementary multilingual analysis that would devote attention to
the situated, cross-linguistic exchanges in which speaking subjects find
themselves—at a loss, not for meaning or words as such, but for *Czech*
words. Faced with the client's overt disapproval at his communicative
competence in Czech, Kafka the surrogate manager disguises his linguistic
discomfiture as a caprice of genius, an earnest fumbling toward the
universally ineffable. This gesture allows Kafka in a pinch to demonstrate,
in plain view of the other participants, that his speechlessness is justified

4. On these five intercultural *savoirs—être, s'engager, comprendre, apprendre,
et faire*—see Byram's *Teaching and Assessing Intercultural Communicative
Competence* (1997): 89.

5. See for instance Steven T. Katz, *Comparative Mysticism* (2013): 11.

by obligations loftier than mere cross-language word recall, sociolectal precision, or tip-of-the-tongue word misplacement.[6] The translingual texture of such "critical language incidents" in Kafka may persuade us to reconsider a few of the axia upon which scholarship has tended to interpret aphasia, allotria, and inarticulacy in his prose writings.[7]

Let us consider the broader context, beyond Kafka's own disparaging self-assessment in this one translingual interaction. Public semiotics in early twentieth-century Prague flourished amid what could be called a double monolingualism, a constellation by which each of two dominant monolingual ideologies (the Bohemian and the German) campaigned to secure institutional misrecognition of the existence of its respective other. The flammable Bohemian–German language politics of the late nineteenth century were, however, more than just the natural hazard of two or more languages abutting one another in everyday life. Conflicts at the micro- and macro-level were rather the outcome of concerted efforts among urban nationalists to establish and maintain linguistically pure spaces. As a rule, major landmarks in Prague bore both a Czech and a German name, and the use of one or the other in conversation functioned as a shibboleth for the social co-construction of belonging in every new speech situation (see Judson 2006; Spector 2002).

This condition of a politicized double monolingualism, however, applied inordinately more to urban spaces than to rural ones. The nineteenth-century Bohemian crownlands of Kafka's forebears had been less a linguistic battleground between German, Yiddish, Moravian, and Czech speakers, than a field of political brinkmanship among urban, modernist monolingualists (whether Czech, German, or otherwise) who found themselves in conflict with intransigent rural, largely non-partisan, and multilingual "anationals." In his study on linguistic borderlands in Imperial Bohemia, Pieter Judson stresses that:

> In multilingual villages, towns, or regions, early political movements attempted to mobilize popular support by demanding linguistic equality for their side. As political conflicts developed around language issues, representatives of each "side" scoured the region for every potential voter, attempting to mobilize nationally indifferent people into nationalist political parties. (2006: 9)

6. On tip-of-the-tongue states, see Ecke and Hall (2013).

7. On "allotria" in Kafka's multilingually inflected *In the Penal Colony*, see Corngold (2001). On "critical incidents" in language learning, see for instance Finch (2010).

The institutional landscape that ushered in Kafka's literary figurations was thus one born primarily of a political conflict between monolingualism and multilingualism, not a cultural conflict between one language and another. In the course of the close-readings that follow, I will claim that Kafka's writerly habitus throughout his career is that of a clandestine polemicist in the midst of that lingua-political conflict.

Languages in search of an author (concept)

Barriers to analyzing how Kafka's day-to-day multilingualism animated and structured his writing still linger in the secondary literature on modernist prose fiction, where "language" still tends to be writ large and singular. The notion that an author's multilingual subjectivity informs and participates directly in his or her textual production has given rise to a hereditary uneasiness in literary studies. The composite legacy of New Critical, (post-)structuralist, Chomskyan, and even Lacanian lines of thought about language bears only meager affordances for an engaged critique of literary multilingualism. Quizzically, the most prominent and frequently cited interventions from theoreticians on the subject are autobiographical or confessional in nature (Derrida 1998; Kristeva 1991). Arising out of the rigors of formalist foreclosure upon the textual artifact itself, and extending to the muscular post-war dictum that "the design or intention of the author is neither available nor desirable as a standard for judging the success of a work of literary art" (Wimsatt and Beardsley 1946, 468–88), this moratorium on authorial readings has scuttled a great deal of potential scholarly speculation about multilingual authorship *within literary studies*—as opposed to in neighboring fields like linguistic anthropology, pragmatics, writing studies, sociology of literature, and applied linguistics—where such a hereditary discomfiture with "intentional fallacy" is not in force.

Wimsatt and Beardsley's conditional eviction of the author from text, however, pre-empted inquiry into the performative bind arising between monolingual textuality and multilingual subjectivity. The "author" icon that traveled from New Criticism to post-structuralism is an enduring legacy of this elision. When Foucault, for instance, sought to articulate a theory of authorship, the problem of language multiplicity did not appear anywhere among the "functional conditions of specific discursive practices" that constituted the core of his findings about the history of literary authoriality (1977: 133).[8] While a general theory of authorial multilingualism is still outstanding, scholarship most often pivots to biographical, allegorical, sociological, historical, or hypotextual modes of analysis, in an attempt to leverage a useful *provisiorium* out of an author discourse created for monolinguals.[9] Steven Kellman's 2000 volume on *The Translingual Imagination* remains one of the most cogent conceptual advances on literary multilinguality, though it is noteworthy that the project predicates itself on the *imagination* rather than on the more traditional literary-theoretical *authorship*. Though classic essays like Meir Sternberg's 1981 "Polylingualism as Reality and Translation as Mimesis" laid out an ambitious agenda for multilingual authoriality, such efforts failed to garner sufficient momentum to alter the course of the (implicitly monolingual) author concept throughout the 1980s and 1990s.

In the case of Kafka (as in that of many multilingual authors), monolingualism is a circumstance of *literary text alone*—not of his "consciousness," his workplace, his father's store, his intimate and profession relationships, Jewish Prague, "primitive Czech territoriality," (Deleuze and Guattari 1975: 16), or the family home.[10] There is plain and ample evidence that, in each of these extra-literary realms of his work, at least two languages were in furtive and contentious cross-pollination with one another throughout his life, vying each moment for a minute toe-hold into political or situated hegemony, in accordance with Prague's politicized double monolingualism (Čermak 1994; Nekula 2003). Literary text, therefore, is the only domain of Kafka's work and livelihood in which the ideal of monolingualism could reign expansive and uninterrupted. His works are thus not a presentation of some aspect of his life; literary text could not be further from the truth of his linguistic subjectivity, his cognitive lexicon, or his symbolic environment.[11] The generic relation between monolingual texts and such multilingual authors as Kafka is almost always apophatic—i.e.

8. For a helpful contextualization, see Catherine Porter's "The Expository Translator" (2014).

9. On the default compulsion to read Kafka biographically, see Edmonds (2010).

10. Michelle Woods's *Kafka's Translated* (2014) offers a detailed and thoughtful guide toward reorienting Kafka scholarship around his multilingualism.

11. On the dynamics of the "multilingual lexicon," see for instance de Bot (2004).

a presence always toiling toward an absence. Literary or intratextual monolingualism is thus less a manifestation of identity, competence, or individual experience than it is a negative reflection of the ways in which agents provisionally consent to participating in a certain form, or a meta-form, of alienation—whether in public dialogue, textual composition, or frameworks of knowledge and memory.

Theorists and critics deal with this absence in varying ways. Celebratory characterizations of a given novel as multilingually heteroglossic are often abetted by the accompanying suggestion that its multilingualism is primarily *hypotextual*—a concept derived from the work of Gérard Genette (1997). This charismatic vision, influential in affirmative studies of literary multilingualism, holds that there are linguistic worlds underneath and beyond the manifest world of the novel's pages, and that those multilingual worlds are somehow submerged though present in the novel—affecting its syntax, style, lyricism, and lexicon in consequential ways. This mode of *apophatic* multilingual critique—one that focuses on an image of multilingualism submerged—pursues figural traces of one language behind or beneath another. In his study of "Yinglish" literature in the U.S., Murray Baumgarten for instance suggests that "If these works are written in English, it is a language with Yiddish lurking behind every Anglo-Saxon character [...] Yiddish, as language and culture, works to make its presence felt in the character, situation, and narrative voice of the story, as it does in the vocabulary, syntax, and morphology of the Western language in which it is written" (1982: 10). Yoram Ben-David has made a similar overture in describing Kafka's work as a primer in "how to write Hebrew in German words" (Suchoff 2003: 271).

The cultural politics of textual monolingualism

The applied linguist Paul Kei Matsuda has raised concern about the recent fervor for so-called translingual writing, claiming that:

> The assumption in this demand is that translingual writing is visible—that negotiation is only acknowledged when it results in mixed language use, leaving out the possibility that negotiation may have led the writer to adopt the apparently dominant choice. But in translingual writing the process of negotiating assumptions about language is more important than the product. Restricting the scope of translingual writing to the end result can obscure more subtle manifestations of

the negotiation as well as situations where writers make the rhetorical choice not to deviate from the dominant practices. (2014: 481)

This desirous search for latent or manifest code-switching is a primary interpretive mode through which multilinguality is brought to the fore in literary studies today as well, and the momentum arising from such analyses indeed offers a testing ground for the epistemology of trans-lingual practice. The downside to these approaches, especially those that focus on conspicuous, manifest intratextual code-switching, is that they draw on a very small collection of exceptional text experiments, which have been able to reach a public readership either because their author had already been prolific in monolingual publishing (Ingeborg Bachmann's *Simultan*; Arthur Schnitzler's *Fräulein Else*), or because the concept of a multilingual text aroused enough academic receptivity to overcome structural marketing barriers (Christine Brook-Rose's *Between*; Yoko Tawada's entire oeuvre).

From Dada to the Spatialists and Anthropophagists, a range of twentieth-century panlingual activists indeed sought to foreground Babelic juxtapositions as a means to critique social inequities and national chauvinisms.[12] Yet these polyglot experiments lie at the outskirts, both of literary publishing and of public awareness. To select such polyglot texts for a literary genealogy of multilingualism results in a *minoritizing* categorization of multilinguality-as-experiment, obscuring the otherwise structurally agonistic relationship between literary monolingualism and social multilingualism. Paradoxically, texts composed in a mix of multiple languages often lack the figural potency to re-enact for the reader precisely this agonism.

Genette's notion of hypotextuality runs conceptually, if not always politically, parallel to literature's uneasily desirous relationship for the multilingual. While a digraphic medium like film (with its subtitles and visual iconicity) can represent milieus where multiple languages are used simultaneously, literary texts are often hard-pressed to give voice to such spaces. Genette's framework is thus provisionally useful in accounting for the fractious and amorous relation between monolingual literary texts and multilingual lifeworlds—a relation in which a single-language text refers, often urgently, to a patently cross-lingual set of signs, oral histories, or collective experiences. Though the term hypotext suggests one text "below" another, Kafka's late parable

12. See for instance Edwin Gentzler's *Translation and Identity in the Americas* (2012): 97.

from 1920, "Returning Home," for instance rumbles with a less-than-lingual, unrepresentable language event happening "in the other room" i.e. *transtextually*. The concept of hypotextuality is most useful if it is understood politically, as a means to figure the suppression of allolingual meanings, even as affirmative close-readings eagerly repatriate them into the interpretive frame.

In "Returning Home," the parable's first-person narrator paces up and down his father's courtyard, where old, unusable appliances block his way to the stairwell. Smelling the coffee coming from behind the kitchen door, the narrator poses a question to himself: "Do you feel at home?" The voice that answers, again his own, begins to falter. "It is my father's house, but each item stands cold beside the next, as if it were already occupied with its own concerns, some of which I have forgotten, some which I never knew. How can I be of any use to them, what am I to them, even if I am my father's—the old landlord's—son?" (1992: 573). Cold "pieces"—the surplus material of heritage-language textuality and orthography—litter the disorderly courtyard, yet the narrator can be of no use to them in the monolingual, German narration at hand. After some deliberation, the narrator decides *not* to knock on the kitchen door, choosing to listen only from afar to the muffled, inchoate voices within. "What else is happening in the kitchen is the secret of those sitting there [...] The longer one stands before the door, the more foreign one becomes" (1992: 573). What the narrator fears most is that someone might come *through* the door toward him, without his having knocked, and ask him something in a language for which he is "responsible" but cannot accomodate in the text at hand.

Neither the text nor its narrator ever enters or witnesses this other room. The monolingual "here" of the narrative must remain outside, increasingly foreign, yet always surrounded by entropic piles of unusable words that nonetheless belong to the narrator by inheritance. Next door to the manifest text is the space of formally interdicted, unpublishable language—of the unruly and mundane admixture of dialectal usages; of Yiddish, Czech, and the local argot of German Prague—which, like the silent appliances in the yard, Kafka could not "be of use to" in his literary fiction. Kafka's literaricity is, in the spatial as well as critical sense, "about" what is being said by the muffled, other-languaged voices in the kitchen, where the coffee is brewing and the hearth is lit.

There can be, however, analytic and political overreach in viewing such hypo- or transtextual gestures as a gateway to multilingualism. Though hypotextuality in this vein may guide readers toward chalk-outlines of a potential "multilingualism of the other" (Kramsch 2011), it does not do more than that, and often renders that multilingualism more exotic and distal in its figural relief than the social world of its provenance would ever bear out. Many texts, including most of Kafka's published and unpublished works, engage less in hypotextual gesturing than with what I think of as a stance of henolingualism—as derived from the Victorian-era scholar of comparative religion Max Müller and his conception of henotheism as "a devotion to a single God while still accepting the existence of other gods" (1878: 707). Lest literary critique contribute to the exoticization of multilingualism, critics can take cues from Kafka's own methodological modesty when faced with the meta-formal constraint of monolingualism.

Suggesting that the modern novel is structurally monolingual, or historically postmultilingual, is also a quite different claim than those Bakhtin-informed visions of "discourse in the novel" that presume monolingualism to be, in the end, impossible in any kind of text, given the heteroglossic nature of secondary speech genres (Bakhtin 1996 [1952–3]). But subsuming multilingualism (or the co-presence of semiodiverse, unregulated scales of linguistic incomprehensibility) under heteroglossia (a socio-aesthetic principle of many-voicedness and sociolinguistic variation that, indeed, sometimes leads to experiences and situations of noncomprehension) impoverishes the usefulness of both concepts. The political import of heteroglossia in Bakhtin's Soviet environment was more akin to a certain kind of civic *monolingualism*, whereby differently voiced articulations of civic subjectivity would present *comprehensible* alternative interventions to those orthodoxies cultivated by the Soviet state. Multilingualism, in contrast, offers no such political expediency or counter-narrative promise. Consider Bakhtin's prescriptive account of heteroglossia in the discourse of the novel, and the conditions of relevance and contemporaneity it foresees: "The novel must present all of the social and ideological voices of its era, that is, all the era's languages that have any claim to being significant; the novel must be a microcosm of heteroglossia" (Bakhtin 1981: 110–11). Semiodiverse multilingualism, by definition, is too diffuse to live up to these centripetal, inclusive criteria of political mobilization and signification. One recent, willful counter-example is Koen Peeters's *Grote Europese Roman* (2007) which, reflecting the fervor for European multilingualization, set its aesthetic sights on winching all twenty-four official European languages into one novel's "microcosm of heteroglossia". This, however, is the epitome of the kind of tempered, postmultilingual "soft multilingualism" (Noorani 2013) that was ultimately inimical to Bakhtin's sense of the political carnivalesque.

A monolingualism artist

While Kafka's early novel *The Missing Person* (1910–14) narrates a comedy of second-language folly, where ambition, waywardness, and escapism propels a young adventurer toward his manifest linguistic destiny, Kafka's later prose harbors an anxious double-bind about mono- and multilingualism. These later texts fail to proceed in a forward fashion, textured and structured as they are by what Bakhtin characterized as a "discourse with a side-long glance at someone else's hostile word" (Bakhtin 1994: 108). Kafka's late protagonists, as in "Returning Home" and in the diary entry with the bookkeeper cited above, oscillate between a compulsion to misrecognize imminent multilingual situations and a vague knowledge that such recognition can only be temporarily postponed. As the authorial Franz Kafka grows older, acquires, maintains, and loses languages—confronting all the while the professional gauntlets of multilingual competency—his prose narratives no longer soar headlong into the various "storey[s] of the inner tower of Babel," but rather tremble soberly outside them (Nekula 2003).

If monolingualism is apprehended as a binding, yet historically contingent *formal temperament*—or, in Barthes's terms, a constitutive myth of modern literatures—then Kafka's own endeavor to project multilingual lifeworlds in variously sillhouetted form over the threshold of "paper German" looks more like a critical ambition than a sin of omission. Kafka chooses not German but monolingualism as his aesthetic medium—as an oil painter might restrict herself to pencil and charcoal instead of oils, in order to render a particular kind of negative figure exquisitely visible. Itself a product of the friction between linguistic multiplicity and monolingual dominance in the high modern public sphere, Kafka's literaricity plays the hegemonic against the anti-hegemonic in ways that free code-switching between languages would be unable to broker.

Before his literary career turned toward a forensics of the monological and the agonic, for which he is most renowned, Franz Kafka tried to write a first novel that would delight in something quite a bit more cheerful: a thigmotactic adventure in literary multilingualism. In biology and theoretical morphology, thigmotaxis is the set of phenomena observed in certain organisms' movement toward, or away from, any object that provides a mechanical stimulus. Dispositionally thigmotactic organisms—among which are Kafka's beloved beetles, cockroaches, and other *Ungeziefer*—tend to conduct their movements along external spatial borders (this is called positive thigmotaxis), and only rarely range away from surfaces of a certain knowable perpendicularity, out into open space (negative thigmotaxis). Scurrying along the baseboard, inching along the wall, thigmotacticians make mechanical, morphological, and institutional peripheries their idiom and their terrain (McGhee 1999: 273).

By the time the traveler Gregor Samsa awakes from troubled dreams in the high-modern, high-nationalist year 1915, the aesthetic space for Kafka's own Central European multilingualism had shrunk from its grand proportions in the Amerika novel (*The Missing Person*) to become nothing but a "room, a proper human room, if admittedly rather too small, [which] lay peacefully between the four familiar walls" (22). Accordingly, the Gregor of *The Metamorphosis* will spend the remainder of his story in the thick of positive thigmotactic survey-orship: "Eating had soon ceased to give him even the slightest pleasure, and so to divert himself he took up the habit of crawling back and forth across the walls and ceiling" (71). Venturing out into open space was inimical to Gregor's anxious disposition, and the haven that walls and crevices provided served also as his platform for the knowable world.

Such, however, had not been characteristic behavior for the picaresque, punkish ingénu of Kafka's 1910–14 novel *The Missing Person*, in which the English-as-an-Additional-Language student Karl Rossmann criss-crosses "America's" open spaces with little regard for the magnetism of walls and perpendicular objects. Liminality is, indeed, an experience that befalls Karl culturally, especially given his structural position in the novel as multilingual immigrant to the United States, but "being liminal" is only rarely his customary, preferred position in narrated physical space. Nonetheless, Karl undergoes a process of thigmotactic metamorphosis just as profound as Gregor Samsa will—not from a bourgeois human into "some sort of monstrous insect," (2014: 21) but rather a transformation into a postmultilingual "freshly minted American" (2008: 46). Whereas Gregor gravitates toward the walls of his "properly human room" (positive thigmotaxis), Karl is drawn out into the wide-open expanses—into all of the social, acoustic, and kinetic din—that constitute multilingual America in the age of Rooseveltian monolingualization (Sollors 1998; Pratt 2012).

Kafka's first novel indeed offers a revealing and often neglected anomaly in his lifelong performative vascillation at the crossroads between multilingual subjectivity and monolingual text. While his later works, like *The Castle* (1924), struggle to measure out endless yet claustrophobic spaces on the "here" side of the monolingual/multilingual literary threshold, Kafka's unfinished debut novel—variously titled in English as *The Stow-Away, The Missing Person, America,* or *The One Who Disappeared*—dramatized an aggressive attempt to steal away from monolingualism and to inhabit the multilingual world "over there," beyond the pale of single-language literary representation. It will be, I claim, Kafka's one and only sustained work of literary fiction that delights in tramping on the "far side" of this divide between linguistic ipseity and linguistic alterity. Later writings, from "In the Penal Colony" (1919) to "Returning Home" (1920), turn to a somber, if often absurdist, actuarial account of monolingual constraint. For its part, the ambition of Kafka's first novel is not to evoke the divide between Prague German and immigrant English *per se*, but rather the divide between textual monolingualism and worldly multilingualism.

In this sense, every scene or venture in *The Missing Person* doubles as 1) a traditional plot development and 2) a metatextual critique of literary monolingualism in an unruly multilingual world. To take an initial example: despite the rough-and-ready second language acquisition adventure that awaits him, the protagonist Karl Rossmann languishes at first in the endless narrow corridors of the ocean liner that has brought him to America—unwilling to disembark into the English-speaking expanse outside. Indeed, and with good reason, he shares this self-undermining hesitation with the text itself. The performative contradiction that must arise between Kafka's assiduous High Prague German and Karl's necessarily hybrid and mutating spoken English throws forth a lingering dilemma of figuration for the text. How can the effects of linguistic mixing and mutual estrangement, of being (dis-)interpellated in a language one does not understand, be indexed or re-enacted in a single-language literary text? Perhaps more difficult still is the possibility of representing partial and uneven proficiencies: one person's capacity to understand but not to speak another's language, or vice versa. Is the literariness of literary language in "the proper human room" of high modernist fiction capable of accommodating these worldly dilemmas in the ceremonial space of Kafka's monolingual texts?

Language learning as narrative problem

Despite Bakhtin's well-loved characterization of novelistic discourse as heteroglossic and centrifugal, based as it was on early modern and nineteenth-century examples, Kafka's early career was primarily animated by a coming-to-terms with monolingualism as a binding, meta-formal constraint upon the publishability of literary texts, in the German-language genres proper to his modernist moment. If we acknowledge monolingualism as a limiting yet contingent constraint for such belles-lettristic "proper human room[s]" as the novel, then it makes sense to think of the Kafka of *The Missing Person* as an emerging "monolingualism artist"—or, to invoke Yildiz's critical-temporal syntax in *Beyond the Mother Tongue*, a postmultilingual artist. This is of course a very different stance than to see monolingualism as either a necessary evil of, or a natural law for, novelistic discourse; instead Kafka identified monolingualism early on as a historic-aesthetic oddity guarded for elites by elites.

The "proper human room" in which Gregor Samsa's writability dwells is one of monolingualism's many lasting inventions—both the imagined social space itself and its literary representation. As a textual experiment, *The Missing Person* indicates how deeply the early Kafka knew already that literature, a primary vocational terrain of nation-building and nation-teaching, was marked by a founding non-adequation between literary texts and the multilingual world. Literary texts that emerge from multilingual lifeworlds like Kafka's must then find a way to index their difficult intimacy with their textual language through an impulse to perform, and to lay bare, the effects of monolingualism, to render it visible for critique. Not only will the non-correspondence between Karl's emerging English and its "translation" into textual German create a patent irony for the paradigmatic axis of language "choice" in the text itself; Karl's speech practices themselves, those of an emergent English speaker, must also generate situations of cross-linguistic pragmatic folly among the characters (on the syntagmatic axis of the text).

Among the consequential questions that will, or ought to, issue from Karl's multilingual, emergent-English self-presentation on the level of the novel's narrative syntax are: Who speaks English and when? With what accents and fluency? And how can the social consequences and symbolic textures that ensue from translingual exchange be indexed in a monolingual German-language text? Or, syntactically speaking: How fast can Karl, fresh off the steamship in New York harbor with only rudimentary schooling in foreign languages, come to speak a standard American English—spectrally backtranslated into German—that will not require the novel's readers to suspend disbelief? How much delay and detour will this problem need to cause for the unfolding narrative? When it comes to "other languages" in *The Missing Person*, narrative coherence and monolingual form appear to be at cross-purposes—already at the outset of the young novelist's career. And yet, this first, paradigmatic operation—of assimilating Karl's hybrid German–English speech into the text's manifest German monolingualism—makes it next to impossible for the text to overcome a second, narrative (or syntagmatic) dilemma: that of depicting "language learning" in any plausible way.

Though the young Kafka has clearly chosen to aggressively fly in the face of these metatextual strictures, *The Missing Person* ultimately appears, somewhat conventionally, to chronicle Karl's carefree love affair with language acquisition in a way that is anything but aporetic in its bearing. The winning tone that characterizes Karl's ambitions vis-à-vis English-as-a-Second-Language soars with the romantic rigor of a summer-immersion language-school pamphlet:

> Learning English was, of course, Karl's first and most important task. When the young teacher from a business school appeared in Karl's room at seven o'clock each morning, he would find him already seated at his desk, poring over his notebooks or walking up and down, committing phrases to memory. Karl realized that when it came to learning English, there could be no such thing as excessive haste, and that the best way to give his uncle great joy was to make rapid progress. (2008: 40)

More like palliative sidebars to the suspicious reader, digressions like these about language learning offer repeated guarantees to readers that Karl's deficiencies in English will be nothing more than a quickly overcome social task for the immigrant hero—and certainly *not* a recurrent logical glitch for the text. In a droll gesture to the novel's monolingual form, the narrative relegates Karl's English language learning to the liminal early hours of each day, before the brass tacks of new-American self-making get underway. And indeed, he succeeds, in ways that later Kafkan protagonists almost never do:

> Although the only English words in his initial conversations with his uncle were hello and goodbye, they soon managed to shift more and more of the conversation into English, which led to their broaching topics of a more intimate nature. (40)

At first, the novel has Karl chaperoned around by an Anglophone beard to smooth over any translingual rough edges. Like a prosthetic device, Karl's English professor is kept at his side to complete his utterances, as the young immigrant briskly graduates from rudimentary speech to semi-proficiency:

> The greater the improvement in his English, the more eager was his uncle to have him meet his acquaintances, and he arranged that during these encounters the English teacher should for the time being always remain near Karl, simply in case of need. (41)

Soon, however, Karl undergoes a rite of consecration as an English speaker, for which he had not yet considered himself worthy. At one of his uncle's get-togethers:

> Occasionally glancing at his uncle, and amid dead silence on all sides, Karl answered at length and, by way of thanking them, sought to make a pleasant impression by using turns of phrase with a certain New York flavor. Upon hearing one such expression, all three gentlemen burst out laughing, and Karl began to fear that he had made a vulgar mistake, but not at all, for as Mr. Pollunder explained to him, he had said something that was actually quite felicitous. (45)

As with the transtextual multilingualism of "Returning Home," Kafka cannot bring himself to say quite what the "phrase with a certain New York flavor" is, as doing so would violate the monolingual contractuality of the text. Nonetheless, Karl apparently delights the locals with the age-old language-learner trick of acquiring regional idioms that are valued as in-group possessions no outsider would have occasion to trifle with.

Acquiring English is further projected into this German-language narrative through a lingua-spatial analectic of circuitous, labyrinthine figures. Karl opts to hold his tutoring sessions on the fly, while driving to riding practice: "Karl then took the teacher along in the automobile, and they drove to their English lesson, mostly via detours, since they would have lost too much time going through the bustle of the main streeet, which led directly from Uncle's house to the riding school" (42), where Karl would meet up with his first English-speaking friend Mack. Again, the dilemmas that speaking English might have posed for Karl (and the novel) are displaced into spatial figurations: detours, indirect routes, and unexpected lateral excursions.

Outsmarting multilingualism

We may be tempted then to say that this novel is hustling from the get-go to dispose, efficiently and urgently, of its own cross-lingual dilemma, through a progressive marginalization of multilingual behavior—so that Kafka's career can get down to what Lawrence Summers might call the "real business" of literary modernism (2012). Friendly as it may have been to polyglot experimentation (with luminaries like Dos Passos, Pound, Joyce, and George grousing multi-lingually around Europe's salons), avant-garde modernist literary criticism had little aesthetic patience for the arduous and unelite nitty-gritty of language *learning*. Thus, if major characters in a modernist novel were, by some necessity, also rudimentary or emergent speakers of a language implicated by the text, their linguistic subjectivity would have to be swiftly transmogrified, without demanding much attention from the novel's plot economy itself. Kafka was most certainly aware of how embodied, emergent bilingualisms were at cross-purposes with elite polgyglot modernism. As he set out to write his first novel, the multilingual twenty-six-year-old Kafka found himself stuck with a monolingual (though heteroglossic) genre that tolerated only the most polite mention of, and tidy expression of, multilingual experience. Yet he chose to compose a novel-length story whose overarching trans-formative movement is that of a "German speaker with no English" who becomes an "English speaker with no German." The question which language is "the one that disappeared" remains a metatextual riddle for this profoundly monolingual text by a profoundly multi-lingual novelist. Why and how did Kafka stake his bid for insinuation into modernist literary traffic on an endeavor that was arguably anathema to the linguistic orthodoxies of his time?

A simple answer is that Kafka was content to finesse this multi-lingual problem by staging his protagonist as a polyglot Horatio-Alger ingénu, a translingual magic-man, thus further fueling his readers' admiration for this and other feats Karl accomplishes along his exotic American journey. Imagine, for instance, how much better readers of *The Castle* might feel about K., if he'd also had to learn a new language upon arriving in the village of Count Westwest? Had this been the case, K.'s lack of preparedness and his disoriented egocentrism upon arrival might be understood—both by the novel's other characters and by its contemporary readers—with quite a bit more empathy toward his efforts at "translingual competence" in the face of the intransigent and inhospitable townsfolk (MLA 2007). Kafka however neither wished for nor delivered a quick fix for the translingual dilemmas of his first monolingual novel and its multilingual characters. Indeed, while explicit thematization of national-language choice gradually fades away over the course of the novel, a distinct pattern of irritations undermines Karl's (and the text's) happy venture toward their respective manifest linguistic destinies of postmultilingualism.

The epigraph that opens this chapter—Karl's discovery that "You simply have to know the mechanism"—offers a sort of intertitle for a moment in which Karl seems to be at wit's end with the daily work of becoming translingually and transculturally competent in a German-language novel about becoming a proper English monolingual. Up until now, he has for the most part toughed it out in good spirits with learning American English: cramming vocabulary, squeezing in tutoring sessions, making friends with an American buddy named Mack, and getting out into the cultural thick of things. But occasionally Karl tires of his new-Anglophone labors, especially in the company of Mr. Pollunder, his first American benefactor. Referring to the man's stately American mansion, Karl complains that Pollunder "talks [...] as if he were unaware of the size of this house, of the endless corridors, the chapel, the empty rooms, and the darkness everywhere" (2008: 69). Meanwhile, Karl's own German-speaking Uncle Jakob's house "seemed to him a coherent whole lying before him, empty, smooth, prepared just for him, and beckoning him with a strong voice" (2008: 71). The two empty residences—one obscure, endless, and unknowable; the other cohesive, servile, and beckoning—index how Karl experiences the monolingual systematicity of their respective English and German linguistic landscapes.

Later in his adventures, when making his way into a hotel, Karl decides to ask for help from the English-speaking clerk, but hesitates. "Karl, who had been eavesdropping, had not yet addressed her when she looked up at him and, interrupting what she was saying and using English that was as clear as a grammar book's, asked in a friendly voice if he was looking for something. 'Yes indeed,' said Karl. 'I can't get anything here'" (104). This precipitously helpful hotel staff-person is for Karl a deputy of English monolingualism as a sublime whole, "clear as a grammar book's." Her pre-emptive address surprises the young man, who had been struggling to muster up the courage to speak to her in an American English register appropriate for the setting. His unwitting and disarmed response does not answer her question at all—whether he was looking for something—but rather describes a broader deictic circumstance conditioning their exchange, both in the hotel lobby and in monolingual novelistic discourse itself: "I can't get anything here." (This translingual breakthrough and disclosure is of the sort that will rarely again transpire in Kafka's later fiction, as we will remember from the narrator's hesitation outside the kitchen door in "Returning Home.")

The "here" where Karl "can't get anything" thus doubles as physical location (the hotel and its lobby) and the always abstract, always concrete domain of literary monolingualism—a domain in which cross-lingual situations, such as the one at hand, are always already dis-figured. Barred from simulating anything but the most nativist styles of speech, the text instead indexes its author's and its protagonist's translingual impasses through spatial-deictic deferral. All these hassles notwithstanding, the hotel clerk immediately comprehends Karl's deictically overdetermined riddle, and she responds by dragging him directly through the polite sociality of the public space of the hotel (and the novel), and deep into its "mechanism":

> "Then come along with me, little fellow," she said; then she said goodbye to her acquaintance, who raised his hat, which seemed like an unbelievably polite gesture in these surroundings, and, taking Karl by the hand, went to the buffet, pushed aside a guest, opened a hinged door in the counter, and with Karl in tow, crossed the corridor behind the counter, where one had to watch out for the tirelessly circulating waiters, and opened a double door that had been covered with wallpaper, and now they found themselves in large cool pantries. "You simply have to know the mechanism," Karl said to himself. (104)

Whom is Karl actually addressing here, with his little aside? What is the epistemic scale of the revelation he is experiencing? While Bakhtin, as we have noted, hopefully theorized the inherent dynamic of the novel genre as heteroglossia, Kafka—through Karl—seems to suspect a more rigid and covert mechanism of operation is guiding it, from within.

An unwelcome breakthrough

Indeed, in *The Missing Person*, Karl's is a very different kind of thigmotactic demurral than what Gregor Samsa practices during his habitual wall- and ceiling-crawls in *The Metamorphosis*. Instead of making do within the familiar four walls, the novel has Karl chaperoned by an

English "grammar book" out of "these surroundings," through a double door that has been deliberately concealed from the guests' social vision. On the other side of the border wall, where Karl is delighted and relieved to have discovered the mechanism behind the social construction of the novelistic milieu outside, his helper grammarian-concierge then however stymies Karl's triumphal mood by posing the fatal question: "So what do you want?" (104–5) It had not occurred to Karl that, once having entered the secret, exceptional space beyond the novel's monolingual confines, he would additionally need to express concrete desires about what kind of linguistic multiplicity is worth appropriating and then taking back with him.

If we follow this line of figural thinking, which must be intra- and metatextual at once, *The Missing Person* appears more and more to be an early-career staging area for Kafka's own transformation into a literary *postmultilingual*. From 1910 to 1915, his prototypical protagonist will metamorphose from a transgressive and triumphal aesthetician of self-translativity (in Karl Rossmann) to moribund thigmotacticians of monolingual space (Gregor Samsa, *The Castle's* K., and the like). Not just agonically entrapped in one specific language or an other, Kafka's actors are entrapped in a condition of monolingualism that is an elective, yet binding feature of literature alone. Karl Rossmann's behind-the-scenes encounter with the "fat, seesawing, and delicate" formation ("*Bildung*" 104–5) of his Anglophone hotel clerk performs that very moment of metamorphosis. Right as Karl discovers the mechanism constitutive of his own textualization, he is immediately made to confront the unanticipated question that follows from transgressive desire: what would one want from a literarily multilingual modernism, if one were building it from scratch? What kinds of nourishment would Kafka and Karl wish to bring back to the "surroundings" of monolingualism from this side-shadowed *Vorratskammer* (provisions closet) of linguistic possibility and semiodiversity, in the interior of the hotel's patently multilingual immanence?[13] Karl stumbles a bit at her question:

> "So what do you want?" she asked, and in her eagerness to help she bent down toward him. She was very fat, with a body that was seesawing, but her face, at least in contrast, had almost delicate features [*Bildung*]. Seeing all the different kinds of food stacked so carefully on the shelves and tables, Karl was tempted to come up with

13. On side-shadowing, see Morson (1998).

an order for a more elegant dinner, especially since he could expect that this influential woman would serve him at no great expense, but in the end he could not think of anything suitable and merely asked for bacon, bread, and eggs. "Nothing else?" the woman asked. "No thanks," said Karl, "but it's for three." When the woman asked about the other two, Karl said a few words about his companions; being asked a few questions like this gave him pleasure.

"But that meal is fit only for convicts [*Sträflinge*]," said the woman, clearly awaiting Karl's further wishes. (104–5)

Karl (and Kafka) know they can theoretically *have* literary multilingualism, even of the non-literary and unpublishable sort, but for what purpose and for how many people/readers? Indeed, unutterable and unpublishable languages in Kafka are often associated, as in this scene, with food: a food housed elsewhere, out of reach from the protagonist's deictic narrative position within monolingualism.

So when Karl gets the chance not only to experience the space of other-language "nourishment," but also to order whatever he wants from it, he defers asking for something specific to his tastes, though his host seems willing to provide it at no extra expense. Instead, Karl shoots far lower than the stars in this heterotopic, heterolingual space, asking only for multiple portions of the same humble dish: bacon, bread and eggs. Tempered by a sense for appropriateness, he opts for enumeration, rather than elaboration. Here we see both the reproduction of what Alastair Pennycook calls "the pluralization of monolingualism" (2010: 12), i.e. the reproduction of identical signs (and syntactical arrangements of signs) in multiple codes, as well as a foreshadowing of what Tim Parks will call the "new dull global novel" (2012; see Chapter 3) one hundred years after *Amerika*. This agile, thick host of other language—ready to provide whatever is available in the cool storage room of affordances—finds Karl's request disappointing; she describes it as an order worthy of only a "convict," but obliges nonetheless.

What becomes of the missing person?

There has indeed been a great deal of scholarly inquiry about whether Karl becomes anything at all in this novel, and whether *The Missing Person* can even be termed a *bildungsroman* in the end. Some scholars focus on his devloping masculinity (for instance Boa 2005), others on his symbolic Zionism (Metz 2004). Indeed, a search for progressive transformation makes philological sense, as this novel and its protagonist seem to offer the last hope in the Kafkan oeuvre for optimistic growth and change of any kind—before his late-era pantheon of ignored hunger artists, indicted everymen, and accidental beetles comes to predominate. One way to read the novel optimistically—for those who wish to—is as an "American Dream" story of immigration, an experiment in cosmopolitanism and multilingualism, which ultimately coalesces with Karl's civic integration into the eternal civic experiment of the Oklahoma Theater. Yet Karl is also "becoming monolingual," both in compliance with abruptly shifting U.S. civic ideologies about immigration between the presidency of Theodore Roosevelt and World War I, but also in compliance with the monolingual meta-form of "the novel" as a high modern genre.

As we have seen with this first novel, it is among the linguistic thigmotactician Franz/František Kafka's preferred textual operations to displace linguistic multiplicity into spatial figures and deictic malaises—into oddly menacing thresholds and neighboring rooms, unreachable and distant surfaces, obscure circuits of hallways and detours, troubling ruptures between "here" and "there." Often, the textual format itself tends to stagger laterally at the level of the syntagm, sentence, or chapter, giving rise to a loose and troubled contiguity, of "many lower, tightly packed [buildings]"—one way the landsurveyor K. beholds the architectural structure of Westwest's residence in *The Castle* (1998: 8). But *The Missing Person* offers a second riddle that departs from this allegorical form of spatial dispacement, turning rather to the history of literary-translational temperament.

The *Amerika* novel is one of the few Kafka texts that stage raucous cross-linguistic stuntwork, where the hero both hungers for and succeeds at "intercultural dialogue"—a rare and often quite frightful occurrence in Kafka. Especially in the later works, the failure to cross—or to be dragged across—such thresholds tends to prevail. But even *The Missing Person*, Kafka's initial experiment in multilingual figuration, was ultimately left unfinished, as Karl Rossmann abruptly absconds from representation at precisely that moment in the narrative when he begins to consort with the infinite chorus of trumpeting angels at the Oklahoma Theater. Ultimately, speaking the angel chorus's standard American English—making the noise of the *Engeln*—becomes Karl's own sacred duty too; he (and the other assimilating angels) assent to the linguistic patriotism that U.S. President Theodore Roosevelt demanded of new immigrant Americans in the advent of World War I.[14]

Karl is swept up into the mesmerizing unison of the ensemble and begins to discover its precious subtleties. "It's so wonderful we'll be together again," cheers his friend Fanny as Karl decides to join the chorus of monolinguals. But she warns, "don't spoil the chorus, or I'll be dismissed." The (German) text of *The Missing Person* trails off soon after, as Karl's contract with English monolingualism is sealed: "Karl began to play; he had imagined it was a crudely made instrument, only for making noise, but it was in fact an instrument capable of producing almost every refinement" (271). Now fully fledged in English and taken up into the communal embrace of its institutions, Karl indeed becomes the *Verschollene,* the "lost one" who leaves behind the text's own medium of production, Prague German. The novel breaks off as Karl, perpetually lost to us readers, is sublated into his new postmultilingual role in the angel-chorus.

Theorizing the "mechanism" of monolingualism

"Generally speaking we ignore historical research entirely."
—Franz Kafka, "Josephine the Singer" (1924)

To consider the Oklahoma Theater scene itself the euphoric/ dysphoric moment of arrival into American monolingualism—into its undeservedly cheerful sociality, its aesthetic monotony, its political self-deception, its oblivion about its own enforced enclosure and immobility—would however leave Karl's story about the mechanism of monolingualism only half-analyzed. Such a reading would also place undue emphasis on American English as the sole culprit of a cultural monolingualism particular to U.S. history, something Kafka was neither particularly knowledgeable about or invested in critiquing. Kafka is after a more formidable opponent than mere jingoistic American-style cultural purism.

In the midst of his own transformation into a well-tempered American monolingual, Karl Rossmann begged his benefactor for a piano, a technology that was, for the first time around 1912, being

14. On President Theodore Roosevelt's political monolingualism, see for instance Vicente L. Rafael's essay "Translation, American English, and the National Insecurities of Empire" (2012): 460.

subjected to industry-standard tuning in *equal* temperament. *Equal* temperament is not the same innovation as *well*-temperament, however; Bach's *well*-temperament system, proposed in the 1720s, had preserved more discord in certain keys, based on the idea that listeners' experience of slight temporary dysphoria would be pleasurably resolved when the player returns to more internally consonant keys on the well-tempered instrument. Karl's freshly delivered piano in the Amerika novel is an altogether different machine than Bach's, tuned with no such scheme of dissonance and resolution among abutting keys in performance. This piano he asks his uncle for is the hard-won historical product of optimized technocracy over sound, cultivated over eight centuries. Its material imperfections of tuning have been tempered into near inaudibility by distributing them mathematically among all keys and octaves on the instrument. Karl is elated about the (equal-temperament) piano's arrival:

> In the first few days, when naturally there were frequent exchanges between Karl and his uncle, he had said that he had played on the piano at home, only a bit but with considerable pleasure, though he had had to make do with the beginner's skills his mother had taught him. Karl was well aware that in telling this story he was in effect requesting a piano, but he had taken a sufficiently good look around to know that his uncle had no need to economize. Still, his request was not granted at once, but about eight days later his uncle announced, almost reluctantly, that the piano had just arrived and that, if Karl wished, he could supervise the move. (39)

This set of feelings and desires Karl is experiencing about piano-playing arises, as we have seen previously, simultaneously with his aggresive attempts to learn English. Whereas Karl will ultimately end up playing the (monolingual) trumpet alongside Fanny and the other members of the largest theater in the world, his process of language acquisition takes place accompanied by a different category of normative instrument. Pianos, clavichords, organs, and other keyboard instruments are categorically different creatures in the history of musical mechanics than are horns, string instruments, and the human voice, because the latter are tuned, effectively, by their players in the process of playing and can be adjusted in situ and ad hoc. The fact that keyboard instruments are bound to the conditions of their pre-performance tuning by a technician (who is not generally also the player) restrains the closed set of discrete tones they are capable of playing before fetching the tuner, but it also co-constrains any other instruments that are to be played in concert with the keyboard. This means that, as keyboard temperament systems underwent innovation from the late medieval to the high modern period, everyone else had to play along. If this sounds like the process of monolingualization—the institution of pre-tuned, panfunctional languages according to which all must play along to one calibrated and coordinated orthodoxy of transposability—then this is not merely an allegorical resemblance. Kafka's novel suggests that musical temperament and monolingualism are historically intertwined traditions in the honing and development of a general paradigm of technocratic meaning-making.

The novel as tempered instrument

As Karl reminisces in the passage above about his prior (allolingual) life in the old country, the performative force of that act of narrating—in the threshold period of 1910–15—was that, "in telling this story he was in effect requesting a piano" (39). That is, the telling of any kind of novelistic story was tantamount to subscribing to a postmultilingual system of *equal literary temperament*. We are thus simultaneously reading a semiotic performance on the level of plot as well as a rehearsal upon the tempered instrument of the monolingual novel. Karl's narrative presence is thus always more than just that of an immigrant making his way through the momentary affordances of multilingual America, but also that of a henolingual cursor making its way through the afforded provisions of a postmultilingual book in an age of equal temperament ideology.

Noting that "telling a story" in a novel effectively means "asking for a piano", Karl then thinks twice about whether his bilingual immigrant uncle indeed has the space and resources to accommodate such an instrument—in a Germanophone domicile within an Anglophone country within a Germanophone novel. That Karl then only needs to take "a sufficiently good look around to know that his uncle had no need to economize (*sparen*)" can be read in several parallel modes: 1) The businessman uncle, bilingual in his enterprises and yet in no need of multilingual literary expression himself, is unaffected by the advent of newly constrained systems of expressive temperament and monolingual literary representation. Like Kafka's father Hermann, the merchant of petty wares and fashion commodities, literary and institutional monolingualisms were of little account in the daily workings of his trade. 2) The same non-concern about temperament and monolingualism applies to the narrated spaces of America itself, where freewheeling market ventures, wide-open spaces, and speculative plentitude offer more spoils than any restrictive system of literary expression could constrain. 3) Karl is "taking a good look around" the novel genre itself, realizing that—given Kafka's already monolingualist mode of artistry—introducing a piano in equal temperament into the mix would not require any greater sacrifice in language than his author had already freely made.

Still, the worldly uncle seems to know better, and announces the arrival of Karl's new piano not quite "almost reluctantly" (39)—as Mark Harman's beautiful English translation has it—but "*fast in der Form eines widerwilligen Eingeständnisses.*" Here, the evocation of "form" is crucial: indeed, the "form of a begrudging confession/concession/ avowal" allows the piano to arrive. Prior to this formal concession, there is even a pause of eight days in the novel's narration, evoking the tuning of a do-re-mi-fa-so-la-ti-do octave in diatonic equal temperament, i.e. the re-tuning of the novel into monolingualism.[15]

(De-)dramatizing transposability

When Karl's new instrument does indeed arrive, his reluctant but accommodating uncle suggests that Karl himself can supervise the "transport" of the instrument into the house, a process described in equally droll terms:

> [Supervising the transport] was certainly easy work, though scarcely any easier than the actual move, since the building had a special furniture elevator that could easily accommodate an entire furniture vehicle, and it was in this elevator that the piano glided up to Karl's room. Karl could have taken the same goods elevator as the piano and the workers, but since the passenger elevator [*Personalaufzug*] right beside it happened to be free, he chose that one instead, keeping himself at the same height as the other elevator with the help of a lever and constantly looking through the glass panels of the elevator at the beautiful instrument that now belonged to him. When it stood

---

15. When the eleventh-century Guido Arezzo codified these names for the tones of the octave, he set them to a hymn to John the Baptist: "<u>Ut</u> queant laxis <u>re</u>sonare floris <u>Mi</u>ra gestorum <u>fa</u>muli tuorum <u>so</u>lve pollute <u>la</u>bii reatum," forever hence linking Western tonality to Christian piety.

in his room and he struck the first keys, he felt such wild joy that, rather than continuing to play, he jumped up, preferring to stand some distance away, hands on his hips, gazing at the piano. (2008: 39)

Kafka is drawing here on a thousand-year history of the laborious transportation of keyboard instruments as diplomatic gifts and emblems of cutting-edge technical progress: first among them organs given from sovereign to sovereign—for instance from an Arab court to the emperor of China—as early as the seventh century. An organ, like that belonging to Winchester Cathedral at the end of the tenth century, was an instrument of territorialization, in that it established tonal values for as far as its sonic prowess would reach. Like the town clock would later become, the organ was the instrument to which all other registers of meaning were tuned. This allowed for a great deal of local specificity in the tuning protocols and harmonic textures of municipal organs and musics. A global practical standard for tone values was on no one's agenda until deep into the seventeenth century, though there were rancorous theoretical contestations long before across Europe about ideal tuning principles.

For his part, Kafka is not known as much of a theorist of music or temperament. In a 1998 essay on one of Kafka's more famous early stories, John Vignaux Smyth points out that music is a much deeper epistemic category for Kafka than apparent at first:

"Investigations of a Dog" [...] goes so far as to bifurcate Science as a whole into "the science of music" and "the science of nourishment"—as though no other valid scientific objects or domains of knowledge could be conceived. Here, "music" seems to be used in almost as extensive a way as it was used by the ancient Greeks when, for instance, they divided Athenian education between music and gymnastics. The first term of this pair may seem to us metaphorical; but for the Greeks themselves, of course, it was no more *merely* metaphorical than music is, I suggest, in Kafka. On the contrary, Kafka embodies a challenge to the discipline of quite "literal" music theory as well as to cultural theory more generally. (169–70)

While such music-theoretical and music-historiographic concerns underpin a great deal of Kafkan figural work, they do so on the level of mechanics, tuning, and temperament, as much as they do in the realm of vocal or tonal aesthetics writ large. Smyth notes that the mathematized formal semiotics of music in the Aristotelian-Christian tradition not only suppressed the threat of social flesh, as Nietzsche described, and "the arbitrariness of the sign run wild" (Smyth 170), but it also invented certain kinds of productive *instruments,* whose performativity still remains relatively marginal in loftier discussions of modern aesthetic philosophy.

Smyth's analysis focuses in Kafka on the human voice and on vocalic instruments such as trumpets, though we may learn just as much from Kafka's keyboard instruments. From a high-modern perspective like Karl's, it would seem nothing less than tragic and parochial to imagine that a skilled keyboard player in the seventeenth century, in the midst of performing a cantata in D, simply *could not* take a flight of fancy into the domain of A—a key which is comprised of all the same white and black keys save one (G sharp). Prior to the rise of well-temperament in the eighteenth century, musicians and composers alike needed to devise clever, practical work-arounds to "hide the wolf" of dissonance in keyboard compositions requiring multiple keys (Lehman 2005), lest the instrument's natural tone proportions reveal themselves to the unsuspecting listener by way of painful and throbbing acoustic clashes. Most musical compositions before 1700 had no wolf to hide, however, as they did not strive to range beyond one key per performance sitting—or did not require a keyboard instrument, as later symphonic arrangements routinely would.

For most of musical history until the Thirty Years War, one could generally assume that a given piece of music would dwell in one musical mode and in one musical key alone. Indeed, the universe of belief that informed medieval music compositions had no reason to accommodate multiple keys or modes. Latter-day developments toward exogamy and transposability in key has few more pure, passionate, and concrete instantiations than the arduous invention of musical temperament systems for piano. The multilingual English-learner Karl, stuck in a German-language novel, is thus "supervising" the transport(ability) of an instrument and its historically hard-won temperament system into his home. But as Karl greets the arrival of the piano and readies himself for the installation process, it proves to be no labor at all. There is no negotiation to do, no Pythagorean commas to be dealt with, and no bickering between defendants of one temperament system over another. There is no battle between empiricists and idealists, no incensed advocate for mathematically pure and proportionally crystalline harmonies over the *alogons*—the boundless, disorderly, incommensurable numbers—necessary for tuning a piano equally, no strategic planning for where to hide the dissonant "wolf fifth" in an otherwise promising composition. There is no Sir Isaac Newton, insisting there was something wrong with scales based on modern, "contrived" proportions in equal temperament, which were for Newton as intolerable as "soiled and faint colors are to the eye" (Isacoff 25).

Feeling at odds with temperament

For Karl, busy supervising the arrival of equal temperament and monolingualism, it all seems a rather simple procedure of pre-programmed mobility, hardly any more laborious than are the efforts of the piano-movers, for whom the house has been built with easy egress and access for such goods in mind. With a lever, Karl calibrates, or tunes, his own parallel ascent in the house's "personnel elevator" according to the speed at which the instrument ascends in the freight elevator next to him, visible through the glass panes. Imagined laterally, Karl and the piano are musical notes ascending the five floors of the house like a musical staff—melodies playing together, with Karl mechanically "tuned" all the while to the new instrument to ensure unison:

> Besides, the acoustics in the room were splendid, and that helped him overcome the slight discomfort he had initially felt on discovering that he was living in a building made of steel. In reality, though, no matter how steel-like the building seemed from the outside, in the actual room there was no sign of the steel components employed in its construction, and no one could have pointed out the tiniest item in the interior design that would have in any way spoiled the overall effect of complete comfort and ease. In his first days there Karl had hoped to accomplish a great deal through his piano playing and was not ashamed—at least just before falling asleep—to imagine that his playing might directly affect his situation in America. (39)

At first, Karl seems to be wary of the instrument and the new range of sound it affords and requires, especially given that the mechanical, inorganic nature of the instrument threatens to engulf the entire steel structure of the house. He is asked by his friend Klara, "Do you want some sheet music?" to which he answers: "No thanks, I cannot even read music properly," indicating his unschooled habitus in orthographic notation systems, as well as his sense of illegitimacy as a performer. This oblivion toward music-theoretical norms, however, allows him to hear social acoustics around him in ways that equal temperament disallows:

> It certainly sounded strange whenever he stood in front of windows opening out onto the noisy street, playing an old soldier's song from his homeland, which the soldiers, who used to lie by the barrack windows at night looking down at the dark square, would sing from one window to the next—but then when he looked down on the street he could see that it had not changed at all and merely formed one small part of a great cycle that one could not actually bring to a halt unless one were aware of all of the forces operating in the cycle. (40)

Here Karl is tempted away from the linguistic and musical temperament ideology immanent in his newly acquired instrument, though he seems to become reassured by the end of the passage. Played in equal temperament on the piano, the soldier's song from his otherly-languaged homeland sounds unlike the vernacular window-to-window transmissions of the soldiers, for whom there is no temperament system beyond the social telegraphy of their own voices. What Karl confronts in his performance is the difference between glossodiversity (as delivered and ensured by his new piano) and semiodiversity (as embodied by the window-to-window soldier songs of his memories). Striving to make his playing correspond with the melodic intersubjective din outside the window, Karl then imagines it all to be part of a great cycle or system (here perhaps the circle of harmonic fifths in which Bach composed *The Well-Tempered Clavier*). Though the cycle is in perpetual, vivid, living, vernacular motion, no one can stop it without mastering its underlying principle of operation: the dream of transposability, of exile without longing, of glossodiversity without difference. The following scene suggests indeed that temperament mechanics and the monolingual novel form collude to suppress awareness of multilingual semiodiversity, as Karl gives up the attempt to perform the melody-from-elsewhere:

> He began to perform his beloved soldier's song, so slowly that the listener's roused desire continually reached for the next note, which Karl held on to for some time and then at last released. As with every song, he first had to glance at the keys he needed but rising within he could sense a sadness that already searched beyond the ending of the song for another ending that, however, it failed to find. "I'm simply no good," Karl said on finishing the song, and looked at Klara with tears in his eyes. (79)

Affectively, Karl's soldier's song is propelled by the maxim of "expressive intonation" attributed to cellist Pablo Casals, namely that "leading notes should lead" (Duffin 2008: 19). This means for instance that, in an ascending melodic line, the notes should be played higher than they are calibrated for in equal temperament, so that the tones themselves express a desire to resolve into the tonic. Like the soldiers singing window-to-window, Karl finds this practice of expressive intonation to be not only natural, but also the hallmark of good music. It is, however, in the process of playing the soldier's song on his new equal-temperament piano that he realizes for the first time that such "leading" tonal expressivity is impossible amid the new acoustic relations that, he has hoped, will "directly affect his situation here in America" (39), and he falls into a state of disconsolation. That the melody he had sought to play on the instrument "searched beyond the ending of the song for another ending that, however, it failed to find" prefigures how the novel—and all of Kafka's novels after it—will break off mid-sentence, failing to find the narrative end it yearned for. Kafkan unfinishability is thus at base a distemper with the mechanics of postmultilingual ideology, rather than a general predicament of the literary ineffable, the troubles of an anguished author, or the dysphoria of a protagonist vanquished by linguistic nationalism. Just as Karl's performance of the soldier's song is scuttled by equal tempermanent, Kafka's figurations are—in a parallel and co-extensive way—scuttled by monolingualism.

The revolution of the clavichord, more than a mere technical innovation restricted to music, is a paradigm shift in meaning itself, or what globalization specialists call "content delivery." Temperament systems transformed *key* from a semiotic system of precise internal coherence to a grid of practical external transposability. By the time Karl supervises the arrival of his new postmultilingual piano, an emic, self-relational, intra-key ecology of sound characteristic of pre-indus-trial musics had been repurposed into an etic, cosmopolitan reserve of ready-to-use transposability. Whatever relation of value obtained in one key, or language, could be practically reproduced in another. This dream of practical reproducibility relied on a new episteme of compromise and consent about the *sign*, resulting in the primacy of transposition over situated essences. This movement could be described as *progressive disimplication,* whereby the value of a given tone was no longer compulsorily implicated in its own discursive habitat or key. Its value and meaning was now a function of exportability—to all other available keys.

The legacy of the monolingual contract

Kafka's covert operations in *The Missing Person* hail for critique a number of customary categories of creative and critical work in ways that post-structuralist literary theory did not find occasion to problematize. What is the analytical relevance of the subjectivity of the multilingual writer, when his or her vocational domain of text-production is so effectively constrained by the mechanisms of (mono)lingualism? How can criticism account for a text that is always lured toward the multilingual world, without ever successfully countenancing it representationally? If the monolingualism of (literary) text is juridical and mechanical, rather than substantive and cultural, how can its constitutive borders be located, from within and from without? Beyond the text, how do affirmative slogans, glossodiverse images, and programmatic rhetorics about being multilingual—both in Kafka's time and ours—foreclose upon the type of meaning-making sesnsibility Karl struggles to recover while playing his untempered soldier's song on an equal-tempered piano? What possibilities for "revolutionary infrastructure" (Boyer 2016) may be possible when technocracies of meaning like monolingualism and equal temperament are finally discovered to be inadequate for human thriving?

In this chapter, I have tried to show how Franz Kafka, in full awareness of the postmultilingual turn in musical temperament and literary logistics, committed himself nonetheless to a monolingual palette. I have suggested that recourse to heteroglossia, and the lure of translingual writing, often overestimate the flexibility of literary genres and the readiness of publishing norms to accommodate the multilingual, semiodiverse world, and that such non-accommodation is a systemic rather than nationalistic epiphenomenon of "lingualism" since the early modern period. Kindred to the work of monochrome painter Aleksander Rodchenko, Kafka's literaricity is "the reminder of the culture [...] we have not been able to create" (Batchelor 2000: 153). This is however no mere admonishment or gesture of despair; Chapter 3 takes up where Kafka's artistry of monolingualism left off—namely with contemporary authors who find ways to make umtempered meaning, from within the postmultilingual literary industry.

Chapter 3

THE PASSING OF WORLD LITERARICITY

My hero is a Turk and therefore no relation of Kafka's; they are
related only in the literary sense of the word.
　　　　　　　—Orhan Pamuk, "In Kars and Frankfurt" (2005)

We can hear the world: it says, "World and World."
　　　　　　　—Peter Waterhouse, "The Sound Valley" (2003),
　　　　　　　　　　　　translated by Andrew Ziesig et al.

A theologian colleague was chatting some years ago with his five-
year-old daughter over breakfast, and she asked him, with prudent
impatience: "Daddy ... what is God doing, *now*?" Seeing both virtue
and urgency in setting aside all the eschatological gambits available
to her from prior conversations about the divine, this kindergartner
instead wanted her father to tell her exactly what God had been
doing in that moment—or, at least, *lately*. Her query—and its implicit
admission, that God may just be too busy right now doing work for
others to have an extra ear for her own predicaments—was surely a bit
of genius, worthy of Aquinas or Ibn Rushd. To this, her father replied:
"He's making *all the things*."

While comparative literature presses on through a third decade
of vigor around defining world literature amid accelerated relations
of economic globalization—discussions which themselves often tack
theological in diction, logic, and grandeur—it might be a prudent
moment as well to ask, in the spirit of this five-year-old's constructivist
itch: "What is world literature doing, *now*?" To this, one provisional
answer might also be: "It's making *all the books*." Indeed, called on as
we often are to satisfy the Goethian or Marxian prompt "What is world
literature?" with a set of requisite traits about world-ready, translatable,
or—more recently—"relatable" literary texts, we might instead find
useful harbor in such an apparently temporizing demurral as hers.
Though it may appear merely an inelegant dodge into the sociologi-
zation of the literary, the choice to descriptively chart the contemporary

relations of world-literary production and reception, rather than any of "its" essential characteristics, may ultimately yield richer insights. David Damrosch has written for instance about why it might be that a novel like Milorad Pavić's *Dictionary of the Khazars* manifests utterly differently in its domestic Serbian political context than it does abroad in translation—a line of thought that leads Damrosch to see a general need for a phenomenology of world literature, rather than an ontology of it (2005: 394). Damrosch is accordingly interested in how this and other novels *manifest* in the world, and in how they are made to manifest in certain travel-ready ways. Accounting for today's infrastructural conditions for world-literary appearance—beyond the character of its individual instances—can help critique world literature's mythic aura of systematicity, coherence, and sovereign intercultural beneficence, without forsaking its poetic promise in the process.

Let us note some contemporary inroads. Pheng Cheah's recent intervention "World Against Globe" (2014) has sought to recover the common sense (from Immanuel Kant to Erich Auerbach) in which worldly literature ought always to be conceived as normative and prolegomenal to humanity as an historical project. For these men, it must be of the temporal world, and not of the spatial map; it must be a moment or momentum of historical becoming, and not merely a wager on commercial extensivity. Otherwise, holds Cheah, the practice and eventual analysis of world-literary writing is left up to global free-market forces alone. "Recent attempts to revive world literature," he claims, "have obscured its normative dimension because they have only understood the world in terms of spatial circulation, the paradigmatic case of which is global capitalist market exchange" (303). Cheah thus calls for an unmapping of world literature, one that is ready to forego the winsome image of the literary text as a flexible commodity traipsing the globe, a neoliberal *bildungsroman* elaborating its own maturation into universal appeal, acquiring surplus value in every new market it touches down in. Not a mere recuperation of high-/low-culture divides, Cheah's essay cast critical light on the current logic of commodity circulation and how it is allowed to pass for world-literary dialogue. This divestment from the capital-accrual schema of world literaricity indeed undermines the triumphalist, wealth-management model of Pascale Casanova, who paints a different picture:

> Literary history rests [...] neither on national chronologies nor on a series of neatly juxtaposed works, but on the succession of revolts and emancipations thanks to which writers, despite their irreducible

dependence on language, have managed to create the conditions of a pure and autonomous literature, freed from considerations of political utility. It is the history of the appearance, then of the accumulation, concentration, distribution, and diversion of literary wealth, which first arose in Europe and subsequently became the object of belief and rivalry throughout the world. (2007: 46)

Here, in contrast to Cheah's appeal, is a Nietzschean moral vision of world-worthy literaricity as that endemic species of capital capable of sustaining a unique, historically contingent, creative counter-nation, a haughty parvenu disdainful of ordinary politics, a self-made myth—passed on from victor to victor amid an otherwise compromised and treacherous landscape of mundane allegiances. World literature for Casanova is the virtuous phylogenetic prerogative to seize and safeguard creative sovereignty.

Devolving world-literary currencies

This logic of a semi-sovereign field of world-literary relations, spatially and institutionally concurrent with political hegemony but diffident toward it, comes in at least two varieties. Casanova's Gallocentric (or at least centripetal) description finds contrary voices for instance in theorists interested in phenomena of interference in the world-literary system, like Roberto Schwarz and Itamar Evan-Zohar, who nonetheless likewise take recourse to economic models and the rhetoric of inter-national monetary subvention. As Schwarz writes in his essay on the importing of the novel to Brazil: "Foreign debt is as inevitable in Brazilian letters as in any other field. It's not simply an easily dispensable part of the work in which it appears, but a complex feature of it" (1992: 50). To this assertion, Evan-Zohar adds that "There is no symmetry in literary interference. A target literature is, more often than not, interfered with by a source literature which completely ignores it" (1990: 62). In the figural landscape of both the Gallocentric and the provincializing versions of this logic, the literary remains a common currency, exchanged, transferred, and allocated concur-rently alongside other forms of diplomatic heft. A "target" literature may put up a fight, but ultimately is found yielding to the mergers and acquisitions dynamics of North Atlantic forms, genres, and narrative conventions. Creative domestications occur, but most often in some lingering tension of debt relationship on the part of what Evan-Zohar calls "source literatures." But what is the underlying currency in which this balance sheet is maintained? Translational monolingualism.

In this model of global circulation, an idiom of source and target, or—as in translation studies—of domestication and foreignization holds sway, maintaining an image of the literary globe as constituted through metonymies of territory (whether those of debtors or targets) by which authors must write as Turkish, Scottish, Gallego, French, or Guatemalan writers, in order to become world-literary. Not pertaining in some reproducible way to one of these metonymies threatens to cause a series of procedural misfires in the prospecting, acquisition, editing, marketing, and reviewing of world-literary texts. Where is this writer *from*, again? What culture(s) is she sharing, and how are editors to shepherd her text's domestication via serial translation into a roster of international markets for readers presumed to be monolingual, or at least monolingually inclined in their reading habits?

This is a particularly troubling dynamic for writers who occupy an adverse relationship to the "lingualism" presumed of them—for instance those who, as John Kerrigan writes in *Archipelagic English*, "are anglophone but not necessarily English and who often have no place in the canon, or, more insidiously, are there on the wrong footing" (Kerrigan 2008: 10). Kerrigan thus calls for a "devolution" of English, in order to rehistoricize Hiberno-English and Scots, a prospect similar in scale and zeal to Makoni and Pennycook's call for "disinventing languages" (2006). Kerrigan writes:

> The incentive to strip away modern Anglocentric and Victorian imperial paradigms to recover the long, braided histories played out across the British–Irish archipelago between three kingdoms, four countries, divided regions, variable ethnicities and religiously determined allegiances is there even for those who are skeptical about the desirability of Scottish or Welsh independence. (2008: 2)

While that project of linguistic devolution is pending, authors writing toward Scots or Hiberno-English will be adversely positioned in the diplomatic system of monolingualisms that understand them to be part of English literature. For Tony E. Jackson, this means that "the novel is the most alphabetic kind of written story" (Jackson 2009: 4–5), in that it requires a constant assimilatory tack toward the metropole's "lingualism". The Scottish novelist James Kelman describes what happens when, for instance, Scots semiodiversity is sought in a novel, beyond what Jackson considers the metropole's *alphabetography*. Kelman writes:

In Scottish the "man" will speak with what is called a "heavy burr." This is what the general run of lower-order Scottish people have in English literature, "heavy burrs." The writers may highlight this within the text. Colonial servants and underlings are integral to English literature and different conventions exist to deal with them. One such convention is the apparent attempt at phonetic transcription. I mean by that the spelling of words to give the impression of sound. I say "apparent" because there is no authentic attempt going on. (2008: 60–1)

Such are some of the literary problems that have emerged most intensively in a period we may choose to call multicultural, post-ethnic, superdiverse, or postmonolingual—a period where ethnicity has ceased to offer satisfying explanatory power as to the provenence or import of a literary work.

From multilingual authorship to postmultilingual world literaricity

This chapter explores how markets have taken refuge in translational monolingualism as the replacement for ethnonationalism in world-literary traffic. I will suggest that this transnational institutional investment in lingualism, over ethnicism—in the fiscal sense of the word investment—has led to the kind of consequences I have described in Chapter 1 as *postmultilingual.* That is, world-literary authors are required in the twenty-first century to "do their language" in a strategically centripetal way, one that eases the process of translation while nonetheless fulfilling the representational service into which ethnicity or national communion were once pressed in the twentieth century. Let us consider an instance in which postmultilingual pressure appears to have been in evidence over the course of one world-literary author's early period of transnational reception.

I first taught Junot Díaz's *The Brief Wondrous Life of Oscar Wao* in Turkey, in 2010, hoping that my English-medium-university students would find in Díaz's kinetic and insurgent code-mixing a vindication of their own multilingual practices, in an educational environment that still conceived of elite discourse as always already belonging in and to English—but always someone else's English, and not their own. In class, my late-teenage Turkish–Arabic–English(–and-now-Dominican-reading) comrades fell instantly in love with Díaz's sentences like "A culo que jalaba más que una junta de buey" (2008: 92), whose single "English" word was the gaunt and indefinite article "a" launching an otherwise robust barrage of sexist metaphor. Díaz's liberty-taking with the still rather stodgily monolingual genre of the transnational novel reminded many of my students of their own translingual syntax, in admixtures of Kurdish, Turkish, English, German, and other languages, while it reminded others among them of Ottoman courtly poetry, which often consisted of strophes with not one historically Turkish word among the Arabic and Persian poetic loan lexicon, despite an underlying Turkish syntactic structure.

The Pulitzer-worthy genius of *Oscar Wao*'s literary multilingualism lay, to my mind, in its disorienting metapragmatics around code-mixing itself: how it pulled the rug out from under readers' anticipatory notions about the reasonable limits of their own interpretive responsibilities (or some would say "competences") while reading a centrifugal, multi-voiced literary text. How much code-mixing was just too much for readability, accessibility, publishability, translatability? When is the limit for multilingualism reached in each of those four cases? How is readerly tolerance diminished when the code-mixes aren't tied to a symbolic investment in the cultural politics of Dominican identity? In *Wao*, for instance, any given unfamiliar word or phrase one encountered could just as easily be found to be of Star Trek, X-Men, or Wagnerian provenance as it could be assumed to be Dominican or pan-Latin@ Spanish, or New Jersey youth vernacular. The ethnic ascription Melnibonian for instance—used to describe a "handsome [read: white]" boy in a Dominican classroom in *Wao* (89)—stemmed from the fantasy writing of Michael Moorcock, and not from any legible mapping of cultural politics in the twenty-first-century Americas. It was through this splicing, dodging, and articulating of various categories of translingual citation—of Melnibonians among Domos among Puertorocks—that Díaz's code-switching repertoire in *Wao* reclaimed for the transnational novel the kind of poetic wonder proper to it, a wonder beyond the functionalist reaches of social romanticism.

But what my students in Turkey found more compelling, even, was how Díaz dealt—indeed multilingually—with the affective predicament of living daily amid Western discursive exportations, and their kitsch, disauthenticating effects on their own lives and life stories in modern Turkey. One Arabic-speaking pious Muslim young woman in my class, raised near the Syrian border, titled her final seminar paper "Santo Domingo was Iraq before Iraq was Iraq," citing the preface to Díaz's novel (4). In the Schwarzian historiographic tradition of "put[ting] our misplaced ideas back where they belong, without ignoring the realities which have caused them to get misplaced" (Schwarz 1992), this one young reader of Díaz took delight and refuge in the pugilistic autoethnographic style with which he explained the ground truths of global American militarism to twenty-first-century Anglophone U.S. readers.

Wao's narrator, who calls himself the Watcher, often glosses items from the *Dictionary of Dominican Things* in footnotes, for instance:

> The pejorative *pariguayo* [...] is a corruption of the English neologism Party Watcher. The word came into common usage during the first U.S. occupation of the DR, which ran from 1916 to 1924. (You didn't know we were occupied twice in the twentieth century? Don't worry, when you have kids, they won't know the U.S. occupied Iraq either.) (19)

In this way, the implied Anglophone monolingualism of *Wao*'s readership is found guilty (by association) of world-historical oblivion, not just failure to learn languages other than English. One partiality begets another, says *Wao*.

But after this debut novel, a major shift occurred in how Díaz approached mono-/multilingual narrative composition. None of the parenthetical footnoting—whether didactic or dismissive—that peppered *Wao* occurs in Díaz's follow-up collection of interwoven short stories, *This is How You Lose Her* (2012), where the linguistic centrifugality of the text is more subdued and circumscribed. The difference in multilingual bearing in these two texts offers us the opportunity to acknowledge how formally divergent the practice of intratextual code-switching in fiction can be, and also to consider how authors' multilingualisms may change according to the success with which their work is distributed and translated.

A comparative case is the German Turkish novelist Feridun Zaimoglu, whose fictions shifted from a combative trilingualism (German–Turkish–English) in his earliest fictional texts from the mid-1990s, which won him in Germany the honorific designation "The Elephant in the Paul Celan Shop" (Droste 1998), to a rather placid belles-lettristic monolingualism in his novels from the late 2000s. In this regard, Zaimoglu's career, from feisty multilingual agitator to a more postmultilingual temperament, reiterates Kafka's own reckoning with the meta-formal confines of literary writing, from 1907 onward. In Zaimoglu's case, his shift in publishers from ID-Archiv to Kiepenheuer & Witsch, and the increasing likelihood that his fictions will be translated (or contracted with translation options in tow), meant that a freely code-meshing writerly subjectivity was no longer manageable from a marketing perspective, even though it was precisely this untempered radical translingual practice that had gained for him his initial profile on the German literary market.

In Díaz's *This is How You Lose Her,* the Brazilian literary theorist Roberto Schwarz's (and my Turkish students') sense for discursive positionality is dealt with as follows: "Santo Domingo is Santo Domingo. Let's pretend we know what goes on there" (10). Less interested in calling out Anglophone monolingualism for its historiographic partiality than *Wao* had been, *Lose Her* is more inclined to submerge untempered translingualism hypotextually, focusing instead on narrating interpersonal dynamics around language use *within the story*—which is indeed a more conventional way to deal with the fact of multiple languages in published narratives, as in the language memoirs of Richard Rodriguez, Eva Hoffman, and others. In *Lose Her,* characters are described as withholding Spanish from each other, young learners of English refuse to help their Spanish-speaking mother learn English along with them, fathers tell their no-good, womanizing sons: "You no deserve I speak to you in Spanish" (4). Are these also metatextual gestures towards an alibi for monolingualism? The narrator discloses his own limitations too: reflecting on conversations with a "campesina ... a *Dominican Dominican*," foreign to his own New Jersey Dominicanness; the narrator finds her language "so demotic I couldn't understand half of what she said—she used words like *deguabinao* and *estribao* on the regular" (101). It seems somehow noteworthy also that, in the graphic-novel special-edition version of *Lose Her,* none of Jaime Hernandez's portraits of the novel's characters show any of them speaking any language at all. Their lips are all but sealed.

Lose Her was one of the first books I ever read on an electronic reader. Among the other new options this format afforded, I was able to click on Díaz's words, like *pulchritude,* and see how online dictionaries would instantly disclose them to me, given their statutory Englishness. But not words like *bwana* and *chupabarrio,* which wouldn't show up in any hypertext dictionary, even if the device were technically willing to link me to meanings in English and Spanish simultaneously. These words of Dominican and pan-Latin@ social extraction are the sinewy and multivalent elements that make up a given sentence in Díaz's fiction thus far, and they continue to predictably go beyond the unimposing cameo code-switching that one often encounters in postmultilingual fiction.

And yet, I am led to wonder whether and how Díaz's multilingual fictions will continue code-meshing from here onward—as the book as a technology changes rapidly under conditions of cognitive capitalism, and as Díaz's international distributors will request more and more easily translatable content and style from him. Will his future narrators browbeat monolinguals in footnotes until we figure it out for ourselves, as in *Wao*, or will we be encouraged to "pretend we know what goes on there," as in *Lose Her*? Put differently, will my students in Turkey encounter in Díaz's future work an excitable position of untempered enunciation, kindred to their own, or a laminated cultural portraiture of otherness? As discussed further below, these are two very different approaches to textual particularity and translingual meaning. And yet the dilemma between them is one that presumptively monolingual best-selling world-literary authors are never asked to face.

Specifying world-literary monolingualism

In most accounts of the endeavor of world literature, a consideration of monolingualism and multilingualism plays only the most peripheral role. The language of composition is regarded as one participatory element in the cultural repertoire of literary creation writ large, and on that specific contextual basis is regarded as a challenge for translation or translatability. But this respective "language of composition" is not afforded a historical profile as that which has necessarily been created, tempered, reduced, or aligned throughout a modern process of linguistic exogamization, panfunctionalization, and isomorphization—in order to be able to appear as such at all. The fact that a candidate text for world literaricity is "written in Dutch" generally garners little interest in how the Dutch language became (and becomes) a unified language, capable of and enfranchised to do commerce with other peer monolingualisms in literary, political, and technological fields.

With clairvoyant modesty, the encyclopedic, big-data student of world literature Franco Moretti has raised this point: namely, that anyone angling to provide a systemic account for world literature is bound to hanker for reductionist approaches to language at some point, lest we feel out of our depth as soon as we pass the last house on the block:

> What does it mean, studying world literature? How do we do it?
> I work on West European narrative between 1790 and 1930, and

already feel like a charlatan outside of Britain or France. World
literature? Many people have read more and better than I have, of
course, but still, we are talking of hundreds of languages and literatures here. (2000: 55)

That Moretti must remind us of the "hundreds of languages" producing
world literaricity is perhaps not so much a scolding platitude, as it is an
ambitious request for the kind of collaborative methodological prepa-
ration that befits those grand, unanswerable questions usually reserved
for theologians. How are scholars to orient ourselves around the
linguistic-translational task of world literaricity, when that task both
flouts and indicts human finitude? What justice can be done, when no
one can begin to know even a tenth of the languages constituting the
world-literary matrix? What happens to the ambition of comparative
philology when acquiring depth in more and more language(s) turns
out to never have been the methodological solution?

Considering these questions of language(s) in world-literary traffic
may also allow us to take stock of the rapidly changing conditions
under which literary artifacts in global circulation are acquired,
prospected, monetized, translated, and consumed in a postmultilingual publishing landscape. As this book is primarily concerned
with the role monolingualism plays in this nexus, we may take the
opportunity to notice that even mentioning these two concepts in
the same breath—monolingualism and world literature—seems to
announce a relationship of anathema, or "antinomy" as Brian Lennon
conceives it in his 2008 essay on "multilingual U.S. literature." This
chapter will, however, suggest that translational monolingualism is
the primary means of production for world literature in its contemporary formats and intensities. Monolingualism is making world
literature, *now*.

Any definition of literary monolingualism that derives from
national chauvinism, a predilection for domination and exclusion,
and/or cultural supremacy relies too heavily on the idea of an organized
pursuit of ideological uniformity. As a structure, monolingualism is
simply ill-equipped for that kind of conscious, intellectual endgame
in pursuit of one imagined community's self-ascribed ideals. We have
learned from Gellner that to stake a historical analysis on the role
of conscious intellectual resolve (for instance the resolve to unify "a"
language) often leads to distortions and overreach in research results.
Slavoj Žižek has added that most powerful forms of ethnocentrism
arise not from a rational preference for a specific set of national values,

properties, or historical narratives, but rather from a shared relation to the "'Nation *qua* Thing,' as Enjoyment, as a *jouissance* incarnated, a vague sense of what is uniquely 'our' way of life" (1993: 201).

Similarly, we ought not be satisfied with any genealogical claim about literary monolingualism that sees it as the result of an ethnocentric program, or a specific rational vision. It would also be immoderate to claim that monolingualism as a social structure follows from the philological or historical-linguistic perseverations of those, like Herder, who saw a special set of capacities in their own national language that other languages did not have. Monolingualism is much more analytically impoverished, and therefore more powerful, than that. In fact, we might entertain the idea that literary monolingualism is not even directly in service of nationalism (or colonization) as such, but of a certain mythic global cartography of panfunctional, discrete languages.

As discussed in Chapter 1, glossodiverse "fast-lane" procedures of translation have, over the past two decades of revolution in mechanical translation, become the primary force shaping what multilingualism means globally, for commercial Research and Development as well as for literary publishing. The civic responsibility to ensure multilingual, democratic access to meaning through translation has correspondingly decamped from the academic, universitarian sphere to the corporate and technocratic sphere. This paradigm shift has brought with it an imagined inevitable future-anterior of translatedness, and correspondingly an ideal of isomorphic, "homogeneous, empty" meaning in any language of global trade in intellectual property (Benjamin [1940] 2010). A given software product from Microsoft Corp., for instance, must now be conceived and developed from its inception with "world-readiness" in mind, such that it can be translated without much ado into an exhaustive roster of national and regional linguacultures. This is now a pre-production requirement, rather than a post-production one—a shift that is equally crucial from an epistemological, aesthetic, or structural point of view. The imperative to optimize semiotic transposability and multilingual content delivery has become the primary site for the production of capital in the age of data-mining and data-obfuscation.

In twenty-first-century trade fiction, the publishability of a given manuscript is also often evaluated based on how many (monolingually imagined) language markets into which the as-yet-untranslated and often as-yet-unwritten work can be exported. A fantastic English-language novel that "won't work" in Hindi, German, or Portuguese (or vice versa) is far less likely to be picked up by a major trade publisher in 2016 than is a generally unobjectionable text that promises "universal relatability" for fifty allolingual readerships. Multilingual, code-blending fictions are particularly left in the lurch, as speculation about how to translate intratextual code-meshes in a novel quickly devolve into a thicket of kitsch culturalism.

Just as temperament systems, which attracted Kafka's attention in his postmultilingual *Amerika* novel, took five hundred years to be effectively developed and disseminated, literary world-readiness—or translational monolingualism—is not the work of any one individual, publisher, work, or oeuvre. Rather, a transformation in the receptivity toward signs and styles must obtain across a vast landscape of literary institutions and readerships, before an aesthetic temperament system can be considered industry-standard. Thus, Ishiguro, Rushdie, and Pamuk are no more responsible for the advent of an aesthetics of literary world-readiness than any other working author. If anything, they are—like early modern symphonic composers—momentary proponents of an ad hoc temperament modality that issues from their own craft context, empirical palette, and market positionality.

Progressive intercultural monolingualization

We might suspect that monolingual constraint upon world literature has necessarily abated in recent decades, amid the rise of transnational phenomena of migration and hybridity. I contend that an opposite trend is in evidence, as new post-ethnic political rationales in superdiverse societies have instead reinvested in translational monolingualism as the coin of the realm, as a structuring lynchpin uniquely capacious and defensible amid the project of global intercultural compression. Scholars working in various contexts of the European literatures have tracked monolingualization processes since the 1980s–90s in their own fields' protocols of literary recognition. Charles Forsdick postulates, for instance, that a recent shift in French Studies, away from the historical framework of Francophonie toward a non-Gallocentric "world literature in French," has resulted in a linguistic centralization of sorts around French as a world language (2015). Reflecting on a 2007 authors' manifesto in *Le Monde* pronouncing the end of Francophonie, Forsdick emphasizes the infrastructure of public literary recognition enabling this shift:

> Far from being a reflection of a new openness [...] the prize system—
> and the editorial practices its supports—in fact reflects conservatism

and centralization in French-language literary production and its domination by specifically French national publishers. (Forsdick 2015; see also Migraine-George 2013)

Across the Rhine to the north, a similar post-ethnic program of monolingualization has been in play since around 1985, bolstered by a progressive though somewhat socio-romantic political investment in literature as a lever-system for the cultural integration of, primarily, German Turks. In a bid to become culturally post-ethnic in ways that its political sphere was as yet unwilling to do (Gramling 2009), West Germany underwent a distinct monolingualization process in its literary scene beginning in the 1980s, a transformation likewise predicated upon promotional prizes for second-language authors of German. Unlike in the French context, however, no major colonial legacy of German empire was at hand that would prompt a latter-day turn away from literature of postcolonialism toward a progressively reconceived "world literature in German" (Gramling 2010). (West) Germany did however have its own transnational legacies in mass labor recruitment, primarily from Turkey and Italy—the literary plank of which was called "guest-worker literature" until the mid-1980s, when the institutional monolingualization of the multicultural German literary field began in earnest. (More recently, multilingual approaches to Shoah literature—from Spain to Turkey—have helped repatriate testimonies from survivors of Nazi rule into German literary history on the model of an empire writing back (Semprún 2003; Aschenberg 1998; Taterka 1995; Oschlies 1986; Jagoda, Kłodziński, and Masłowski 1987).)

Where transnational guest-worker writers' efforts in the 1970s had generally focused on expanding political expression through poetic (and journalistic) means *in any language*, 1980s institutional discourse turned to the depoliticized task of commending stylistic achievement in German as a foreign language, as academics and critics began to respond to the multicultural civic imperatives of the late 1970s. Harald Weinrich, the founder of the Adelbert von Chamisso Prize for second-language writers of German, described the provenance of this new impulse in 1986 as follows:

> The creation of the Adelbert von Chamisso Award for authors with native languages other than German should be a signal that this literature, coming from the outside, is welcome among us Germans and that we can appreciate it as an enrichment of our own literature as well as a concrete piece of world literature. And

even if we sometimes are not sure how to address these half-foreigner, half-native authors who often do not have a German passport but do have a German pen, we are momentarily absolved of our linguistic confusion when we name them "Chamisso's grandchildren." (Göktürk et al. 2007: 390–1)

Such was the opening salvo of a politically progressive monolingualization process that would last until 2000 at least. A fascinating set of gestures, Weinrich's progressive literary paternalism combines several performative elements: a) promoting West German guest-worker literature to the status of world literature; b) using literature as a proxy domain with which to sidestep the imperative to pursue *political* transformations in solidarity with non-citizen writers; and c) taking recourse to a phylogenetic logic of inheritance under which to subsume these writers and their "confusing" multilingualism. This erasure would be less problematic if the writers themselves had generally opted for German as their literary language, but they did not. Novelists and poets like Güney Dal and Aras Ören, luminaries of the early literature of migration (Adelson 2005), wrote primarily in Turkish for an internationalist audience. Their work fell subsequently out of favor among scholars and reviewers alike over the course of the 1980s and 1990s, amid the monolingualization of post-ethnic German-language literature.[1] That the namesake of Weinrich's prize for second-language writers, Louis Charles Adélaïde de Chamissot, was a French multilingual aristocrat driven into German exile as a youth by the (monolingualist) Jacobins, begins to suggest the ironic discrepancy—and yet provocative historical dialogicality—between these multiple world-literary positionalities.[2] In deciding to confer the label "Chamisso's grandchildren" upon writers primarily of transnational mass-labor-recruitment backgrounds, Weinrich awkwardly used Chamisso's own aristocratic journey of literary monolingualization as an aspirational prescription.

This progressive monolingualization of national literary-institutional milieus since the mid-1980s—arising out of attempts to overcome extractive colonial or mass-labor-recruitment legacies, as well as to tamp

1. On Aras Ören, see Gezen (2015). On Güney Dal, see Göktürk et al. (2007): 419–21.

2. On precisely this constellation between "revolutionary monolingualism" in 1790s France and "reactionary multilingualism" in the contemporary European Union, see Moore (2015).

down what conservatives see as the excesses of multiculturalism—is however not the only major recent monolingualization trend in the relations of production for world literature. Shuyo Kong's illuminating book, *Consuming Literature: Best Sellers and the Commercialization of Literary Production in Contemporary China*, details how translation publishers in mainland China have created booming new markets for two types of aggressively marketed Western "classics." James Joyce's *Ulysses* has, in the Yilin Publishing House's translation by Xiao Qian, been advertised as an accessible and fun read, worthy of the kind of best-seller status it could never expect in the West. In the final chapter of *Ulysses*, Xiao for instance divides up Molly Bloom's disorienting thought-prose, smoothing away the kind of aestheticist offroading that would have prohibited effective marketing in translation (Kong 2004: 135). Meanwhile, novels like Colleen McCullough's *The Thorn Birds* and James Waller's *The Bridges of Madison County* are up-marketed as Western classics, with culturalist prompts on their dust jackets like "Why do Americans love this book so much? What does it tell us about the mind of contemporary Americans? Reading it will help you find the answers!" (Kong 140).

While a predominant "politics of untranslatability" continues to evolve in the Euro-American scholarly sphere (Apter 2013; for a vociferous objection, see Venuti 2016), Chinese trade publishers have in the meantime found optimistic and lucrative detours around even the most daunting ostensible predicaments of translation. At Yilin Publishing House, the relations of production for world literature are fueled by a complete reorganization of literary hierarchy, a refunctionalization of the notion of a "classic," and an intensification of the value of intercultural, interlingual accessibility, as it is presumed to inhere in a good literary work. Good is, now again, that which travels well, and which brings news (Brown 2003). It would be both an analytical and a political mistake to take the Parisian discourse of untranslatability as normative, while pursuing the Beijing counter-practice under a sociological aegis alone. Indeed the Yilin Publishing House's advertising platform—with its values of intercultural inquiry, love of readerly discovery, and accessibility—subscribes to a great many of the humanistic ideals that have always characterized Enlightenment-based cultures of reading.

We have just now considered two planes of production upon which the global nexus of world literature is currently "making *all the books*," both of which hinge on the kind of literary-technical *tempering* we described in the previous chapters as "translational monolingualisms." These two planes are: 1) a chiastic reordering, in major non-Anglophone markets like mainland China, of the upmarket/downmarket

logic of "challenging classics" vs "dramatic page-turners," by way
of a commercial translation culture predicated on disambiguation
and hyperdomestication; and 2) a post-ethnic monolingualization
of national literatures in Europe, accelerated by promotional prize
landscapes, designed to ameliorate domestic "linguistic confusion"
arising from decades of mass labor migration, postcolonial migration,
and superdiversity. Both of these programmatic models make explicit
claims about the world literaricity of the texts they shepherd and those
texts' unique potential for achieving intercultural understanding. Both
of these modes of production retain, equally explicitly, their claim
on the literary and aesthetic nature of their commitments. Both,
furthermore, arose in the 1980s and gained commercial predominance
in the 1990s.

Soft multilingualisms, dull novels

These are two of the ways world literature comes to matter and
comes *into* matter, primarily through changing relations on a field
of translational production—a field where hundreds of (historically hybrid) lyrical, generic, rhetorical, orate, and literate traditions
vie for translational legibility amid the inherited regularities of an
Anglo-Franco-German cosmopolitanism and its publishing houses.
A candidate text for world-literary circulation and legibility must be
prospective in its translational readerly address, able to "be relatable"
for ever new abstract publics of cosmopolitan monolinguals: more
or less worldly readers, sometimes of multiple languages, who are
addressed nonetheless in the language presumed of them. Such a focus
on the industry and industriousness of world literature—including its
pre-production and post-production moments of linguistic disinter-
mediation—might move us closer to an account of the relationship
between world literaricity and monolingualism.

   In his essay on transformations in Arabic poetry from the nineteenth
to the mid-twentieth centuries, Yaseen Noorani offers an account of
what a genealogy of monolingualism—or what he terms "soft multilingualism"—might offer for comparative world-literary study:

   The development and dominance of modern national languages has,
   perhaps paradoxically, entailed powerful tendencies toward linguistic
   equivalence and interchangeability where formerly, difference and
   incommensurability were more the rule. This is not to say that

linguistic distance was in the past untraversable or that such distance has now been eliminated. It is nevertheless clear that languages have been profoundly altered by the process of modernization and nationalization, such that they progressively conform to a common communicative template. Multilingualism may now be more accessible than ever before, but it is increasingly "soft" multilingualism, in that it remains within the confines of familiar linguistic norms. "Hard" multilingualism, which requires reckoning with formerly existing radical linguistic difference, is more and more confined to the learning of "dead" languages. The advancement of soft multilingualism has been a key factor in enabling many of the processes of contemporary globalization, and has in turn been furthered by them. (2013: 8)

By distinguishing between soft and hard multilingualism, Noorani is able to postulate that translatability, far from being the moral ballast of humanism or another kind of transhistorical constant, had to be induced in the early Arab nationalist movements of the 1920s. Arabic courtly poetry in the nineteenth century was still what might pass as radically untranslatable (though nonetheless often translated), relying as it did on traditions of classical topoi of artful description—*wasf*, or ekphrasis—topoi which were intertextually enmeshed in a visual-semantic hierarchy specific to that courtly tradition and therefore so endogamous so as to be impervious to translation.

In contrast, Arab nationalist poems of the mid-twentieth century, for instance the poem "The Village Market" by the Iraqi poet Abd al-Wahhab al-Bayati, "assimilate to the international norms of poetic expression that became dominant in the wake of modernist poetic movements, like imagism and surrealism in Britain, France, Germany, and other European countries" (Noorani 2013: 12). Though al-Bayati's poetry was explicitly nationalist and ideologically oppositional towards Europe's colonial aggressions, his rhetorical nationalism was readily readable as such by others in translation—amid a system of newly, globally translatable forms and rhetorics of nationalism and national feeling. This twentieth-century development, which Noorani calls "soft multilingualism," has become a prohibitive precondition for cultural production and political legibility in the early twenty-first century.

The suggestion that soft monolingualism, or what I term translational monolingualism, took hold most effectively in eras of poetic nationalism undermines the presumption that nationalism is predicated on purism in the face of foreign elements, and that monolingualism is a nationalistic commitment. Nationalism under

Noorani's schema appears to be an exogamous idiom designed to dock, exchange, and communicate in a mutually accommodating way with the metalanguage of other parallel nationalisms. Latter-day world literature may also be understood as a productive domain tempered into translatability by monolingualism and "soft multilingualism." Like software programs marketed globally in hundreds of languages by Microsoft's World-Readiness team, fiction and poetry can be tempered for literary world-readiness as well, made easily transposable from a source language toward imaginary monolingual end-readers in a roster of national languages. This logic of perpetual prospective circulation destabilizes the logic of Lawrence Venuti's famed heuristic dichotomy of domesticating vs foreignizing translations (1995), long before such translations are even to take place.

Accordingly, the aesthetic conditions of production, or publishability, for such candidate texts are pre-keyed towards translatability and exogamy. As Tim Parks writes in "The New Dull Global Novel":

> Writing in the 1960s, intensely engaged with his own culture and its complex politics, Hugo Claus apparently did not care that his novels would require a special effort on the reader's and above all the translator's part if they were to be understood outside his native Belgium. In sharp contrast, contemporary authors like the Norwegian Per Petterson, the Dutch Gerbrand Bakker, or the Italian Alessandro Baricco, offer us works that require no such knowledge or effort, nor offer the rewards that such effort will bring. More importantly the language is kept simple. Kazuo Ishiguro has spoken of the importance of avoiding word play and allusion to make things easy for the translator. Scandinavian writers I know tell me they avoid character names that would be difficult for an English reader. If culture-specific clutter and linguistic virtuosity have become impediments, other strategies are seen positively: the deployment of highly visible tropes immediately recognizable as "literary" and "imaginative," analogous to the wearisome lingua franca of special effects in contemporary cinema, and the foregrounding of a political sensibility that places the author among those "working for world peace." (2010)

As a literary connoisseur, Parks is disappointed in a world literature industry that, he claims, is impatient with anything but wall-to-wall pre-translatedness and aesthetic exogamy. As such, his diagnosis is a more condemnatory one than is Noorani's, in that Parks ascribes to the new world literaricity inferior quality, monetized transparency, and easy consumption, while Noorani remains circumspect on these questions of criticism and competence. Rather than diagnosing aesthetic translatability as the dysphoric result of a flattening process, it is possible to view this contemporary development as a rather *early* moment in a long process in the invention of translationally monolingual literary temperament, one that gained conjuncture around Kafka's high modern era, and continues in newly critical forms in today's global novels.

Artisans in the linguacene

Such a historicized conception of literary temperament need not presume a decline in quality, complexity, or singularity. Indeed, Bach's *Well-Tempered Clavier* is often cited as a quantum leap in aesthetic complexity, in that it exploits the multiplicity of tonal permutation in ways that predecessor composers had never had the technology to imagine. Temperament systems herald not the end of creativity and particularity; they recalibrate and redirect aesthetic virtuosity from the endogamous to the exogamous plane of articulation. In a corresponding spirit, world-literary texts in the early twenty-first century are often wrangling with the emerging literary temperament systems of the linguacene, including with their exogamous attenuations and endogamous nostalgias.[3]

Non-Anglophone authors who find themselves in the prospective catchment area of world literary (re)production often deliberately hone and harness rhetorical resources that obfuscate or dilate the channels of translatability through which they are selectively incorporated. In the structure of translational monolingualism, or what Noorani calls "soft multilingualism," authors from Kafka to Pamuk have been increasingly poised—as Karl Rossmann says in *The Missing Person*—to "know the mechanism" (104) of monolingualism, in order to render it visible for critique and expressive elaboration. Indeed, in contemporary global literary traffic, such texts are made to *pass* in a certain way, precisely by eliding or suspending aspects of what we might, with Emily Apter, consider their "right to untranslatability." (2013)

This conception of passing draws implicitly on discourses within critical race studies and LGBT studies, and on histories of "passing" as something one is somehow not, or not allowed to be. In LGBT/queer

3. For an illuminating take on "conspicuous multilingualism" as a foil for monolingual authorship, see Yuliya Komska (2015).

studies and in indigenous, ethnic and critical race studies; "passing" is often used pejoratively, but has a range of general vernacular uses.[4]

Reflecting on her beloved friend Clare, the protagonist of Nella Larsen's 1929 novella *Passing*, Irene Redfield, has this to say about Clare's decision to pass as white:

> It's funny about "passing." We disapprove of it and at the same time condone it. It excites our contempt and yet we rather admire it. We shy away from it with an odd kind of revulsion, but we protect it. (185–6)

Artisans working in the new world literaricity seem also to seek recourse to historical strategies of passing, passing by, brushing with, skirting—a thigmotactic disposition that diverges sharply from the rhetorics of contact, transformation, mutuality, interculturality, exchange, and translation that have primarily informed the world literature debate in recent decades. Faced with industrial world literaricity as a temperament system of translational monolingualism, a new mode of fiction-making is afoot—as exemplified in the works of Orhan Pamuk, Terézia Mora, James Kelman, Horacio Castellanos-Moya, and Peter Waterhouse—one that itself incorporates the contemporary relations of production of world literature and aestheticizes them to critical ends.

This strategy requires more than mere postmodern language play, since the hyperobject being contested is not the grand narratives of language or logocentricity themselves, but rather a particular translational infrastructure that is beginning to obtain in the incipient linguacene. This is an infrastructure that above all needs to ensure semiotic coordination among world languages. Literature—as the golden calf of language-based semiosis—is an especially prized epistemic testing ground for that infrastructure. World-literature debates are thus always also a latent proxy discourse about ostensibly non-literary movements toward a controlled global glossodiverse multilingualism. Untempered texts threaten to break or de-justify such an infrastructure, and—within the cultural politics of soft multilingualism—it falls ironically to literary translators to strive more than

---

4. This line of thinking was inspired by the comparatist Jacob Emery's use of the phrase "passing for World Literature" during an informal roundtable discussion at the American Literary Translators' Association in Bloomington, IN, October 2013.

ever for universal serial translatability. In the idiom of Skopos translation theory (Nord 1995), the function of the world-literary translator
becomes maintaning the coherence of world-literary traffic, rather than
ensuring the political appearance of a given text.

Consider a text by the contemporary Turkish–Kurdish author
Murathan Mungan, whose 1984 short story "Love's Tears, or Rapunzel
and the Drifter" (Turkish: "Aşkın Gözyaşları ya da Rapunzel ile Avare ")
features a transgender character who transitions from man to woman
over the course of the short story. Turkish does not have pronominal
gender, an absence that induces certain pragmatic effects on the social
discourse within the text, affordances that the psychologist Dan Slobin
calls "thinking for speaking" (1996). The two main characters are Efkâr (a
male name) and Ümit (a pangender name). Efkâr drives a group taxicab
(dolmuş) in Ankara, on which Ümit is a frequent passenger. The elapsed
time of the story is about three years, at the end of which Efkâr, by this
time in love with his passenger, asks Ümit to undergo sex reassignment
surgery. Before that point, the reader has no pronominal indication of
Ümit's statutory or experiential gender—though both characters are
quite often feminized or masculinized respectively in the text by intertextual links to a host of well-known Arabic, Persian, and Anatolian
folktales that feature tragically star-crossed heterosexual couples.

When bringing this text into world-literary traffic, the pragmatic
affordances of translating transgender promise some trouble. Should
someone translate this at all, given the symbolic violence required to
perform pronominal gender on a text (and a fictional person) who
doesn't have it? Whose perception of things does the translator side
with, and therefore compel readers to side with?—with Efkâr, with
Ümit, with the author, with the reader, with Western transgender
activists and theoreticians, with Turkish and Kurdish transgender
activists? It is impossible to consult the fictional person Ümit directly.
The only agent in a position to commit or abstain from that kind of
linguistic manipulation in this case is the translator, since pronominal
gender is profoundly absent in the original.

While Ümit is unconcerned with whatever unspecified gender Ümit
is bodying forth, Efkâr's demand that Ümit become a woman mirrors
and presages the demands the translator performs upon the text. Ümit's
particular linguistic (un)genderedness would need to be translated out
of the story in order for it to enter the traffic in meaning that constitutes
world literaricity under the episteme of global translatability. Ümit
would have to be made to pass (in Anglophone translation) as a trans-
sexual, as a gay man, or as post-operative heterosexual woman, because

that is how the episteme of translatability trans-codes Ümit, despite all intratextual pragmatic implicatures and counter-evidence.

Strategies for passing

But cannot the effects and affects of a multilingual world, the code-meshing and mutual linguistic estrangement, the normative essence of being (dis)interpellated in a language one does not understand, be openly indexed or re-enacted in their full complexity in a single-language literary text? Perhaps more difficult still is the possibility of representing partial and uneven proficiencies: one person's limited capacity to understand but not to speak another's language, or vice versa. Is the literariness of literary language capable of spiriting these worldly dilemmas into the "ceremonial" space of monolingual text? Literary texts that emerge from multilingual lifeworlds are most often compelled to index their difficult intimacy with their own textual language—by laying bare the effects of monolingualism *by way of monolingual text*. Some watershed endeavors in scholarship, like Doris Sommer's ludic readings of Chican@ lyricism in *Bilingual Aesthetics* (2004) or Steven Kellman's explorations of polyglot writers in *The Translingual Imagination* (2000), highlight cases in which manifestly code-switching fictions do indeed make it into published form. Yet dealing with the problem of monolingualism in literature requires more than this: namely, to analyze the often hypotextual relation between multilingual language events and their unrepresentability in "single-language" text, and to continually insist on the latent possibility of writing a world that deals, thinks, and feels outside of monolingualism.

The remainder of this chapter surveys, in brief, various attempts in recent world-literary writing to pass amid the requirements of transla-tional monolingualism, or as Noorani describes it, "soft multilingualism." This project often takes the form of critical doubling, monolingual drag, or an otherwise performative divestiture from the unmarked doxa of literary monolingualism. The predominant categories available for describing world-literary exchange—"host culture," "receiving culture," "foreign material," and "home tradition"—speak of entities that these texts actively work to disarticulate, to fend off, and to aestheticize for critical purposes. Furthermore, these texts are leavened on the struggle between translational monolingualism and semiodiverse multi-lingualism, turning those two metaliterary planes into narrative and aesthetic resources for the novels themselves. Often these authors' texts turn upon themselves, straining against what Morson calls "the bias of the artifact" (1998: 599) endemic to the novels of national literary canons. They endeavor to perform—not describe—the multilingual world, a matrix of thought, meaning, and feeling from which their writing is nonetheless formally exiled. Meanwhile, monolingualism has sought to secure an aura of universal receptivity and complicity from its multiple-language publics, even if this means sacrificing the dominant language to routine invasion and impurity, as Kafka imagined in a parable:

> Leopards break into the temple and drink to the dregs what is in the sacrificial pitchers; this is repeated over and over again; finally it can be calculated in advance, and it becomes a part of the ceremony. (1992: 117)

In Kafka's spatial story, the temple ritual proceeds symbiotically with that which, as a matter of course, enters unauthorized and desecrates it. The creatures that break into the ceremonial space in the off-hours leave traces of having been there, of what they have taken with them. Their participation is regular and expected—and yet unratified and radically foreign. The "other language" is made hauntingly present through an evoked distance from the "here" of narration—either through spatial, deictic, or syntactic displacements. The other language is the apophatic, the "elsewhere."

Under such conditions of monolingualism, this figural relation between languages and space in the literary context is a kind of lingua-spatial analectic—a coded dispersal of (cislingual) *heres* and (translingual) *theres* by which multiple-language social phenomena can become figurally modeled in relief in monolingual text. Though the concept of an analectic derives from the debate among David Harvey, Henri Lefebvre, and Edward Soja about a Marxian socio-spatial dialectic (Soja 1980), the term "analectic" stresses that a collection of multilingual utterances cannot be recuperated into a totality of meaning as expressed in one language alone, that they defy the reconciliation and transparency that translation seeks to proffer.

Gary Saul Morson proposed that Tolstoy and Dostoevsky developed ways to resist the compulsory, forward progression of their own works—to overcome "Lessing's curse"—through narrative techniques he calls *sideshadowing* (1998). While Morson seeks to discover the lateral, spatial fissures of open-endedness in a text, this simultaneity also manifests spatial figures that index a multilingual world beyond the pale of the single language on the page, gazing back at the reader. Straining against their monolingual contract with the implied (monolingual) reader, these texts point to other spaces, where multiple, living codes mix and countenance one another without meta-formal constraint. The thresholds to which these texts point are ominous, tempting lines that create a split in the space of the narrative: The cramped "here" of the manifest text has, at its margins, the "elsewhere" of its multilingual hypotext.

Hana Wirth-Nesher provides an early example of the ways trans-lingual authors have found it necessary, and even productive, to "pass" in the world-literary system. Mary Antin, one of the English-writing allophone authors Wirth-Nesher surveys in her monograph *Call it English*, puts it this way: "I was born, I have lived, and I have been made over […] I am as much out of the way as if I were dead, for I am absolutely other than the person whose story I have to tell" (Wirth-Nesher 2008: 50). There is a certain sovereign haughtiness in this stance, as Antin further projects: "I shall turn the aliens' ridicule into sympathy. This I can do, for I am both of you and of them. I speak both your languages" (2008: 52). Wirth-Nesher also speculates that Antin is invoking in her rhetoric of authorship the ceremonial practice of reading Torah: "Since I am called to the forum, I pray that no error passes my lips. This is the only success I long for" (2008: 52). Writing perfectly, passingly (in English) becomes a sacred ceremonial goal, one that requires Antin to align herself with the requirements of a tradition that is not her own.

Translation in the snow

Perhaps more than anyone on the world literature circuit today, the narrators of Orhan Pamuk's novels—some of whom are named Orhan Pamuk—return again and again, happily, to questions of passing. The European Union, for one, plays a complex intra- and extratextual role in his 2002 novel *Snow*. The novel itself was in part the result of sweeping pro-E.U. political reforms in Turkey in the late 1990s that dismantled and reorganized censorship statutes to the extent that Orhan Pamuk could publish a political novel about contemporary Turkey, which highlights—if not always by name—the Armenian genocide, the ongoing war in Kurdistan, domestic phone-tapping, the Turkish secret police bureaucracy, and Islamist fomentation in Germany. Pamuk sought legal counsel in examining the manuscript line by line to ensure the novel would pass muster with this new, liberalized censor. (Lau 2005) The resulting text is, to a great extent,

itself thus an artifact of post-Schengen European integration and
E.U.–Turkey accession agreements.

Such moments of compliance and alignment, I contend, hint at a
larger epistemological project in Pamuk, one that has literary-theoretical
and literary-didactic designs, rather than merely self-promotional ones.
For one, Pamuk's self-implantations disrupt the notion that the novel
exists primarily in order to depict something representative about
contemporary Turkey. While Kafka assiduously cleanses his texts of all
social deixis and local reference, Pamuk proceeds in the other direction,
diving into a detailed investigative forensics of an ostensibly "local
landscape" in Kars. Yet for every clause that describes or meditates
on local meanings in the northeastern provincial city where the novel
takes place, another clause ruminates on how those meanings are
circulated—often internationally before they are circulated nationally.
Snow's narrator routinely plots out for its readers the international
order-of-operations for the novel's own content-distribution:

> A number of correspondents for French and German newspapers,
> however, did pick up on the item, and only after they had gone [...]
> and published stories in the European press did the Turkish press
> begin to take an interest: at this point, quite a few Turkish reporters
> paid visits to the city. (14)

As this account mimics the publication conditions and consequences
of the novel *Snow* itself, it induces a kind of *mise en abyme* of publishability, a conical structure at the center of which is nothing but "the
silence of snow"—a hypotextual index of formal and semiotic erasure.

In a remarkable piece on "Reading Pamuk's *Snow* as Parody," Sibel
Erol points out how:

> The most notable aspect of *Snow* is the discrepancy Pamuk creates
> between the claims of the characters, who define themselves in
> one-dimensional extremes and through their differences, and
> the multi-dimensionality of interlinkings and similarities created
> through intertextuality, to which the characters in the novel
> themselves are not privy [...] The parody in *Snow* resides in this sad
> humour. (2007: 413)

As Erol suggests, the characters in the novel—including Ka—recite
and uphold exclusively national personae, despite the transnational
affiliations that both undermine and underwrite those identities.

Especially among *Snow*'s bureaucrats, activists, political leaders, and artists, any conspicuous bonds to Germany and Western Europe that might compromise a character's public image as a devoted Turkish national are comically suppressed—and often in vain. In this sense, the novel and its characters perform what Elisa Martí-López describes as a "preoccupation with autochthony" (2002: 45).

While the omnipresent veil of snow in the novel intimates the constitutive absence of the city of Kars on any world-literary map, snow also offers a functional conceit for the novel's artificial autochthony—a "pathetic fallacy" for the glocalist gaze:

> The weather office has announced that cold air coming straight from Siberia and the accompanying heavy snowfall will continue for three more days. And so for three days, the city of Kars will have to do as it used to do during the winters of old—stew in its own juices. This will offer us an opportunity to put our house in order. (30)

Extraordinary conditions of blinding white compel the city to close in on itself, to give an account of its home-grown attributes and devices, though many of these come from elsewhere: Frankfurt, Istanbul, Ankara. This predicament (both for the novel and for its protagonists) could have been avoided, we are told. On his way eastward, the ambitious author Ka, seeing the oncoming snow, "might have realized that he was traveling straight into a blizzard; he might have seen at the start that he was setting out on a journey that would change his life forever and chosen to turn back" (3–4). This, again, is an authorial index about the figural status of the novel itself: its expendability, its utter literary-historical contingency, and the unlikelihood that it would be written or published under ordinary, i.e. non-exceptional, circumstances like the E.U.–Turkey accession negotiations, the West Study Group's postmodern coup of 1997, and other moments of profound upheaval in national governance in Turkey.

The formal effect of the snow throughout the blizzard is negative: "Ka came to feel as if they had entered a shadow world. The rooms were so dark he could barely make out the shape of the furniture, so when he was compelled to look at the snow outside, it blinded him—it was as if a curtain of tulle had fallen before his eyes" (13). But this is not merely a matter of perceptual distinction and personal observation; snow is structurally linked throughout the text to publishability and mediation: "At that very moment, the electricity went off. As the printing press whirred to a halt and the shop fell into an enchanted darkness, Ka was struck by the beautiful whiteness of the snow falling outside" (24). The staging of these nationalized local stories, designed and produced for the sake of international circulation, plays a central role in the narrative. Consider the intricate heterogeneity on display at Kars's "national theater" variety show, where the exile Ka, having returned from West Germany, is expected to read a poem:

> The show, which was watched by the entire population of our city, included republican vignettes, the most beautiful scenes from the most important artistic works of the Western Enlightenment, theatrical sketches criticizing advertisements that aim to corrode our culture, the adventures of Vural, the celebrated goalkeeper, and poems in praise of Atatürk and the nation. Ka, the celebrated poet, who is now visiting our city, recited his latest poem, entitled "Snow." The crowning event of the evening was a performance of *My Fatherland or My Scarf* (*Çarsaf*), the enlightenment masterwork from the early years of the republic, in a new interpretation entitled *My Fatherland or My Head Scarf* (*Türban*). (29)

Importantly, Ka has written no such poem at this point in the narrative, and yet the title the newspaper gives to the poem is *Snow*—the principle of both the fetishization and the erasure of the local. The transmission of the theatrical performance—which is to include this as yet unwritten poem by the Westernized, secular bourgeois Ka—is depicted in cartoon-like proportions that dramatize the nitty-gritty work of banal nationalism (Billig 1994):

> Kars Border Television worked tirelessly to organize this first live broadcast in its two-year history so that all of Kars would be able to watch the splendid performance. Although it still does not own a live-transmission vehicle, Kars Border Television was able to stretch a cable from its headquarters in Halitpaşa Avenue the length of two streets to the camera at the National Theater. Such was the feeling of goodwill among the citizens of Kars that some residents were kind enough to take the cable into their houses to avoid snow damage. (For example, our very own dentist, Fadıl Bey, and his family let them take the cable in through the window overlooking his front balcony and pass it into the gardens in the back.) (33)

This reference to snow damage in the context of media distribution reinforces the notion that Pamuk is working towards an understanding of the transnational circulation in certain forms of narrative and of the negative spaces left by the reproduction of those forms. As David Palumbo-Liu suggests in another context:

> The fissures and gaps that trouble the conversion of Form [are a] problematic situated in an eminently worldly space and time, one that is characterized by migration, displacement, and the inhabiting of the modern world by new forms and ideologies. Under these circumstances, Form becomes freighted with the obligation to encase an as yet unsettled and indeterminant admixture of projected desire and repressed fear. (2008: 202)

In *Snow*, as opposed to Kafka's *The Castle*, the Form-giving element is snow itself. Like the blank page, upon which only selected world-literary narratives are published, snow is both potential enunciation and abject unspeakability at once. It is, to cite Bhabha on Fanon, the "zone of occult instability where the people dwell" (2013: 303). In fact, the word zone applies aptly to snow; it is neither a place or a space, but a quadrant of erasure in an economy of exhaustive semiosis, a fissure of suppressed representations in a roaring enterprise of world literature: the "great unwritten" tempered out of publishability. Fazıl, a former student of Kars's Islamist academy and one of Ka's most pensive informants, addresses this literary economy explicitly:

> "I can tell from your face that you want to tell the people who read your novel how poor we are and how different we are from them. I don't want you to put me in a novel like that." "Why not?" "Because you don't even know me, that's why! Even if you got to know me and describe me as I am, your Western readers would be so caught up in pitying me for being poor that they wouldn't have a chance to see my life. For example, if you said I was writing an Islamist science-fiction novel, they'd just laugh." (410)

This exchange is an instance of what Edward Said described as a self-reflexive "way of describing the author's position in a text with regard to the Oriental material he writes about." (2007: 86) Fazıl finally demands that "his author" Orhan Pamuk—whom Azade Seyhan calls "the unofficial interpreter of Islam for the American public" (2005: 209)—inform readers that nothing said about Kars in the novel is true.

The aphasic polyglot

Composed in the same year as Pamuk's *Snow*, Terézia Mora's debut novel from 2004, *Day In Day Out* (German: *Alle Tage*)—an implosive and granular anti-hymn to linguistic Europeanization—treads a similar path of linguistic precarity and statelessness as Ka in *Snow*, though her main character Abel takes on a diametrically opposed strategy for linguistic passing in the age of European postmultilingualism. Set amid the whirling reconfigurations in the wake of the war in former Yugoslavia and the early days of borderless Schengen Europe, Mora's story stages a polyglot protagonist, Abel Nema, whose multiple language proficiency is both the telos and the nightmare of monolingualism. His mother-in-law says: "Everything about him is just fine: he's a quiet, polite, good-looking young man." She then continues:

> And at the same time, everything about him is all wrong. Even if you can't put your finger on it. There's something *suspicious*. The *way* he's so quiet, polite, and good-looking. Though maybe that's what comes of being highly gifted. [… H]e can do things. He speaks a few languages. Or so they say. Because in fact he hardly says a word. Now that may be a symptom. But it's not the cause. (9)

In Abel Nema, we encounter a (post)multilingual subject who, as a complication arising from a near-fatal gas leak in a Berlin apartment, can acquire languages with instrumental ease, by "learn[ing] sound by sound, analyzing frequency charts, rummaging through phonetic codes, painting his tongue black to compare imprints. It's starting to look like punishment: drinking ink or eating soap powder. The word *laboratory* appears in a new light: the technological comes first, the human second. You'd think he was creating a homunculus there in the night, except that his consists exclusively of language, the perfect clone of a language between glottis and labia" (99).

Indeed her son-in-law Abel, an undocumented refugee her daughter had "rescued from the fire" in "Transylvania" (i.e. from the tumultuous post-Soviet republics of southeastern Europe in the early 1990s), has come to speak ten languages perfectly. At a previous engagement, Professor Tibor B. countered the mother-in-law's discomfort about Abel's uncanny disposition:

> He has the same problems as any emigrant […] he needs papers and he needs language. He's taken care of the latter: he's mastered

the language, mastered ten, and to such perfection that you'd never believe he'd acquired most of his knowledge in the language lab, from tapes, so to speak. I wouldn't be surprised to learn he'd never spoken with a single living Brazilian or Finn. That's why everything he says is so, how shall I put it, *placeless*, so uniquely clear—no accent, no dialect, nothing: he speaks like a person who comes from nowhere (*nirgends herkommt*). (10)

Regaining consciousness after his near asphyxiation, Abel is resurrected as a higher being who can understand and reproduce most any language in the most clinical and instrumental form:

He had said no more to Bora than three broken sentences, and now he was internalizing every word, every sentence he heard, and even if he did not understand everything he could tell where they made a mistake; he could picture the constructions as if they grew out of his fellow patients' mouths in the form of branch-like patterns. He stared at them./I don't know why, Grampa muttered to the Third Man, but I don't like the way he keeps staring at a single point. (72)

This intergenerational observation echoes Pennycook and Halliday's misgivings about glossodiversity, and its tendency to use all languages to convey a single set of global cultural values. As such, Abel is the perfunctory embodiment of the European Common Framework of Reference for Languages: able and competent in eliciting, understanding, and producing meaning in multiple languages when necessary. He spends his nights practicing fricatives and other sounds in his "language laboratory," while his transnational flatmates wait at home for him to communicate anything of value to them, which he never does.

Another party to the conversation about Abel, his landlord Konstantin, says:

He's a lucky duck [...] I said to him, You're a lucky duck! And he stared at me as if he hadn't understood. And that's supposed to be what he's best at. Which makes me think the thing he's really best at is getting people to take an interest in him without lifting a finger. You think you've got a handle on him, but by the end you're upset because all the time you talked he looked only at your mouth, as if the only thing he cared about how you produced your fricatives. And all the rest—the world, the whole caboodle—didn't concern him in the slightest. (10)

Abel thus functions as a sort of temperament device for translational monolingualism: registering or misrecognizing the words of other (non-native) speakers of German like Konstantin, according to the relative translatability or vernacularity of their expressions. Unlike Konstantin and the other war refugees (from sub-Saharan Africa and southeastern Europe), Abel is able to wield his linguistic mastery to obtain patronage from local foundations and benefactors, who grant him multicultural stipends and promotional funding for him to continue his self-fashioning labor as a living testament to intercultural understanding.

> Everything that had theretofore played a role in his life—the swarm of memory and projection, of past and future that blocked the passengeways and filled the rooms with their hullabaloo—was stowed away, in secret closets somewhere, and he, now empty, was ready to accept a single brand of knowledge: language. Such is the miracle that befell Abel Nema. (73)

Nema's genius competence in glossodiversity does not last, however, and he eventually falls into a catatonic state that indicates, perhaps, the telos of translational monolingualism: a blank affirmativity toward anything and everything:

> What he most likes to say is still: That's good. The relief, no, the joy he derives from being able to say it is so palpable that his loved ones give him every opportunity to do so. He always utters it with gratitude: That's good. A last word. It's good. (418)

So ends Mora's epic novel, with the once polyglot Abel Nema only able to confer equivalent and undifferentiated value on whatever is presented to him. Such are the contemporary figures of postmultilingual world literature, straining to critique the translational means of production by which they are to come to readability on the international market.

For its part, Europe is depicted as a group of homeless men sitting in a city park outside the courthouse:

> They sit there all day and all night in a semicircle of stone niches, more or less symmetrical, six to a side. In the middle sits a fat man in splendor, one knee to the southwest-west, the other to the southeast-east, the putative commander of this raggle-taggle Olympus, a paved sun at his feet with a fountain at its center. It is broken. (77–8)

Mora's follow-up novel, *The Only Man on the Continent*, picks up the issue of the dark side of European multilingual technocracy and its effects on individual speakers, but in a different fashion. The monolingual Anglophone image of the protagonist's London-based chief of European affairs, Anthony Mills, hovers threateningly in the distance throughout the novel. Darius Kopp confesses to the reader a preference for "the boss's boss, Mr. Bill Bower, *Vice President Global Sales* [...] the complete opposite of Anthony, a nice man with a warm voice. He can sing too. At the last *Sales Meeting* we sang *Sweet Home Alabama* in the Karaoke-Lounge, and everyone cheered us on" (29).[5]

Because of his inclination toward the unencumbered, anti-hierarchical communication culture of this equally absent figure Bill Bower in Sunnyvale, California, Darius regularly goes around the chain of command of his London-based bosses, a strategy that leads to such telephone conversations with London as follows, which begins with a ritual humiliation in English from the other end of the line:

> *Oh, I am sorry*, says Kopp with despondence in his voice. *I did not want to hurt you.*
> *You did not hurt me.*
> Kopp was once again *sorry*, in case that was the wrong word. You know, Englisch *is not my mother tongue.* Perhaps I meant *harm you.* No, that was also wrong. I can't really harm you at all. You know what I mean: I express for a third time my remorse. I promise on to be good from now on. *But please, Anthony, never ever talk to me like this.*
> At which point Anthony once again ended the conversation by hanging up. (29)

After this gruff transnational exchange, Darius Kopp, the company's "only man on the [European] continent," finds he needs to grumble to himself for a bit longer: "Even though the little number at the end wasn't bad—I'm a poor, terribly confused *bad english speaker*, I can't really have intentionally said that you are a vainglorious dirtbag, who gets artificially up in arms for nothing—it didn't console Kopp as much as he had hoped." (30) Mora's urbane post-postmodern protagonist is not seeking intercultural understanding or reconciliation between the

---

5. English words in the original are italicized here, though not in Mora's primarily German-language text.

linguistic self and other, but rather seeks a life in which the whole world could sing *Sweet Home Alabama* together during paid work-breaks.

Terézia Mora thus offers with her *Only Man* a critical status report on multilingualism and literature. As in her previous novel, the otherwise unimpeachable values of language learning, heteroglossia, and plurilingualism offer neither political salvation nor aesthetic revelation. Darius Kopp's advanced competence in English brings him no societal opportunities; it rather subjugates him to precarious transnational labor relations that (linguistically and structurally) undermine the erstwhile (monolingual) discourse fields of the German social market economy. In the social landscapes of the novel, no multilingual meanings are sought in the philological sense; rather, one longs for globally recognizable contact zones like business karaoke, which can tame and level relations among nationally and linguistically diverse colleagues. The novel is thus a dramatization of what Emily Apter calls the "deaestheticizing jaws of globalization" (Apter 2013: 1), multilingualism-as-sing-along.

Mora's novel shows not only that personal multilingualism promises no immediately advantagous (creative or commercial) basis of existence, but also that societal-global multilingualism has long escaped the hallowed sphere of philology. Why does the globalized, urbane, multilingual, pragmatic, adaptive performer of the twenty-first century, in the figure of Darius Kopp, find multilingualism so unsatisfying? Not merely because he is not a literary scholar or researcher of social pluralism. Nor because he is secretly xenophobic or ideologically monolingualist in a traditionally nationalist sense. Rather multilingualism in the free market economy is no longer for him an idealist abstraction of progressive geopolitics, but rather a bodily interpellation, one that conscripts him compulsorily into newly unregulated labor relationships.

Translating human rights

In another contemporaneous case, the novelist James Kelman, in his 2000 novel *Translated Accounts,* dramatizes the banality of collecting, recording, disseminating, and presenting genocidal brutality in a twenty-first century where "human rights" are tantamount to "the right to have one's human rights translated, and translatable, globally." Kelman introduces his novel with the following dispassionate preamble, worth citing the at length:

These "translated accounts" are by three, four or more individuals domiciled in an occupied territory or land where a form of martial law appears in operation. Narrations of incidents and events are included; also reports, letter-fragments, states-of-mind and abstracts of interviews, some confessional. While all are "first hand" they have been transcribed and or translated into English, not always by persons native to the tongue. In a very few cases translations have been modified by someone of a more senior office. The work was carried out prior to posting into the computing systems. If editorial control has been exercised evidence suggests inefficiency rather than design, whether willful or otherwise. [...] A disciplined arrangement of the accounts has been undertaken. Some arrived with titles already in place, others had none and were so assigned. Chronology is important but not to an overriding extent, variable ordering motions are integral to the process of mediation that occurs within computing systems and other factors were taken into consideration. It is confirmed that these accounts are by three, four or more anonymous individuals of a people whose identity is not available. (2001, ix)

This is how the novel begins—with stacks and stacks of passive-voice, boiler-plate, automated prose that records but does not communicate trauma. Most interesting here is how Kelman's twenty-first-century poetics around trauma turn toward the technical, the procedural, the obfuscatory, the duplicated and duplicitous, the automated and collated, the translated and truncated status of narrative—in a world-system of trauma communications.

Copy-editing atrocity

A further example of this trend obtains in the Salvadoran author Horacio Castellanos Moya's 2004 novel *Insensatez* (*Senselessness*), in which a Central American intellectual, in exile from his home country, is hired for $5,000 in a neighboring country to copy-edit 1,100 pages of a report collating the narratives of hundreds of survivors of, and witnesses to, massacres perpetrated in the throes of so-called armed conflict between the army and the guerillas. Says the narrator to himself:

I would only have to look it over, a final proofing, it was really a great gig, five thousand dollars just to [...] polish and touch up the final

version, although of course I had carte blanche to change anything
I thought necessary, without of course altering the focus—and his
trust in me was such that it wasn't necessary to go into much detail.
[...] Three hundred of those pages were lists of massacres and
victims' names, and the other eight hundred were very well written,
as I was soon to discover. (15)

Despite the greatness of the gig, the narrator spends far less of his three
months as a copy-editor copy-editing, and much more of it drinking
beer in the afternoons across the street from his office and trying to
convince acquaintances of the striking poetic virtuosity of the first-
person accounts he is going over. On one such occasion, he seeks to
deflect his beer-drinking partner's impression that he "had read those
sentences out of my notebook to convince him of the righteousness of
a just cause I was committing myself to, when what I really wanted [...]
was to show him the richness of the language of his so-called aboriginal
compatriots, nothing more, assuming that he as a poet might have
been interested in their intense figurative language and their curious
syntactic constructions that reminded me of poets like the Peruvian
Cesar Vallejo" (20).

Now on a different level than Kelman's defamiliarizing procedures
of collation and automation around translated narrative, Castellanos
Moya lays bare the hungry aestheticization that can befall survivor
testimony, and the lure of a poetic "surplus value" that might elevate
such narratives out of the red tape that conditions these trauma testimonies' prospective entry into the translated historical record.

Provincializing the European crisis in language

Writing in German, the British-Austrian translator Peter Waterhouse
composed "The Sound Valley" (2003), which comprises one, extended,
single-paragraph, fourteen-page utterance, which is said to take place in a
"sound valley" ["Klangtal"], rather than in for instance a "word valley" or
a "language valley." The five-year-old narrator's mother explains to him:

"The Valley we are looking into now is called Sound. It is the
Sound Valley. All the sounds are true. Everyone screams there,
and sings, squeaks, scratches, croaks, knocks, shouts, bellows." The
harmony was more direct, more fluent, more glowing, more feverish
than words. The words "tears" and "eels" became sounds. Crying

and pain were an immediate, flowing, ringing thing. His mother said: "I traveled here into pain, out of the world, disembodiment, Austria, culture, corruption, states. In fish pain, animal pain, pained screams, tiny pain, body pain, sadness glows and wafts and rings. Not Weltschmerz, but the opposite. Village-schmerz. Path-schmerz. Muscle-schmerz. Tiger-schmerz. Scorpionsting-schmerz. Snakebite-schmerz. Malaria headache. Also snakebite language. Tiger language. Body language. Village language. Bird language. Tongues. Air-and-spit language, non-dictionary language. We are right in the middle of physics here." (7)

This sound valley the mother speaks of is not only a homophonic caprice of metaphor, but also a location in Malaysia, southwest of Kuala Lumpur. This is where the mother and her son reside throughout the course of the prose-poem, which is narrated entirely from the perspective of the five-year-old Heinrich, whose Austrian family has been living in post-war exile in Malaysia. Heinrich has next to no image or conception of Europe or Austria, and he appears also to have no claim on "homeland" whatsoever. He does not understand national borders and possesses no stable "mother language," particularly since his mother continually undermines the political coherence of her own language. She reads "English letters" aloud, which were apparently not even composed in English. Despite the fact that Heinrich has never visited Austria nor Germany, the text—which is actually a conversation between mother and son—thematizes all manner of phenomena that animate contemporary German philology and cultural history: travel narratives, bilinguality, the Third Reich, the cultural life of the city of Vienna, the Cold War, the Adolf Eichmann trial, county fairs, ferris wheels, the Austrian *Hutweide,* deceased grandfathers, Donald Duck, and the Steiermark. In an agglutinating and unsentimental way, the narrator Heinrich relates all of these ecologically and discursively accumulating associations, which he encounters second- and third-hand in Malaysian exile. Out of these, Heinrich creates manifold syntheses like the following:

His nose was fruit—that is, a bud, fruit: his nose traced the fruit that lay along the street for sale or for taking, but his nose was itself the fruit. Pineapple, Malayan nanas, wafted out, and his nose was pineanose. The child tickled his nose, the tickling was like tasting, it was a tickling "tasten"; it was like the English "to taste." In German the child swept his nose with a handkerchief corner, or "touchcloth," but in English it touchclothed also. (3)

The psycholinguistic, material, and poetic situatedness of the young Heinrich among "his" many languages, which themselves appear not to acknowledge the existence and potential for meaning of the others among them, corresponds to the childhood experiences of the poet Peter Waterhouse, son of a British officer and an Austrian mother. His own binationality and multilinguality came about in and through the catastrophic events in 1940s Central Europe. The postmodern predicaments of his own symbolic subjectivity as a binational poet in the twenty-first century are intimately demonstrated in this prose-poem, without the tendencies toward kitsch pedantry that often plague translingual experimentation.

Through intertextual references to the (also) multilingual Austrian poet Hugo von Hofmannsthal, Waterhouse undertakes in "The Sound Valley" a radical divestiture from some of the most prized visions of European aesthetic-political modernity, as well as from the famed "discontent with culture" (and language) that this modernity tended to proclaim at the outset of the twentieth century. Against this backdrop, it is noteworthy that the letter the mother reads to Heinrich is called "A Letter"—that is, "an English letter that was not written in English," which reportedly treats of a child named Katherina and a fish. This letter is, of course, one of the most famous letters in European philology, serving each year in literature proseminars as proof of the Central European crisis of language and "language skepticism" around 1900. The text was published in 1902 by Hugo von Hofmannsthal in the Berlin newspaper *Der Tag* and is often referred to in literary historical contexts simply as the "Chandos Letter," as its fictional epistolary conceit holds that it was a letter written in 1603 by Phillip Lord Chandos to his colleague and friend Francis Bacon, in order to apologize for and explain his years of literary inactivity.

The Hofmannsthal text is thus a fictive letter in many senses, which nonetheless seeks to diagnose not so much the psycholinguistic condition of the English letter-writer in the early seventeenth century, but rather that of the entirety of Viennese *fin-de-siècle* modernity. The text is accordingly written not in English but in German, although readers are expected to assume that it was, in its fictive compositional context, written in English, and furthermore (fictively) that it has been translated into German for the readers of *Der Tag*. Or, readers must at least act as if there is no relevant distinction between the two languages. Nonetheless, the bilinguality or translatedness of this letter, one of the most important philological-didactic texts of the twentieth century, remains un-problematized to date. It is this strange circumstance that

Peter Waterhouse reanimates in his text, which was composed exactly 100 years after the Hofmannsthal text, and published exactly 400 years after the fictive Englishman Lord Chandos is supposed to have written it, in apology for his literary silence.

Of course, this vainglorious philological jubilee is of no import to the five-year-old child Heinrich, and he has no grounds for curiosity about such a convoluted translational fiction as this. The text is thus a narrative of the child's attempts—psycholinguistic, philological, episte-mological, and ecological as they may or must be—to come to terms with the apparently binding categories of knowledge the (European) adults present him with. These are, for Heinrich, adults who write and recite English letters written in German without mentioning or acknowledging the translatedness or the translatability of said text, adults who apparently suffer from the following kinds of linguistic problems, which Heinrich in his displaced exile context finds either ridiculous or incomprehensible. Chandos writes to Bacon:

> At first I grew by degrees incapable of discussing a loftier or more general subject in terms of which everyone, fluently and without hesitation, is wont to avail himself. I experienced an inexplicable distaste for so much as uttering the words "spirit," "soul," or "body." I found it impossible to express an opinion on the affairs at Court, the events in Parliament, or whatever you wish. This was not motivated by any form of personal deference (for you know that my candour borders on imprudence), but because the abstract terms of which the tongue must avail itself as a matter of course in order to voice a judgment—these terms crumbled in my mouth like mouldy fungi. (Hofmannsthal 1952 [1902]: 133–5)

So, in the most elegant and belles-lettristic terms possible, Lord Chandos insists on the unrepresentability and incommunicability of ideas, and the powerlessness of language vis-à-vis a phenomenal world full of passionate experiences, sublime diversities, and symbolic recal-citrance. Chandos concludes his letter thus:

> The language in which I might be able not only to write but to think is neither Latin nor English, neither Italian nor Spanish, but a language none of whose words is known to me, a language in which inanimate things speak to me and wherein I may one day have to justify myself before an unknown judge. (133–5)

With these words, the linguistic subjectivity of this exemplary multi-lingual writer of European modernity is silenced. For anyone involved in contemporary twenty-first-century models of linguistic competence, whether the ACTFL standards or the Common European Framework of Reference for Languages—we could ask ourselves: Where would we rank Lord Chandos and his speechlessness in the communicative language assessment protocols of our day? For instance, in the upbeat, indivualistic "I can" sociality of the CEFR? Would we perhaps need to conceive of a new assessment rubric for uncertain, insatiable, stubborn, despairing non-speakers, for multilinguals who have given up on all of their languages, because they no longer believe in the represent-ability of the world? Perhaps something like Z.2.2: "The learner has, as Hofmannsthal writes, 'lost completely the ability to think or to speak of anything coherently." (133–5) How else may we go about assessing linguistic subjectivity in Hofmannsthal's modernity and Waterhouse's postmdernity, by way of the child Heinrich? Which linguistic subjec-tivities in the twenty-first century will be celebrated and promoted as relevant civic models? Which linguistic worldviews will be made conse-quently unrecognizable under the conditions of a neoliberal market?

One is then led to ask, in current parlance, whether Chandos—with the many classical and modern languages he reads, understands, and creates meaning with—is communicatively incompetent? Is he a multilingual "more-languaged" person, or is he "less-languaged," as David Martyn formulates it? (2014) Or perhaps the languagedness ("*Sprachigkeit*") of Lord Chandos is that of an "enlightened monolin-gualist," as Wolfgang Butzkamm coined the term in 1973? Let us, however, return to Heinrich in Malaysia, the latter-day oral interlocutor to Hofmannsthal's woes, who then begins to naively recombine them by way of his vernacular, situational virtuosity. The child's interpretive tactics recall the question Hito Steyerl and Encarnación Gutiérrez Rodriguez posed in 2003: "Can the subaltern speak German?"

In the opening lines of the prose-poem, we encounter the first index of a much more radically multilingual worldview in Heinrich and Waterhouse than Hofmannsthal's and Chandos's melancholic retreat a hundred years prior. After hearing the German-languaged English letter aloud, the narrator claims that this is proof enough that English and German are "one"—not "the same" or "alike," but "one." (3) Immediately after this discovery, the child finds himself hypnotized by the joyful trees above. Yet the sentence structure—through which this hypnosis is entextualized and experienced in the story—is of a sort that is only possible in German, namely through extended participial clause. One would have to completely reformulate these sentences into subordinate clauses in English translation. In this translingual doubling of possibilities (extended participial constructions next to subordinate clauses) readers are in fact confronted by two kinds of trees or "treenesses." In the one case, the sentence grows (in German) and extends through participles from the sentence's trunk or base; in the other, subordinate clauses branch out laterally (in English).

In the compositional world of the text, the (un)translatability of its contents thus remains fully unproblematized and yet potentiated, and the two versions of the tree (translated and untranslated) partner one another into representation. This hypotextual affinity offers the child a unified theory vis-à-vis the multilingual world. No mere substitution or replacement of one symbolic system by another, the translatedness of the trees is potentiated in the child's own vision. (Considering, for a moment, this translational capacity on the table of the Common European Framework of Reference for Languages, one might ask what kind of translingual competence Heinrich's perception demonstrates: namely, the competence to operate simultaneously in two symbolic systems, the German and the English.) The narrator continues in this vein:

> Thinking needs no concepts, just geography. Not thoughts; but geo-thoughts. Not song; geo-song. Many of the poems I like to read are translations, and they bring two halves together. And the world, I believe, is brought together in rhyme and rhythm. (5)

In this moment, one could suspect the narrator of a romantic universalism or a kind of Platonic ideal of the ultimate commensuration, reconciliation, and harmony of worldly linguistic differences. This would be, I suggest, a too simplistic reading of the text, and the particular use of the word "*gleichen*" or "liken" in the story suggests another approach:

> The things were alike, the booths along the street resembled [glichen] one another, the varieties of fruit wafted and shone and resembled one another, the spicy and sweet odors drifting out of the snack stalls resembled one another. (3)

Here, the child Heinrich develops for himself an understanding of the word "liken," grasping it as a kind of performative practice, rather than a principle of logical identity, ipseity, or equivalence. For Heinrich, "likening" is something one does: an activity, a desire, and not a circumstance of nature or a norm. Things become alike in the moment they actively liken themselves to one another, or allow themselves to mutually liken. Being "alike" in this sense becomes a kind of creative practice of semiogenesis, in which the principle of neighboring possibilities returns to the fore. That is, words and concepts accumulate in the moment of translation, rather than disappearing through replacement, and this accumulation yields a translingual syntax in which multiple bearers of meaning can emerge simultaneously. This syntax of neighborliness sheds further light on the difference between glossodiversity (a multiplicity of codes for common meanings) and semiodiversity (a multiplicity of meanings) in M. A. K. Halliday's sense (2002). As Heinrich recognizes no practicable boundaries between national languages, he is left with a semiodiverse aperture on the world. At the close of the text, the mother asks Heinrich:

> "When are you happy Heinrich?" Her child: I am happy when I have to guess. For example, like when I went to the Indian's little newsstand that had this aroma. And I had to guess what it was. I had to guess, I couldn't see what smelled. I guessed the flowers and cakes and hairspray and the birthday candles. The Indian knew what it was. And I didn't know. (11)

This is the final sentence of the prose-poem. Here, "having to guess" and "liking having to guess"—capacities which Heinrich must cultivate within himself in his multilingual environment—are capacities that Lord Chandos cannot muster in his moment of language crisis. He (and a great deal of multilingual, monolingualist European modernism) preferred the certainty of skepticism, which does not threaten his social and epistemological hierarchies. Lord Chandos admits as much, as he writes:

> The good and strict education which I owe to my late father and the early habit of leaving no hour of the day unused are the only things, it seems to me, which help me maintain towards the outer world the stability and the dignified appearance appropriate to my class and my person. (133–5)

In Chandos and Heinrich, then, we face two very different approaches to languages: Chandos, the authoritative skeptic who seeks to maintain his class and person; and Heinrich, who is happiest when he has to guess, when he is unsure which path to follow. This happiness is perhaps a component of what Claire Kramsch (1997) calls "the privilege of the non-native speaker." Heinrich's mother, for instance, explains to him how it was when they first came into exile in Malaysia and were no longer among native speakers of "their" unified national language, suddenly finding themselves amid the postcolonial multilinguality of the Clang Valley. She performs this circumstance in memory:

> When we came to Malaysia, melodies began. My forest became loud. My words became loud. My speaking spoke. Moan, groan, bang, squeak, fizz, kaplop, miaow, uff, bomp, sniffle, pow, wap, urks, ratsch, spin, splash, snarl, scoff, klong, bang, raaah, screech, groar, adieu you beautiful world, haps, hiss, grrr, yelp, boo-hoo, munch, splutter, rapfoooo, I began speaking like Walt Disney's people, hach, faff, kricks, uff, oye, vrrrr, vropp, ah, mommy, ow, oh, crunch, I spoke like that ever-aghast Donald Duck and the speechless things in the comics: What, what, what, bong, zoing, drop, shhpp, yaps, swupp, I rhymed myself together, I sang myself together, I pulled myself together. Blessed be our house on the Ewe Boon Road 35a in Singapore. If you listen to me closely, Heinrich, if you listen to your comics Mother closely, then you too will be a writer, a Donald Duck poet, one who pulls and rhymes it together. A duck who hears the spoken language and saves Europe. (8)

It is Heinrich's untempered, unruly multilingualism—his Donald Duck language—that may, more than any other political strategy or ideological solution, be able to "save Europe."

Passing in monolingualism, beyond the literary

Though the preceding examples of world-literary texts suggest various strategies of critical passing in the global system of translatable monolingualisms, it is not only literary texts that find themselves in such a predicament. Individual speakers face similar dynamics, as a former student from Turkey illustrates below in a testimony about his study abroad experience in California, circa 2009:

> [The International House] was a hub of Englishes. All exchange students spoke English—albeit at varying levels of proficiency—but did so with a particular accent and mannerism that marked them

as outsiders. I wasn't a Californian, I had only lived there a while ago. I wasn't exotic cause I was too darn fluent. The Californians thought I was trying too hard (Dude, chillax homie. Speak in your own accent.), some were convinced it was an act (Aha! You mispronounced that!), the Brits hated my accurate grammar (How come you speak that correctly and still sound like a Yank, mate?), the French were furious that I had no accent (Zis iz absulutely krazie!)—though I would trade my entire knowledge of English phonetics for a slight French accent any day—and the Spanish were displeased with my diction (Stop using hard words on us!). The sentiments eased a bit over time as they noticed I struggled with English at times (No way you got a C on an essay!) and wasn't perfectly assimilated to every element of the culture (You hate the pace too?). I was never a full member of the multilingually English speaking, multiculturally American bubble that was the ILC [International Living Center] (Why won't you put together a Turkish Culture Night?). I have to admit, at times I wished I had a strong, indecipherable, impenetrable Turkish accent and had all the mannerisms and clothes to make me a proper "Turk" (whatever that is) just to be relieved of the double-agent status (Hello my friend, My name Nazim Korkmaz. I am Turkish from Ankara. It is capital. I have big mustache and camels. I pray to Allah in Arabic 5 times in a day. I sell carpets. I drink tea. I am proud person. Thank you).

Here, this exchange student expresses frustration with being expected to act representatively toward his perceived culture of origin, a task often presumed of world-literary texts as well. In the following chapter, we will explore how a new juridical logic of a *ius linguarum*, or "right of languages," prescribes and curtails certain modes of speaking for multilingual world citizens like this student.

Chapter 4

A RIGHT OF LANGUAGES

> Our colleague here can't speak German anymore, since he got the German passport.
>
> —Kebap stand employee,
> Schlesisches Tor, Berlin, July 2007

It has been suggested that the story of German citizenship reform since 2000 is, in the end, "much ado about not-very-much" (Green 2012). After an initial peak in new conferrals of citizenship to foreign nationals (at around 190,000) in the year 2000, naturalizations have been steadily declining among eligible residents, while the average length of residence in Germany among non-citizens has increased. Naturalizations in Germany among E.U. nationals, who enjoy privileges of mobility and employment that their parents' generation could only fantasize about, have held at below 1.0 percent since 2000. Among non-E.U. nationals, one might suspect that the liberalization and streamlining of home-country protocols over this period regarding release from citizenship would have led at least to a significant uptick in German naturalization applications (Green 2012: 180). Turkish citizens, for instance, no longer have to contend with labyrinthine inheritance and military service burdens before acquiring German citizenship, as they had in the 1990s, making the nitty-gritty of the application process less daunting. The fees for becoming a German citizen, though they have increased significantly, are still in the mid-range among peer countries. So why, among those eligible, have there been so few takers?

The blithe answer is that citizenship is a bygone technology, and that Europe's various naturalization procedures are working through a lame-duck period of decreasing relevance, general civic divestment, and policy-level recalibration around new principles of belonging and borders. The casual remark cited above, from 2007, tells a different story. The speaker, a Kurdish-Turkish non-citizen resident of Berlin, made this quip to me while we chatted (in German) at the counter of her döner-kebap shop in the traditionally Turkish/gay/anarchist neighborhood of East Kreuzberg. Whether as an apology to me or as a sidelong dig at her male colleague, she explained—in his presence—that his apparent unwillingness to join us in our idle banter was a consequence of his "getting the German passport." Her word choice reflects several discursive consolidations particular to the epoch and place. "Unser Kollege" ("our colleague") symbolically positions the co-worker as a respectable, upstanding member of an organized workplace, rather than—for example—as a friend, casual acquaintance, fellow countryman, or comrade-in-arms. She describes him, however, as having "gotten" ("gekriegt") "the" ("den") German "Pass" ("passport"), rather than for instance receiving "*his* German passport" or "German *citizenship.*"

This mundane symbolic gloss—of "getting" a German passport like one "gets" a can of soda out of an ill-maintained vending machine—is quite standard imagery and tone in vernacular discourses on citizenship in Germany, where the passport artifact itself bears higher value than the intangible apparatus of citizenship (*Staatsangehörigkeit*). The next clause of her explanation is however something new, and goes to the heart of this book's exploration of the mono-/multilingual system in its recent technocratic instantiations. Given all of the rhetorical resources one might choose in accounting for an acquaintance's grumpiness, standoffishness, or silence in a situation that seems to warrant some linguistic form of polite communication, this speaker took spontaneous explanatory recourse to what in the U.S. would be referred to as her co-worker's "citizenship status." She then intuitively aligns the normative range of casual conversation practices in semi-public or commercial settings alongside a corresponding spectrum of citizenship status—as naturalized, documented, permanent resident alien, refugee, asylum-seeker, and the like. This is a complex symbolic procedure, reflecting a particular narrative about one's right—in a purportedly post-ethnic society—to volunteer certain kinds of speech or silence in a wide range of semi-public interactions.

Whether begrudgingly, in jest, or both, the non-citizen resident volunteering phatic speech to me in this interaction assumes the role of the spokesperson-deputy, who assumes by habit or principle that it is "good to talk" (Cameron 2000)—and to talk *in German*. Her colleague, in turn, is regarded as having earned—or "gotten"—the right to be silent, to be unforthcoming with language, to not speak when implicated in a conversational frame. The passport-holder is in this regard exempt from a certain mode of interpellation, or at least from certain soft forms of it in apparently non-consequential, non-official settings. Citizenship reform in Germany since 2000, as elsewhere, has however effectively dissolved the distinction between official and nonofficial, and between consequential and nonconsequential settings, following the securitarian anticipation of an ever-emergent, ever-potential moment of civic terrorism. Consider for example the generic role of the multilingual speaker in the dramaturgical scenarios laid out in Germany's 2005 Act to Control and Restrict Immigration. This first-ever Immigration Law (*Zuwanderungsgesetz*) stipulated German language competency as a probationary condition of legal residence in the following specific way:

> Integration efforts on the part of foreigners will be supported by an offering of integration courses. Integration courses include instruction in the language, the legal order, the culture, and the history of Germany. Consequently, foreigners should become accustomed to the living conditions in federal territory to the extent that they will possess the necessary self-sufficiency to handle all aspects of everyday life from a third party. (Act to Control and Restrict Immigration: 190–1)

Notice the orderly bundle of integration desiderata, which begins with language and end with German history. Taking as a given the successful completion of these integration courses, candidates for naturalization or permanent residency will "consequently" be able to do certain things—things that are, interestingly, seldom regularly expected of autochthonous citizen-residents. Handling "all aspects of everyday life without assistance from a third party" is quite a high bar for citizenship as such, one that was not even among the bold requests Immanuel Kant made of the citizens of his day, should they wish to come out of "self-imposed immaturity" (1983 [1784]: 41).

Mythologizing the multilingual citizen

What kind of broad investment in language is occurring in this new law? Susan Gal and Kathryn Woolard (1995) stress that such political efforts directed at language are often symbolic proxies toward the valorization of other, non-linguistic goals. Indeed, the transformative ritual foreseen in this narrative-become-law is a new staging of citizenship as such, not of the immigrant citizen specifically, but of the linguistic citizen at large: informed, responsible, competent, and ready to handle just-in-time linguistic tasks in a rapidly changing civic marketplace. Language (and *not* the domains of legal order, culture, and history made subsequent to its competent command) is made the arbiter of successful transformation. As Bourdieu famously argued about ritual, it is not the transformation of *x* into *y* that is prized—here from foreigner to citizen, from non-speaker to speaker, or in Bourdieu's example from boy into man—as much as the reaffirmation of the boundary crossed (1991: 117–18). Indeed, an extraordinary amount of political energy has been invested, since the kebap stand employee's birth circa 1985, in getting citizens and non-citizens to speak in certain ways rather than others. The non-citizen has become the mythic testing ground, primarily because he or she can justifiably be subjected to more invasive assessments of bodily/linguistic comportment, whether multi- or monolingual, while birth citizens maintain at least the legal-constitutional basis to dilate in either "white linguistic disorder" (Hill 2008) or intransigent silence.

In his comparative analysis of the 1794 decree on language from the French National Convention and a 2007 European Commission "think piece" on language diversity, Robert Moore comes to the following conclusions about the mythic deployment of "language" in both contexts:

> The specter of miscommunication, caused perhaps by speakers with less-than-perfect fluency in the Standard, and/or through their use of an inherently flawed verbal instrument, is viewed with undisguised horror, and is seen as a threat to governance and social cohesion. Both texts offer, interalia, brief potted narratives of malaise, variously involving social chaos, feudal oppression, unfreedom (slavery), social disintegration, war and bloodshed, religiously motivated terrorism narratives, in other words, of how bad things were "before" (the Revolution; the establishment of the EU), and/or of how bad things will be in the future, if the prescriptions contained herein are not followed. Most important of all, in both texts citizens are exhorted to make a free choice that is nonetheless compulsory: to abjure some communicative media (and, by implication, the communicative practices associated with them), and to "adopt" others. What emerges from the comparison is a remarkably consistent picture of what "linguistic diversity" looks like when seen by a specifically European state (latterly, supra-state). (Moore 2015: 20)

This securitarian dynamic, of promoting reactionary multilingualism to the helm of domestic politics, adds a newly complex layer to what Rosina Lippi-Green (1994) describes as the suppression of linguistic variations in favor of, in the British case, Received Pronunciation. With twenty-four constitutive languages to manage, the customary hierarchy of intralingual diversities (in Polish, French, or Suomi/Finnish) is inflected with the European Commission's valorization of standard variations, such that the envisioned multilingual lexicon favors an attenuated selection of high-value standard repertoires.

In the German context, this new juridical discourse about how to monitor and assess immigrants' familiarity with German culture-in-language has departed starkly from the salutary neglect of the Kohl years, when the federal government had aggressively promoted the maintenance of heritage cultures, befitting the ethnonational logic of the *ius sanguinis*. Residents of Turkish descent, whether or not they had ever spent much more than a summer vacation in Turkey, were expected to be, at some point, "ready to return."[1] In an abrupt departure from even the late 1990s in post-Reunification Germany, the early 2000s saw a rapid proliferation of laws and protocols that made social assistance and visa renewals directly dependent on an immigrant's progress in German language and integration courses. Intake and assessment procedures that had previously been agnostic about an applicant's language competence were rewritten to gauge longitudinal progress and demonstrable effort in learning German. Meanwhile, political defendants of federal and provincial "integration" curricula insisted that German language proficiency was not a compulsory state directive, but rather a civil right, ensuring gender parity and economic opportunity for low-income and middle-class transnational residents alike.

A 235-million-Euro language package for non-E.U. nationals, for instance, was framed as a social welfare initiative that might redress a heretofore unjust and ethnicized system of immigrant enfranchisement, in which heritage-German resettlers from the former Soviet Union had been granted no-cost integration courses, while Turks and Arabs were forced to go it alone. Through this rhetoric of redress, speaking German "without the assistance of a third party" was resignified as a social justice imperative and civil right. Relieved in this way of its dubious countenance as a state mandate, the right to speak German

1. See for instance West German Chancellor Helmut Kohl's first campaign platform statements in, among others, "Koalition der Mitte: Für eine Politik der Erneuerung" (2011 [1992]: 69).

acquired the political aura of a win–win solution for migrants, post-migrants, and non-migrants alike.

Indeed, considering how the early guest worker program (1955–73) had systematically depended on non-German workers' *lack* of German language proficiency when wage and workplace disputes arose, the advent of a new public idea about language learning (Pratt 2003) in the early twenty-first century was no less than a watershed civic–political moment. Fifty years after foreign nationals had been invited en masse to work in West and East Germany, their descendants and latter-day counterparts were now being encouraged to partake of the symbolic capital that the German language offered. The old rumblings of ethnic nationhood—juridically untenable in this New Europe—were being translated into an ameliorative language politics that might correct the injustices of the past.

Language assessment deputies

A sea change in citizenship statutes at the end of the 1990s announced Germany's long-overdue departure from its Imperial "right of blood," *ius sanguinis*, toward a French-inspired "right of territory," *ius soli*. The rather sudden policy change, unveiled by the ruling Red–Green coalition government in 1998, signaled a milestone in transnational residents' quest for civic recognition, one that had been forged in fits and starts in the Federal Republic over most of the preceding thirty years. Turkish newspapers from the Kemalist weekly *Cumhuriyet* "The Republic" to the tabloid *Sabah* "Morning"—each known for hawk-eyed criticisms of German naturalization policy—quickly recognized the import of the Federal Republic's retreat from ethnic communitarianism with headlines like "Bravo Almanya!" and "Yeni Vatandaşlar Hoşgeldiniz" ("Welcome, New Citizens!") (Gottschlich 2007 [1998]: 168).

When asked in 2006 to clarify how the various generations of immigrants already living in Germany, as well as their family members abroad, might best ready themselves for the federal government's language policy reforms, interior minister Wolfgang Schäuble responded:

> I'm just now beginning to think about that. But we can see that it doesn't make sense that children come to primary school without knowledge of German. So they have to learn it beforehand. And

in concrete cases I have immediately asked: How do you propose to do language courses in Anatolia? But there are also audiovisual possibilities. The test can be done on the telephone. We're trying that out here in the Interior Ministry. For late resettlers [ethnic Germans from Soviet territories] we've been doing language courses prior to their arrival for a long time now. What we can expect of ethnic German late resettlers, we can perhaps also expect from Turks, who want to come to Germany. (Carstens and Wehner 2006)

In this upbeat, impromptu gloss, the interior minister described his agency's linguistic challenge with a mix of procedural experimentalism and conceptual vagary. Of course, high-level partisan politicians (in the legislative as in the executive, on the national as on the European level) do not tend to have practical or theoretical training in second language acquisition methodology. Neither do many of them have extensive personal experience with *struggling* to access the opportunity to learn a language under duress or pressure, as refugees, asylum seekers, and migrants seeking regularization routinely must and do. (Neither, for that matter, do many academics like myself, who research the politics of linguistic citizenship, possess both of these experiential characteristics.) This means that, across the board, the statutory prose outlining the mandates of language learning under conditions of what Moore calls "reactionary multilingualism" often vastly overestimates the prospective results of formal language learning programming, while vastly underspecifying the long-term resources necessary for providing and assessing those services. At Schäuble's optimistic behest, German consulates around the world were nonetheless instructed by the Federal Office of Administration to advise visa petitioners that spouses and children of legal residents could not join their next-of-kin in Germany without achieving the following level of language competence:

Basic knowledge of the German language are on hand [*vorliegen*] only when the main features of the German language are commanded in speech and writing, so that familiar, everyday expressions and very simple sentences, which serve the satisfaction of concrete needs, can be understood and used. The person to be incorporated [*einzubezie-hende*] must also be in a position to introduce himself and others as well as to ask other people questions as to their person, for instance where they live, which people they know, or which things [*Dinge*] they possess, and must be able to answer these kinds of questions. They must be able to make themselves understood, when a dialogue partner speakers slowly and clearly and are prepared to help. They must furthermore be in a position to inquire after or reproduce information from everyday life in short communications, for example in forms, short personal letters and simple notes. (Bundesverwaltungsamt 2005)

The forensic scenarios of linguistic exchange envisioned and codified here dovetailed with post-9/11 security imperatives and federal law enforcement's strategic deradicalization programming, for which multilingualism presented both a procedural impasse and a symbol of cultural resistance. While thousands of consular officials beyond Germany's borders were suiting up for complex language-assessment responsibilities for which they were generally undertrained, the political imperative at home remained uncannily simple: *learn German if you want to stay here.* Interior minister Schäuble formulated his expectations to this effect in a March 2006 interview:

What can we expect from foreigners, who are living here permanently? We can expect that they want to live with us here. They ought to learn German and take part in the life of civil society *in its diversity.* They ought not to intend to live as if they weren't here. (Carstens and Wehner 2006, my emphasis)

Speaking German was thus resignified as an escape route out of unilateral heritage-cultural bonds—figured in deictic terms as "not being here"—toward civic diversity and "being here." This rhetorical superimposition of place deixis, linguistic territoriality, and civic communitarianism indicated how the ideal of a publicly monolingual (though privately multilingual) German polis was acquiring a panacean valence in policy-making spheres. One year after Germany had passed its first-ever Immigration Law and declared itself an immigration country, language(s) had begun to *mean* in a new and politically binding way (Göktürk et al. 173–93). Reflecting on the French National Assembly's decree from 1794, Moore points out that such pronouncements about the liberty-guaranteeing nature of language learning were in evidence in their campaign as well. The decree asseverated for instance that:

Citizens, you have the good fortune to be French, and yet many of you lack an essential element to merit fully this title. Some do not speak the national language at all, while others know it only imperfectly.

There are entire departments where French almost never enters into the interactions of civil life. Nonetheless, the knowledge and the exclusive use of French are intimately linked to the maintenance of liberty, to the glory of the Republic, that is to say, your happiness, since its interests are your interests. (Moore 2015: 21)

The silence of the kebap-stand employee, in the face of Schäuble's interpellation, is the silence of the former language-learner under duress, the applicant required to acquire and perform the German language in order to "get the passport." He has in a sense graduated from this thickened and symbolically precarious sociolinguistic mode of citizenship conferral I understand as a *ius linguarum*, or *right of languages*.[2] In this juridical model, languages are decidedly in the plural, in the form of organized, plural monolanguages, administered by a technocracy like the European Commission in consultation with a complex constellation of other European and non-European institutions. This citizenship paradigm is not a *ius linguae*, or right of language (in the singular), as it does not rely on traditional Jacobinist, Rooseveltian, or Kemalist notions of linguistic purification and exclusion, along the lines of Karl Marx's revolutionary pronouncement about bilingualism in *The Eighteenth Brumaire*, that:

Man makes his own history, but he does not make it out of the whole cloth; he does not make it out of conditions chosen by himself, but out of such as he finds close at hand. The tradition of all past generations weighs like an alp upon the brain of the living. [...] Thus does the beginner, who has acquired a new language, keep on translating it back into his own mother tongue; only then has he grasped the spirit of the new language and is able freely to express himself therewith when he moves in it without recollections of the old, and has forgotten in its use his own hereditary tongue. (2001 [1852]: 11)

Under such a *ius linguae*, doubling, borrowing, translating from already existing material (here, called "tradition") is feared and rejected. It is not yet clear whether Marx's species-wide psychopathologization of translingual practice is to be understood as historically contingent or rather as humanity's semiotic original sin. In either case, Marx's conceptual dilemma here finds affective kinship in Ilan Stavans's 2001 memoir *On*

2. For an initial account of the "right of languages" see Gramling (2009). On the "thickening of citizenship" see for instance Smith (1999).

Borrowed Words, in which Stavans stages a conversation with the classic bilingual memoirist Richard Rodriguez. The latter, or his fictional double in Stavans's own memoir, asks: "What does the switch from one language to another really entail?" Stavans's response is:

> "My English-language persona is the one that superimposes itself on all previous others. In it are the seeds of Yiddish and Hebrew, but mostly Spanish." I invoke the Yiddish translation of Shakespeare's *King Lear,* which, in its title page, read "fartunkeld und farveserd"— translated and improved [...] "You know, sometimes I have the feeling I'm not one but two, three, four people. Is there an *original person*? An essence? I'm not altogether sure, for without language I am nobody. Language makes us able to fit into a context. And what is there to be found in the interstices between contexts? Not silence, Richard—oh, no. Something far less compelling: pure kitsch." (2001: 251)

It is this last, dramatic revelation that reminds of Marx's inaugural disdain for translingualism in the *Brumaire.* After all, most of the acts of borrowing that Marx cites to ground his hypothesis about failed revolution and squandered justice are translingual ones: nineteenth-century French from thirteenth-century Italian, sixteenth-century German from ecclesiastical Latin, revolutionary French from imperial Latin; it is this act of taking, without disclosing having done so, that demotes tragedy to farce for Marx, essence to kitsch for Stavans.

Brian Lennon (2011) analyzes Stavans's jeremiad for code-switching as an awkward genuflection to monolingual editorial conventions, as an ill-conceived social mistake—or in Lennon's language, "a tropism or a solecism that must remain opaque to the reader" (12). Marx's distaste is for failure-by-copy, for the feckless revolutionary who—clothed in the inevitability of *Rückerinnerung* (remembering back)—commits a venial misdemeanor of anaphora against his own political moment. Just as code-switching is seen as pre-condemned to indefensibility in literary prose, it is keyed to precocious, infantile folly in political action. And, as for the *Brumaire* text itself, this is only the beginning. Marx enlists several semiotic domains—(national) language, situational *parole,* tradition, dramaturgy, kinship, clothing, and political tempo-rality—more or less interchangeably in diagnosing the recalcitrance of sustained political consciousness. The main distinction Marx draws is not between monolingualism and multilingualism as such, but between one political moment's ability to forget its (often translingual) semiotic references from the past, and another political moment's compulsion to remember, to see itself as a "cognate" of a precedent event:

> The nation takes on the appearance of that crazy Englishman in Bedlam, who imagines he is living in the days of the Pharaohs, and daily laments the hard work that he must do in the Ethiopian mines as gold digger, immured in a subterranean prison, with a dim lamp fastened on his head, behind him the slave overseer with a long whip, and, at the mouths of the mine a mob of barbarous camp servants who understand neither the convicts in the mines nor one another, because they do not speak a common language. "And all this," cries the crazy Englishman, "is demanded of me, the free-born Englishman, in order to make gold for old Pharaoh." "In order to pay off the debts of the Bonaparte family"—sobs the French nation. (12)

This particular text shows how a distaste for symbolic doubling is embedded in Marxian analyses of means of production, a distaste that will tend to preclude multilingual and translational analyses of culture among Frankfurt School theorists. The result is that, in an era where meaning—literary, informational, visual, musical, political, and civic— is being monetized across language frontiers at an asymptotic pace, we are left with few Marxian tools for approaching a political economy of multilingual citizenship. Simply forgetting heritage, regional, and auxiliary languages, as Marx suggests, was never not a palatable option for a European Union whose founding idiom is *diversity in unity*. What is explicitly sought however is the management and functionaliz- ation of this diversity for particular mythic conceptions of European behavior. Silence, aphasia, and non-communication—as chosen by my newly naturalized non-interlocutor in Berlin in 2007—had no place in this intercultural idiom.

A *protohistory of the* ius linguarum

It is not a particularly novel insight to point out that non-citizens often find, or conclude, that they ought to watch what they say for fear of incurring swift and arbitrary consequences either from the state or from those it enfranchises. Prior to penning her 1943 essay "We Refugees," Hannah Arendt had herself arrived in New York from Portugal on an illegal visa just two years earlier, and though she had already begun publishing in English by the following year, she nonetheless continued to pen essays in German throughout the 1940s for the anti-Nazi journal *Aufbau,* and also in Yiddish—though less frequently—for the New York daily *Morgen Zshurnal.* Here is how the undocumented Arendt describes her and her refugee compatriots' orientation toward multilingualism in her would-be host society:

> After four weeks in France or six weeks in America, we pretended to be Frenchmen or Americans. The more optimistic among us would even add that their whole former life had been passed in a kind of unconscious exile and only their new country now taught them what a home really looks like. [...] With the language, however, we find no difficulties: after a single year optimists are convinced they speak English as well as their mother tongue; and after two years they swear solemnly that they speak English better than any other language—their German is a language they hardly remember. (111)

A spellbinding and beautiful essay in itself, the candor of Arendt's "We Refugees" as regards multilingual practice under political duress is often overlooked, in favor of more general observations about refugee status (see Agamben 1995). Contemporary in some important sense with later theorists of bilingual identity like Richard Rodriguez and Ilan Stavans, Arendt depicts English as a necessary, auratic talisman, a harbor promising a future life of stability, anonymity, and—as the kebap stand employee suggests at the opening of this chapter—the prerogative to remain silent or illegible in public. English offers the early Arendt the dream of being left alone. She continues on to describe the political scene in which her customary linguistic practices become newly performative in semi-public encounters:

> Once we were somebodies about whom people cared, we were loved by friends, and even known by landlords as paying our rent regularly. Once we could buy our food and ride in the subway without being told we were undesirable. We have become a little hysterical since newspapermen started detecting us and telling us publicly to stop being disagreeable when shopping for milk and bread. We wonder how it can be done; we already are so damnably careful in every moment of our daily lives to avoid anybody guessing who we are, what kind of passport we have, where our birth certificates were filled out—and that Hitler didn't like us. We try the best we can to fit into a world where you have to be sort of politically minded when you buy your food. (115)

Contrasting this line of thinking with her later more programmatic works of political theory, we may reflect on at least a few features of this passage: 1) how the subjective experience of "language choice" is understood as arbitrating political status, even in the absence of explicit state interpellation; 2) the prescience of this line of thinking for identity-political debates in the 1980s; and yet 3) how language, proficiency, accent, and speech are not mentioned here explicitly, but are implicitly that which might betray one's presumptive back-story, or which might allow one to be detected. That Arendt is both circumspect and insistent, at once, that this kind of situation is indeed "political" indexes an emerging multilingual theory of rights that her later work did not explicitly bear out. The essay further prompts us to inquire what the social effects of a *ius linguarum* are in the broad range of historical situations implicated in the 2005 German Immigration Law, according to which multilingual non-citizens "will possess the necessary self-sufficiency to handle all aspects of everyday life without assistance from a third party."

Ius linguarum *as myth*

In exploring the forms that monolingualism can take in social and political life, the preceding sections might seem to assent to the idea that monolingualism and its embodied forms do indeed exist. This is a position that many if not most sociolinguists, philologists, anthropologists and philosophers of language would not readily underwrite. Particularly Michael Holquist has taken pains to demonstrate the impossibility of monolingualism as an ontological category:

> The language of those who are said to speak only one language, in this everyday sense of the term, is already immersed in the ineluctable disunity and formal multiplicity that are the necessary condition for having any language at all. Failure to perceive the systemic multiplicity that is at the heart of any spoken language is a linguistically uninformed view that historically and politically is eventuated as linguistic monism. (2014: 8)

While Holquist is no doubt *analytically* correct in his bid to dissuade scholarship from embracing "monolingual" and, for that matter, "multilingual" as actionable, substantive categories, monolingualism can nonetheless 'exist' through its discourse effects, without having an ontological claim of its own. Here we can take recourse to how Roland Barthes described the signifying power of myth. As I claimed in Chapter 2, literary artisans like Franz Kafka have been variously compelled to strike an irrevocable bargain with monolingualism-as-myth, *despite* its ontological baselessness—a bargain that resists elective divestiture, particularly if one wishes to publish books. In this vein, we may recall how Barthes described Maupassant's disgruntled intimacy with the Eiffel Tower:

> This pure—virtually empty—sign is ineluctable, *because it means everything*. In order to negate the Eiffel Tower (though the temptation to do so is rare, for this symbol offends nothing in us), you must, like Maupassant, get up on it and, so to speak, identify yourself with it.[3]

Maupassant's choice for radical, myopic, and yet disdainful identification with the tower aptly figures Kafka's own literary habitus vis-à-vis monolingualism.

Indeed, one of the ways scholarly research has been able to dispose of monolingualism before conceptualizing it is to designate it as a "myth." The alliterative notion of a "myth of monolingualism" brings together two touchy words, each of which comes bearing its own high-voltage and ambiguous history of use. Both words conjure a mood of peripatetic belatedness, angling in each case to expose something that appears to have worn out its welcome, luxuriating in the plain sight of theory and practice alike. *Myth* and *monolingualism* hail forth for critique two intersecting planes in the same system of regulatory social physics. They attempt to mark the ways in which institutions (in the Bourdieusian sense) self-justify and self-naturalize through forms of speech practice (or what Barthes would call *parole*) that are generally taken to be shared, commonsense, or nonideological. Once invoked—though always somehow retrospectively—both words put their newly adopted objects *on notice*.

Despite this apparent critical kinship between *myth* and *monolingualism*, the rift between the two begins with a glance at the morphology of the words themselves. Whereas the first term, *myth*, comes to us in most languages in a lexical form that is earthy, protocultural, and hardly one syllable in length, the six-syllable latter term, *monolingualism*, sounds about as engineered, cloying, and parvenu in any vernacular vocabulary

---

3. Barthes 1982: 237. "C'est signe pur—vide, presque—il est impossible de le fuir, *parce qu'il veut tout dire*. Pour nier la Tour Eiffel (mais la tentation en est rare, car ce cymbole ne blesse rien en nous), il faut, comme Maupassant, s'installer sur elle, et pour ainsi dire s'identifier à elle" (1964: 27).

as words ever allow themselves to be. The word *monolingualism* looks recently unpackaged—shipped in from a university laboratory.

I do indeed consider monolingualism to be a myth, not in the commonsense social-diagnostic sense of the word myth, but in the sense Roland Barthes proposed was at work in post-Vichy France. Like other myths in the Barthesian sense of the term, monolingualism's mythic effectiveness rests on its familiarizing self-disclosure and its reassuring transposability. Like Kafka's Oklahoma Theater, all monolingualism wants in return from modern subjects is a particular kind of belief in planetary linguistic order(liness) and a concomitant disattention to the fact that such an order did not exist before the seventeenth century. Barthes's famous example of second-order signification, *quia ego nominor leo*, from a Latin grammar book, is "mythic" in Barthes's view because it suppresses and mutes its first-order meanings and their historical and social contexts—Who is this bold and proud lion? Whom is she speaking to? Why is she speaking, anyway?—replacing them with the mythic, second-order message: "I am a grammatical example demonstrating correspondence between subject and predicate in Latin." With *quia ego nominor leo* as a heuristic template, monolingualism-as-myth may be understood as performing a different, equally mandatory second-order signification. Under the episteme of monolingualism, *quia ego nominor leo* becomes: "I am Latin. Latin, like *your* language—you *have* one, right?—can say anything. Don't worry about it too much. We can get it translated." Its systematicity promises to be exhaustive and serviceable at once, leaving nothing of note behind.

For an item of speech to qualify as *language* under the myth of monolingualism, it must pertain to at least one among a set of sovereign, equal, non-overlapping, transposable, possessible, federated, panfunctional integers of systemic languageness—like Dutch, English, or Igbo. (The mythic logic of monolingualism does not even require linguistic territorialization anymore, though Yildiz makes a strong case that it indeed once did, 2012.) In *Mythologies*, Barthes writes: "Myth [...] is a language which does not want to die: it wrests from the meanings which give it its sustenance an insidious, degraded survival, it provokes in them an artificial reprieve in which it settles comfortably, it turns them into speaking corpses."[4] If we

---

4. Barthes 1982: 244. "Le mythe est au contraire un langage qui ne veut pas mourir: il arrache aux sens dont il s'alimente, une survie insidieuse, dégradée, il provoque en eux un sursis artificiel, dans lequel il s'installe a l'aise, il en fait des cadavres parlants" (1964: 241).

are to conceive of monolingualism as a kind of speech that has been indentured to a certain mythic structuration, then the conditions, terms, privileges, relations, and effects of that exchange must be brought to light. Citing Hobsbawm and Wallerstein on the "invention of tradition," Makoni and Pennycook (2006) have claimed that the "invention of languages" took place first by fashioning innumerability among discrete African and Latin American languages, in the context of colonial consolidation, making languages countable like solid items. According to Pennycook and Makoni, what we have inherited in the form of "languages," all languages in fact, are artificially named and fashioned unities, which latter-day linguistics can only truly critique by "disinventing" them, through a careful, empirical awareness of the divergent, centrifugal speech practices that constitute them—a commitment that Yngve (2004) describes provocatively as "hard-science linguistics." This constrained plentitude is abetted by an ideal of translation as isomorphic *adequatio*, a domesticating transposition of the Saussurian signifier-signified relationship onto the translingual correspondence between one language and its potential other, the unity of which empties the other language of its conceptual content and relational values. Translation then is pursued, under the episteme of monolingualism, as a substitution, rather than as an articulation.

Myth-busting?

In terms of the invention of discrete, transposable, panfunctional languages, or what I would prefer to call monolingualisms, it was not only the coerced enumerability of discrete languages under colonialism that needs analytical undoing, but also the transposability hypothesis of the late seventeenth and early eighteenth centuries, manifested in Johann Sebastian Bach's *Well-Tempered Clavier* in the 1720s, i.e., the ideal that a given melodic composition can and should be transposable from any one key into any other key, without significant delay or adjustment to the instrument—an imperative that ran counter to nearly every stylistic, aesthetic, spiritual, and moral orthodoxy of medieval music. Approaching monolingualism not as the *prima facie* exclusion of "other languages," but rather as the ideal of expedient translation as isomorphic *adequatio*, we may conceive the technological moment of monolingualism rather as the idea that language(s) are languages primarily because they can be translated into other languages, that a language *means* to the extent that it can also mean, readily, in German,

French, or English translation. In a sense, this is, again, the translingual superimposition of the Saussurian signifier–signified relationship onto the translation-ready correspondence between one language and its other. Monolingualism was translingual structuralism, two hundred years before structural linguistics.

While the mid-century Barthes was animated in part by his dismay at what appeared to be indomitable, because anachronistic, myths of French imperial rectitude, he was careful to pursue myth not in terms of the particular substances under its sway, but rather in terms of myth's signifying structure. Indeed, Barthes asserted that myth was a structure that functioned with a relative lack of interest in the precise historical substance of the meanings it conscripted. Everything under the sun was and is equally susceptible to mythologization, and no myth—whether Frenchness, femininity, or monolingualism—is eternal. Barthes indeed sought to provide what amounts to an absolute grammar of myth, one that was indifferent, universalist even, in its relation to the cultural materials of a particular age.

Under the specific myth of monolingualism, language artifacts—if they are to be considered "language" at all—inform their interlocutor about the nature of the bounded system from which they issue, and reassure that interlocutor that the spoils of said system are accessible to him via transposition or translation. Kafka's famed parable of Odradek dramatizes a scene in which such a candidate linguistic artifact behaves badly vis-à-vis the monolingual episteme that has textualized it: instead of providing documentation of its linguistic provenance when prompted by the patriarch, the creature merely retorts: "*Unbestimmter Wohnsitz*" ("Residence unknown") and laughs at the myth, contented with its own drag performance of monolingualism. He does not say "I don't know where I come from," nor "I won't tell you," but rather responds to the linguistic census-taker in the census-taker's own language.

Myth, as we mentioned, is a broad and unwieldy term. I would propose that a commonsense use of the concept myth—along the lines of: "It's an (urban) myth that military dolphins armed with anti-terrorist lasers are loose in the Gulf of Mexico"—leads us immediately into a cul-de-sac when thinking about monolingualism. Tinged as it is with a general admonishment toward naiveté, this use of the word *myth* sets up two classes of people—believers and critics—who deal with myth in ways that are fundamentally at odds with another, but are in some ways mutually reliant. Myth-believers are held under myth's sway and are therefore unchanged and unchangeable in their stance toward myth. Myth-critics have, in contrast, furnished for themselves a lateral glance at the myth, are able to minoritize its role in their lives, and are therefore changed in their general apprehension of the world. This evangelical approach envisions a threshold of conversion by which a myth-believer can become a myth-critic when she divests from the myth, at which point she is no longer beholden to its *parole*. I suggest that any such apprehension of monolingualism as myth, one that underwrites a temporal or intellectual threshold between participants and critics, or that relies on the notion of "divesting" from monolingualism through critique, is inclined to underestimate the mythic power and structure of monolingualism—misapprehending it as a small-minded, coercive, and propagandistic ideology that should have been debunked long ago.

Furthermore, to pan the myth of monolingualism as an outdated custom (say, in the Netherlands) or as a jingoistic farce (say, in the United States) would disavow the many things this myth has been effective enough to invent and institutionalize over the past three centuries—including highly advanced popular literacy, mutual comprehensibility between states and their citizens, technical stand-ardization, the publishing industry as we know it, and also, indeed, ethnolinguistic nationalism. As a historically contingent episteme, monolingualism has brought forth a bundle of inventions that even the most vigorous celebrants of multilingual subjectivity would have a hard time doing without. Thus if a discourse on monolingualism (as myth) pursues as its primary analytical objective the relative truth or falsity— or the ontological status—of monolingualism, that discourse will be forced into a stalemate of rebuking, rebutting, or correcting positive claims, by replacing them with other claims that, nonetheless, still avail themselves of the myth's originary terms—essentially impugning the said myth with items borrowed directly from the myth itself.

For instance, we could indeed choose to take a vigorous debunking stance toward monolingualism as myth, such as: a) monolingualism has never actually existed in human language practice, given the dialogical, centrifugal nature of speech itself; or b) speech commu-nities, particularly those emerging over the eighteenth and nineteenth centuries from war-nationalized societies in northwestern Europe, *became* monolingual by force but never were monolingual in *essence*. We could continue with: c) Anglophone U.S. Americans do not on average prefer to remain lifelong speakers of one language only, and they in fact vigorously oppose English-only legislation; or d) learning and mixing multiple languages does not aggravate children's develop-mental aptitude and educational achievement; poverty and exclusion do this. These we could call respectively the ontological, historicist, corrective, and redistributionist arguments toward debunking the myth of monolingualism, and there is assuredly ample evidence and scholarship to defend each of those interventions. Having done so, however, we encounter the problem that "debunking myths" may indeed lead to gradual policy changes and consciousness-raising, but tends to leave the generative matrix that makes and remakes the factual distortions of monolingualism relatively durable and untouched. As a matter of course, we also are then compelled to take refuge in logical premises produced by that generative structure itself. In the case of monolingualism, myth-debunking projects require us to make affirmative counter-distinctions, using terminology such as multilingualism, plurilingualism, "codes," "switching," and the like—namely, constructs that take as their justifying basis a natural or heuristically sound cleavage between monolanguage and multilanguage.

The statutorily multilingual European Union, for instance, now finds itself several decades into just such an experimental dilemma around hundreds of language pairs (for twenty-four member languages), such that the *socially* multilingual United States can only wonder hopefully at the whole affair. And yet, such state-centralized planning around universal trilingualism compels policy-makers—at each turn, and often against their better wishes—to essentialize, delimit, individualize, and institutionalize categories of speech experience and linguistic identity that often have only the most tenuous historical grounding themselves. Compelled by civic expediency and technological urgency, *monolingualism* and *multilingualism* remain the heuristics of choice—absent other categorizations that might enjoy more subtlety in social analysis while retaining sensible applicability in public affairs.

Similar and notoriously freighted double-binds persist in how the U.S. Census Bureau reports ethnicity/race, whereby a given respondent's civic desire to "be counted" as something relatively commensurate with who they are often conflicts with the principles of enumerability, singularity, and individuality with which s/he is interpellated as a citizen/denizen. Even when laid bare as violently inaccurate, such myths of category remain central, untroubled, and authoritative. Both the compulsion to produce evidence of a documented language and a documented ethnicity/race tend to effect "a kind of *arrest*, in the physical and legal sense of the term" (Barthes 2012 [1957]: 235).

Given how swiftly these umbrella categories of *multilingualism* and *monolingualism* are being operationalized for the purpose of statecraft, any scholarly analysis that instrumentalizes the one to debunk the other—or that affirmatively elevates the one as a civic or moral virtue over the other—will suffer a certain methodological top-heaviness and fragility. What's more, the *kind* of multilingualism that is often idealized in order to stave off or "de-competence" ostensibly monolingual parochialism is often deeply at odds with existing popular multilingualisms, leading to new discourses of verbal hygiene for postmulticultural societies (Cameron 1995, 2013; Levine 2014; Warner 2015). It will be equally insufficient, however, to debunk the multilingual/monolingual binary wholesale as a "myth" or logical fallacy, because this option contents itself too quickly with the idea that these categories, once discovered to be ontologically untenable, are also therefore *ineffective,* or will soon grow to be so, as the work of debunking them marches forth.

A recent Coca-Cola commercial featuring a multilingual version of "America the Beautiful" appears to be celebrating language diversity and multiethnic, multiheritage U.S. citizenship. And yet, when the symbolic subjects of the video, the children, dive to the bottom of a pool collectively, their arms reach out for the same thing: a Coke bottle cap. Such is the structure of glossodiverse monolingualism: the pursuit of identical, monetized meanings in multiple codes. What use is multilingualism for the world if all of its multiple-language speakers are pursuing the same bottle of Coke?

Regardless of their truth or falsity, myths are, if anything at all, *effective,* and it is precisely myth's effective, modest, friendly, and yet insuperable performativity and interpellary stride that distinguishes it from other things: natural orders, fables, stories, tales, rumors, ideologies, pleas, policies, legends, polemics, pathologies, movements, backlashes, alibis, or orthodoxies. I would suggest that monolingualism is indeed none of these latter things, and that notions of monolingualism that see it as one or the other among them both over- and underestimate its signifying logic. Rather than a program of ethnolinguistic supremacy or a movement of *ressentiment,* monolingualism is a relatively humble signifying structure—in Barthes's characterization, a *kind of speech* or "parole"—which will use anything at its disposal to preserve its appearance of timeless and pacific self-evidence. Indeed, to do so, monolingualism will continue to marshal all the resources of multilingualism, multiculturalism, diversity, plurality, and democracy as the source materials for its own second-order signification.

De-mythologizing monolingualism

In responding to such divergent approaches to language plurality, humanities and social science research may pursue a sustained critical focus on the unmarked term at the heart of it all: the *mono* that has made *multi* thinkable and then practicable, and compulsorily so. Theories of monolingualism can call on the critical spirit, if not always the rancor, of previous struggles to define *whiteness, maleness, hetero-sexuality, cisgender,* and *metropole*—positions that have likewise gone without saying for most of modernity.

What these predecessor questions shared was a commitment to carefully enumerating how racialization and gender subjectification have sedimented vernacular and dynamic arrangements into durable expert institutions, in Bourdieu's sense of the word—institutions that are as intricate as they are defeasible, as consequential as they are undefined. And in each case, a broad research commitment to name the unmarked term (whether *white, male, heterosexual, cisgender,* or *metropole*) arose only *after* the emergence of ethnic studies, women's studies, gay and lesbian studies, transgender studies, and post-structuralist ethnography. There is ample space to think of monolingualism not as a mere debunkable myth, but as a discursive system arranged in antisubstantialist fashion, such that ontological arguments about it will routinely underestimate its power.

Monolingualism is not the idea that one language is preferable to another; it is too busy being monolingual to bother with ideological domination or rancor of that sort. Rather it is the idea that anything, absolutely anything, can be reasonably done, said, or meant in any one particular language, given the proper circumstances. From this point of view, monolingualism becomes, over the course of modernity, an irresistibly efficient, enfranchising, and even pleasurable civic base, which Kafka clearly had in mind when he closed his *Amerika* novel with the chorus of angels (English speakers) in the Oklahoma Theater. The embrace of monolingualism in the age of Theodore Roosevelt was, for Kafka, essentially that of a vast glee club, with an endless number of potential participants, and from which there was no desirable egress. In the endless chorus of Oklahoma, monolingualism is an artificial plenitude, a communitarian ubiquity that renders a single, centripetal, and heterodox universe of signs recognizable—and has no need for others.

Meanwhile, as research initiatives and advocacy organizations pursue *language rights* for underrepresented and precaritized speech communities, the UNESCO Universal Declaration of Language Rights insists that the major threat to most endangered language communities is a combination of the following structures of endangerment: a lack of self-government, a limited population or one that is partially or wholly dispersed, a fragile economy, an insufficiently codified language, or a cultural model that is opposed to the dominant nation-state form— all of which are assumed to be responsible for the fact that some languages appear unable to survive and develop within the twenty-first-century "world-language system" (de Swaan 2001). This means that whatever global public resources that happen to be available for language rights and language justice initiatives are being dedicated, overwhelmingly, to bringing dominated language(s) "up to speed" with dominant languages, to retrofitting threatened language communities with the fully formed panfunctional chess board presumed by structural linguistics. What is thereby left unquestioned is the *concept of languageness* that these advocacy efforts presuppose (Makoni and Pennycook 2006). Pekel (2009) describes this form of multilingual advocacy in the political arena of language rights as *monolingual multiculturalism*.

Since the liberalization and de-ethnicization of citizenship law in 2000, Germany has hosted an intensive mobilization of innovative myths for assessing the practices, opinions, and languages of candidate citizens. Though the procedures of previous decades were no less interested than contemporary institutions in how well-suited one was to become a German citizen (Wernicke 1989), the *ius linguarum* of reactionary multilingualism is a new caliber of organization and control. In contrast to its predecessor models that explicitly assigned a singular and distinct "blood" or "soil" to a given citizenry, the newly evolving linguistic model of civic belonging was not designed to engineer or maintain a uniform civic essence *per se*. Rather, a *ius linguarum* implicitly acknowledges the plurality of languages spoken among a given populace, but resorts to segregative strategies in order to minimize the effect of multilingualism on public life. Upholding cultural diversity while discouraging the substantive public use of heritage and nonstandard languages, the *ius linguarum,* and its culture-political substrate cosmopolitan monolingualism, is reactive in nature as a public policy strategy—rooted, paradoxically, in the recognition that multilingualism has become a societal norm (Vertovec 2007, 2010).

You are Germany

Following two turbulent centuries of ethnic nationhood, civic discourse in twenty-first-century Germany has sought to liberalize and transform what it means to be, or become, German. Premiering in simulcast on almost all domestic television stations on September 26, 2005, the Bertelsmann-funded "Du bist Deutschland" ("You are Germany") campaign presented viewers with a multicultural collage of spokespersons who both embodied and advocated an inclusive civic vision of the Berlin Republic (Jessen 2005). In the original television spot, spokespersons of African, Asian, Middle Eastern, and Southern European descent extemporized in German on this open-ended vision—that anyone who answers the call to active civic participation on a neighborhood and national level embodies Germanness itself. It was no longer ethnic culture or historical communitarianism that arbitrated belonging, but rather how one pitched in to the emergent project of pan-ethnic German public life. Despite the cascade of internet parodies that followed, the campaign held fast to its proposition that Germanness was no longer a shared ethnic heritage, but rather the sum of the vitality and diversity of an interculturally oriented citizenry in an era of global mass migration and European integration.

The fact that went unthematized in the upbeat television spot and on the ubiquitous subway placards that accompanied it throughout 2005 and 2006 was that the inclusive address "Du bist Deutschland" both performed and prescribed a doctrine of public monolingualism. An ideal of cosmopolitan linguistic unity (in German) has superseded the multiculturalism debates of 1990s Germany, leading to various forms of performative monolingualism in social policy and everyday life. The threshold of belonging—indeed of civic presence or "being here" in Germany—has, implicitly shifted from ethnic heritage to linguistic practice, a shift that now places corresponding conceptual demands on teaching professionals and language studies researchers. Here, I have chosen the term "performative monolingualism" to describe the symbolic practice of speaking German (as opposed to one's other heritage languages), in postmulticultural Germany. By speaking German exclusively in the public sphere, multilingual speakers of migration backgrounds comply *de facto* with a set of civic ideals that have become codified in German law, promotional culture, and statutory discourse since the late 1990s.

Indeed, the public use of multiple languages among Germany's labor immigrants and postimmigrants had been a cause for parliamentary discord since the mid-1970s, but national immigration politics did not undergo a coherent "linguistic turn" until century's end. Aiming to bolster former labor migrants' "readiness-to-return," *Rückkehrbereitschaft*, to their countries of ancestry, the Kohl government (1983–99) had funded heritage language-learning programs on the basis that "Everyone has a right to live in *his own homeland.*" The *ad hoc* institutional multiculturalism of the 1980s was thus fueled in part by political visions of an eventual exodus of recruited guest workers and the families they had formed in Germany. When the Soviet Union's collapse and the war in Bosnia gave immigration a more broadly humanitarian mandate in reunified Germany, a series of multiparty commissions convened to decide what it would mean for Germany to "come out" internationally as an immigration country. Five years later, the Independent Commission on Migration, headed by former Bundestag President Rita Süssmuth, delivered its findings:

> The tendency to seek naturalization is not great among migrants who came to Germany before the 1973 recruitment ban. Apparently the requirements for naturalization were unattainable for them. In recognition of the far-reaching integration efforts of these people, the Commission feels a more generous position on multiple citizenship is appropriate for this group of people. *These immigrants, as well as German society, have neglected the acquisition of the German language, because they were expected to have a limited period of residency.* During naturalization procedures, the blame for this situation should not be ascribed to these law-abiding immigrants who have worked hard since their arrival in Germany and who have raised their children here. (Süssmuth 2007: 184, my emphasis)

The inadequate linguistic subjectivity of veteran labor migrants—and particularly of German Turks—was thus recast as a symbolic failure of the guest worker system. But despite the commission's push for magnanimity in the realm of linguistic assimilation, a broad Center-Right legislative alliance had already begun to resignify the German language not as an inherited ethnic possession but as a pan-ethnic lingua franca. From this post-ethnic standpoint, the twenty-first-century German language took on the political valence of a syncretic "guiding language," whose centripetal power would render the specters of classic multicultural doctrine— parallel societies, mutual indifference, and cultural relativism—obsolete.

However, in an era when states are taking on superdiversity and multilingualism as a matter of design, a very different model from the classic *ius soli* appears to be taking hold. Globally, *ius soli* is on the decline, as nation-states that had previously based citizenship on territorial birthright sought to restrict this entitlement to those born to legal, permanent residents: Australia in 1986, Cambodia in 1996, Chile in 1980, the Dominican Republic in 2004, Hong Kong in 1997, Ireland in 2005, New Zealand in 2006, South Africa in 1995, Thailand in 1972, Great Britain in 1983. India and Malta abolished *ius soli* altogether in the 1980s, citing immigration and population booms as they adopted *ius sanguinis* systems.

This means both that Germany's adoption of limited *ius soli* in 1999 runs counter to the general global trend, and also that, since the 1980s, more and more countries are exploring ways to strategically manage generational citizenship growth based on the switchable vs specific assets of candidates (i.e. parents) who, due to their own citizenship, will predictably teach their children the state-favored language and civic values. Indeed, the systematic juridical presumption that individuals born on the national territory are or should automatically be citizens, regardless of the language they will or will not speak, appears increasingly to be a thing of the past. The following section explores one setting in which performative monolingualism has been effectively elevated into a political myth of the *ius linguarum*.

In the schoolyard

No institution without a space of legitimation.
—René Lourau (1974: 141)

It was standing room only. The international press corps—from the *Frankfurter Allgemeine Zeitung* to *Al Jazeera*—turned to face the front of the room, where the teenage student council representatives were taking their seats. An immigration activist in the crowd called out to class president Asad Suleman, pressing him to describe what it felt like to be "a victim." Amicably poised, the sixteen-year-old answered back: "I don't understand the question. Could you be more precise?" The room broke out in laughter (Lau 2006b).

Ninety percent of the students at Herbert Hoover High School in Berlin's northern Wedding district grew up speaking multiple languages—switching mid-sentence and mid-experience from Urdu, Polish, or Turkish into German, and back, as a matter of course. In early 2005, the school administration had made a splashy debut in national immigration politics by implementing a German-only language policy on its campus. The policy's jurisdiction extended well beyond the classroom—into lunchtime, recess, class trips, and all interactions on school grounds.

Over the next nine months, as monolingual school policy and the multilingual habitus of its students collided with one another, the school became a high-profile mirror-space for twenty-first-century Germany's civic self-image. Advocates of cultural integration and scholastic achievement for youth with migration backgrounds quickly elevated class president Suleman to an almost oracular status, as a maverick defender of the German-only (*Deutsch-Pflicht*) policy. In a measured tone that nonplussed beat reporters of all political persuasions, the teenager spoke plainly of the practical benefits of the monolingualist policy: "Our German has improved in the last year, and the aggressions are subsiding, now that everyone is trying to make themselves understood in one language" (Lau 2006a).

Suleman's schoolyard realpolitik inflamed the Turkish daily newspaper *Hürriyet*, whose editors dubbed the school a "forced Germanification asylum" (*Zwangsgermanisierungsanstalt*). Class president Suleman is of Pakistani descent, and some conjectured that his advocacy for German as the school's lingua franca had arisen out of experiences of social exclusion at the hands of the Turkish-speaking plurality of the school's student body (Lau 2006a). Seconding *Hürriyet's* vivid condemnation was the prominent Berlin Green Party legislator Özcan Mutlu, who rebuked the Hoover language compact as part of a tide of integrationist policies unfit for a self-professed cosmopolitan city like Berlin. Mutlu took stock of the affair as follows: "It's no coincidence that, after the tests of conscience (*Gewissenstest*) directed at Muslims and the desire to tighten immigration law, there is now in the province of Berlin a prohibition against speaking one's mother tongue in school" (Lau 2006a). Mutlu's inductive gesture—projecting the school's strategic monolingualism upon Berlin as a whole and, by easy extension, the Federal Republic itself—indicated the Hoover debate's underlying political mood: one that, for some, added up to a "new German patriotism" in the Berlin Republic (Lau 2006b).

Within weeks of its implementation, Herbert Hoover's German-only plan had become a political test case, not for the wholesale suppression, but rather for the spatial partitioning of lived languages in an aspiring cosmopolitan society. Though classes and conversations went on as regularly scheduled, the school had become an emblematic space for surveilling national immigration policy at work—a "crisis heterotopia"

(Foucault 1984) where law, language choice, and nationhood would converge at lockers, bicycle racks, and soccer scrimmages. Christian Democrat parliamentarian Robert Heinemann went so far as to suggest that "Those who defy the rule should be made to sweep up the schoolyard" (Öymen 2006).

Herbert Hoover's students were, however, among the least concerned about the arrival of performative monolingualism to campus. When the federal commissioner for integration Maria Böhmer arranged a visit to interview students about the pledge they had been asked to take, the young people took the opportunity of their conversation with her to push beyond the piquant topicality of the international press battle, calling Böhmer's attention instead to less politicized institutional needs: reducing class sizes to twenty-five students, increasing the minimum application quota for foreign-born teachers, improving access to extra help and tutoring in German, guaranteeing post-secondary trainee-ships for graduating students, and facilitating students' advancement to college-preparatory courses at *Gymnasium* (Varli 2007).

None of these concerns that the students raised had played a consequential role in the unfolding press debate, because these issues appeared tangential to the mythic proposition that multilingual students should only speak German when at school. Some students concluded that the Hoover monolingual contract amounted to little more than window-dressing. A group of Turkish-speaking students assured the *Hürriyet* newspaper, in Turkish: "There has been this decision to prohibit other languages at school. But it is not enforced. In the schoolyard and in other places we still speak Turkish among ourselves. In fact, we often even speak Turkish in class. The prohibition doesn't work" (Varli 2007).

Consider also the stoic insistence with which Herbert Hoover class vice president Halime Nurin dismissed the charges of linguistic hegemony that were being leveled against her school: "We weren't forced. We ourselves want to speak German. There's no punishment either if we switch into our mother languages once in a while" (Lau 2006a). Here, Nurin champions the spirit of the German-only pledge, on the basis that it only coincided with and confirmed her own preferred language practices. In the same breath, however, she asserted her and her friends' ultimate autonomy from the policy. Given these students' testimonies, it would be somewhat heavy-handed to diagnose the Hoover policy and the new statutory role of language use in German society as a draconian curtailment of the personal freedoms guaranteed in Article 3 of the Basic Law. Nor would it suffice, however, to view the state's recourse to linguistic unity in civic policy-making as a loose collection of ad hoc initiatives, or a reflexive retrenchment into parochialism in the course of Europeanization.

In 1994 the intercultural pedagogy researcher Ingrid Gogolin had described the ritual misrecognition (yet incorporation) of multiple-language subjectivity as "the monolingual habitus of the multilingual school," highlighting how even the most interculturally inclined domains of the German educational system tended to pre-empt the use of Turkish, Arabic, and other languages as bearers of knowledge, while continuing to valorize English and French in their stead. The events at Hoover demonstrate how Gogolin's hypothesis—of the super-imposition of monolingual ideology upon the patently multilingual social space of the German school—was being expanded in the 2000s to a national policy doctrine.

The Hoover school's German-only policy resonated profoundly in public discourse, galvanizing the preconception that migrants' and post-migrants' demonstrated proficiency in the German language is and should be the primary bellwether of their "will to integrate" (*Integrationswille*) into German (and thereby European) society. The crowning indication of this broad national investiture in linguistic unification came six months after Asad Suleman's press conference, when the embattled Herbert Hoover school community was honored with the annual 75,000 Euro prize of the German National Foundation (*Deutsche Nationalstiftung*). On its website in 2008, the prize selection committee commended the Hoover project in the following terms:

> Toward the improvement of a common school life that does not exclude anyone [...] the students, parents, and teachers have agreed after intensive discussion and without governmental assistance upon German as the school language. The school's proactive initi-ative underscores the significance of language as a precondition of integration, without hampering the cultural roots of the partici-pating people. Far beyond the borders of Berlin, the development has become an example of discovering one's own best interests (*Interessenwahrnehmung*) in the context of an active civil society. (Deutsche Nationalstiftung 2006a)

Officiating the prize-conferral ceremony, Bundestag president Norbert Lammert praised the school's students and faculty—along with Germany's 2006 National Soccer Team—as standard-bearers of successful integration. He assured the skeptical audience that:

You'll find no one that opposes dialogue, and absolutely no one who
is against tolerance. The question, under which conditions both can
come to be, is much less frequently posed [...] Each society [needs]
a minimum inventory [*Mindestbestand*] of common convictions
and orientations [...] No political system can maintain its inner
legitimacy without a cultural foundation of commonly held convictions. (Deutsche Nationalstiftung 2006b)

For Lammert, the Hoover school's commitment to multicultural
monolingualism exemplified a kind of integration avant-garde, leading
the republic back toward its "inner legitimacy." Speaking exclusively
German in the schoolyard would, according to this model, nourish a
shared minimum inventory of national values and core commitments,
including civic diversity, gender equality, and religious tolerance.
It is worth noting that, in his 2,500-word congratulatory speech,
President Lammert explicitly mentioned language just three times.
Foregrounding "shared convictions and orientations" as the ultimate
"meaning" behind language, Lammert subsumed linguistic practice
under civic communitarianism. The resulting policy doctrine—a *ius
linguarum*—was presumed to carry out the symbolic labor of civic
unification that a multi*cultural* politics of recognition had been unable
to broker since the 1970s.

   In his speech, Lammert echoed Jürgen Habermas's reluctant defense
of monolingualism as the key to a cosmopolitan patriotism in his
lectures on the future of the Berlin Republic:

If the manifold forms of communication are not to spread out
centrifugally and be lost in global villages, but rather foster a focused
process of shaping will and opinion, a public sphere must be created.
Participants must be able simultaneously to exchange contributions
on the same subjects of the same relevance. It was through this kind
of communication—at that time conducted by literary means—
that the nation-state knitted together a new network of solidarity,
which enabled it to some extent to head off modernism's drive to
abstraction and to re-embed a population torn out of traditional
life-relationships in the contexts of expanded and rationalized lifeworlds. (Habermas 1997: 177)

For Lammert, it was no longer tenable, in the age of migration and
Europeanization, to consider German language as an ethno-cultural
treasure (*Kulturbesitz*), that should be promoted for its own sake.

Rather, German would serve a social function as a *de facto* common language of the multiethnic student body, uniquely capable among the other languages of de-escalating conflict and aggression. Lammert's stake in the centripetal social power of speaking German reiterated the 2005 Immigration Law, in which proficiency in the German language was codified as a prerequisite of civic subjectivity. Speaking German meant that one would be finally in a position to cross over from subcultural "parallel societies" (*Parallelgesellschaften*) into both "the world" and "civil society in its diversity." Pledged to a unitary language on paper but simultaneously violating it in practice, the students at Herbert Hoover High School stand in a long line of German code-switchers who have been raised in a necessarily adverse position vis-à-vis monolingual doctrines. Having grown up negotiating with both a state-sanctioned, territorial language and one or more "minor" heritage languages, the students at Herbert Hoover are the heirs to a long-standing tradition of adverse multilingualism in German-speaking lands.

Beyond German borders, throughout the European Union's supernational experiment with civic integration, ethnic heritage is being replaced by linguistic practice in twenty-first-century citizenship reform (see Gal 2006). This Aristotelian vision of political engagement through what Wolfgang Butzkamm (1973) called (in a different methodological context) "enlightened monolingualism" presumes that the state's pan-ethnic lingua franca will "enable their members to live a good life by participating in public affairs for the benefit of the whole (*bios politikos*)" (Schaap 2011: 24). In this way, cosmopolitan monolingualism—a public procedural monolingualism that mythically promises transparency and equal access to security and justice—has gained a great deal of traction in societies tired of coping with the intransigencies of multiculturalism. This new view—tied as it is to a future anterior of successful language learning among new citizens on the one hand and of cohesive, communicative communities on the other—fulfills all the characteristics of neoliberal self-making: horizontal, voluntaristic, entrepreneurial, opportunity-rich, privatizable, decentralized, team-oriented, and at turns hopeful or mute about structural poverty and other forms of socio-economic precaritization.

Transnational trends

We live, ever more mandatorily, in what Deborah Cameron calls a "communication culture" (2000), as opposed perhaps to an "essence culture" or a "hard culture"—an age of cognitive capitalism in which languages are increasingly encouraged to act exogamously, i.e., in opportunistic and competitive relation toward other languages. One of the ambitious and optimistic aspects of the European Union that I find admirable, from my perspective as a teacher and researcher near the U.S./Mexico border, is Europe's official stance on universal civic trilingualism—i.e., that Europeans should be "competent" in two European languages other than their first language. The assessment procedure for figuring out how competent one is, the Common European Framework of Reference for Languages (CEFR), is billed as stressing communicative competence rather than grammatical prescriptivism.

In the U.K., and particularly in Germany, the naturalization game has moved from territory to language, such that we may now speak of an ascendant civic model in Europe of a *ius linguarum*. Importantly, this "right of languages" in the plural is most often multilingual and not ethnonationalist in its rhetorical design; it does not ask naturalization candidates, as U.S. president Theodore Roosevelt and Turkish president Mustafa Kemal had both done in the early 20th Century, to forsake their languages for the benefit of a linguistically standardized citizenry. Instead, it asks multilingual candidates to demonstrate competence in the public language and discourses of the state, and then funds and assesses their progress toward that goal. *Ius linguarum* frames political participation in one post-ethnic lingua franca as a civil right, which ostensibly protects new citizens from the occult precarities of their multilingual lifeworlds. The *ius linguarum* is, admittedly, a difficult state endeavor to criticize, because its visions of community cohesion are abetted by an even more unassailable rhetoric of human rights and autonomy.

This new jurisprudential principle of a right of languages, i.e., about who gets to speak European and how, is framed around when and how potential Europeans use their (multiple) languages in public—thus the plural genitive *linguarum* rather than the singular *linguae*. We may consider this hierarchy of multilingualisms and translatabilities in terms of an admittedly crude heuristic of fast and slow lanes in the translingual traffic in meaning (Pratt 2002). Let us take the fast lane first: this is what I consider the *glossodiverse lane* of European translation. Let's say this first lane facilitates and optimizes discussions on, for instance, European constitutional values and other supranational matters that cluster around E.U. domestic referenda and accords, the distribution of European parliamentary documents, the implementing of institutional schemata for foreign policy, immigration, education, and the like. One constitutive affiliate of this glossodiverse lane is the paralinguistic performative utterance of Euro banknotes, which feature the iconography of the bridge, promising that it *will have been* the civic rationale of Europeanization to establish translatability as a founding predicate: i.e., *Europeanness is/as translatedness*. Facilitating traffic wherever any consumer, investor, or migrant in Europe travels, this first lane of meaning-making exhibits a mode of multilingualism that Halliday (2002) has named *glossodiversity*, by which he means the mobilization of multiple codes in the service of common meanings.

In the *centripetal* project of Europeanization, this glossodiverse mode of multilingualism makes a great deal of sense, as it serves a civic logic to which its member states and, in some cases, its populaces have assented by treaty—sometimes vigorously, sometimes belatedly. While European statutory discourse is co-constructed and disseminated in a glossodiverse mode, by way, for example, of Estonian and Maltese public policy-makers and translators, other Estonian and Maltese meanings may be seen to be just as happily "stuck" in the constellations of their historical use, just as they had been before European translational performativity arrived on the scene. We could call this salutarily neglected, semiodiverse lane of meanings, quite simply, the slow lane of European translatability.

Paradoxically, it is this slow lane, this ecology of viscous cultural particularities, that serves not only as a primary mythic reservoir for European pride, i.e., "unity in *diversity*," but also as a primary source of parliamentary debate and statutory consternation in Brussels and Strasbourg: i.e., whose champagne can be called champagne, who gets to call themselves Macedonian, etc. But these are only the tip of the iceberg of the slow lane, these luxury items and geopolitical denominations. These constellations of meaning in Europe's Slow Lane—though in no way themselves closed, pure systems after centuries of mercantile migration, capitalism, and international socialism—remain relatively indifferent and unmoved by most forms of European glossodiverse bridge-laying. In the slow, semiodiverse, viscous, and agglutinating lane, languages continue to exercise all of the frictions of social deixis and autochthony that abetted their own claim to *languageness* in the early modern and protonational periods, thereby reflexively resisting the pluralist-incorporative imperatives of European integration.

Conclusions

The foregoing chapters have suggested that today's linguistic "new world order" is not primarily one of deep ideological ties or affective entrenchments between speakers and their own native languages, as was perhaps still plausibly the case when the first major theoretical texts on nationhood made their claims (Hobsbawm 1991; Anderson 2006 [1983]: 36). Rather than adhering to a map of entrenchments, particularities, and incommensurabilities, nations and nation-like enterprises now renovate themselves most efficiently on a grid of global translatabilities: civic, literary, political, and indeed ideological. Even the most doctrinaire purveyors of religious, securitarian, or nationalist self-design are today often working as hard on their translatability logistics as they are on the fundamental axia of their existence (Irshaid 2014). In her study of Islamist university students in Turkey and their use of Anglophone slogans at political demonstrations, Ayşe Saktanber theorized a predominating "panoramic narrative of modern faiths, global assertions, and local values that Islamic youth creates, both to build an identity and to represent their otherness" (2002: 255). Though it is not the task of this book to re-theorize the national community in the age of global algorithmic translatability, this chapter has considered how monolingualization processes in citizenship reform since 2000 reflect a general adaptation to a new order of translatable nationalisms under conditions of "soft multilingualism" (Noorani 2013).

What has been assumed in these past few centuries—economically, infrastructurally, literarily—to make translatability an orthodox *civic* virtue, and then a planetary mandate with its own technical systematicity, especially amid the asymptotic acceleration of mechanical translation in recent decades? We can further ask whether translatability is *essentially*—despite its opportunity costs—a public good and a civic virtue worth defending today at all costs. And if so, what are we to make of dissent and counter-evidence about it? One hint of counter-evidence is how vigorously normal it is to preserve certain terms as untranslatable—like Allah, which could just as well be translated in English as God, but is not. This was the focus of an art installation by the Palestinian-born artist Emily Jacir entitled simply "Translate Allah". It calls attention to the fact that, even for a globalist metaculture that favors translation, some items are made to occupy a ritual position of iconic untranslatability, particularly if their familiar kind of foreignness serves an indispensible political function.

I have attempted to set aside deliberation upon the ever-polemicized, ever-alluring question of "translatability" itself (Apter 2013; Crépon 2015; Cassin 2015), as all good challenges find their challengers in one way or another. Rather, we have been interested throughout this book in the grid upon which such translatability is ensured, tempered, perfected, and performed—and in becoming able to describe that grid as structural monolingualism. This is a shift away from the question of how lay and certified translators countenance and situate themselves vis-à-vis various discrete translation efforts, challenges, feats, and difficulties, and toward how other technicians and innovators are employed to produce and refine global interlingual systems of content-transfer infrastructure. This shift requires us to divest from the idea that translating in the twenty-first century is primarily a conscientious aspirational intercultural activity; that intercultural translating is the heir of humanist metaphysics in the era of globalization. Rather, we have asserted that translating (on the structural grid of monolingualism) is primarily and intensively a business enterprise, relying on complex and evolving modes of supply-chain management. This is an order predicated on organized, monetized, idealized transposability—and its precaritized and opaque discontents. In the context of this order, forms and lifestyles of cosmopolitan monolingualism are amply available for mobile global citizens bearing translatable intellectual property. Sometimes the bearers of such property—like Lawrence Summers—do learn languages and become somehow multilingual, but more often than not the globalized monolingualism available to them throughout the course of that learning remains unchanged.

This is, however, not an Adornian argument. I am not suggesting, for instance, that postmultilingual writing, speaking, or even translating is somehow trapped within a monetized echo-chamber of interlingual reiteration, along the lines of Horkheimer and Adorno's claim that "All laughter in the culture industry is always the laughter of derision" (Adorno and Horkheimer 2003 [1994]: 163). I am indeed of the opinion that human speakers are always less and more than monolingual, and that the speech practices of individuals and communities are always less amenable to structural monolingualism than are personal beliefs toward the charisma of ideology generally. Here we may rely on the enduring finitude of the human mind and body to prevent any true collusion between structural monolingualism and the linguistic habitus of individual speakers. The work of Alison Phipps in applied linguistics on "linguistic incompetence" (2013b) and Mireille Rosello in comparative literature on "rudimentariness" (2011) reminds us how world citizenship may inhere precisely in experiences of failure to comply with monolingualism in its glossodiverse forms. In Chapter 3, we suggested that world-literary authors are both participants and critics within this enterprise, and that they work within the myth of monolingualism, issuing promissory notes toward a truly postmonolingual, postglobal world that we as yet can hardly imagine. Their bid to pass as monolingual in the world-literary scene, and their illustrious failures at it, provide hopeful evidence that monolingualism is a technocracy that will fail in ways that capitalism, for instance, has not done. Whereas Chapter 3 drew primarily from published literary sources that have garnered international renown, this chapter on linguistic citizenship responds to an unpublished constituency—students, workers, teachers—whose assessments both complement and critique those world-literary endeavors.

Despite (and because of) postnational and supranational trends in policy-making, business logistics, and market behavior, nation-states have found they need newly artificial means for distinguishing between acceptable forms of linguistic belonging and participation. Contrary to thirty years of public discourse on cultural difference, globalization, and migration, and despite the fact that nation-states from Germany to China are tarrying with post-ethnic self-stylizations, monolingualism is indeed a political technology and civic gatekeeper on the rebound. We are witnessing literary industries and state institutions—for example in postmulticultural states like Germany—aggressively reinvesting in the technologies and civic logics of monolingualism, as they had once done amid the renationalization campaigns following the transnational inferno of the Third Reich. Renationalization strategies today, articulated in post-ethnic or pan-ethnic terms, are calling on "common language" rationales in more aggressive terms than ever before, prompting us to consider what translational monolingualism means for citizens in the twenty-first century.

AFTERWORD: INTO THE LINGUACENE

In 2012, we say, "It has become a faint dream of nights long past
that at an international conference the participants had to use
an earphone to listen to speeches translated 'simultaneously' by
man-machinery behind the scenes."
—Yasujiro Niwa, "Multilingual Communication" (1962: 596)

Taking stock of the definitional, rhetorical, and pragmatic distemper
that the word *monolingual* itself has brought about in recent decades,
this book has attempted a juxtaposition of contemporary civic and
scholarly uses of the word, alongside previous endeavors to "mark the
unmarked" in humanities and social science research (Ellis 2006). The
foregoing chapters have suggested several interlocking domains in
which monolingualism has taken hold as an actionable, dependable
means of production, while other traditional means of production in
the service and industrial sectors obsolesce. From its initial, ideational
forms in the seventeenth century, monolingualism has grown into a
structure capable of producing its own kind of literatures, citizens,
competencies, translingual compliance protocols, and indeed also
corresponding ideas about the proper conduct of multilingualism. In
contrast to some contemporary trends in scholarship, I have suggested
that the purchase and promise of monolingualism is currently under-
going a growth spurt amid the convulsive reorientations of economic
globalization, such that, as global markets discover multilingualism as a
monetizable field of commerce, national governments accordingly also
reinvest in certain normative visions of the flexible, optimized speaker
in post-ethnic logics of citizenship. While each of these two developments appears to be affirmative of *multi*lingualism in the emancipatory,
humanistic sense often associated with that concept, these new market-
and citizenship-oriented logics (of translatable intellectual property
and civic self-translation, respectively) are won through intensified
prescriptive attention to the underlying monolingual ideal, from
which a derivative notion of multilingualism is then achieved through
multiplication.

With good reason and even better motivation, literature is often seen as a time-honored haven for multilingual experimentation, while contemporary Europe is admired for its 1 + 2 initiative towards universal civic trilingualism. In twenty-first-century Europe, however, a citizen is welcome and encouraged to be and become multilingual, provided that one has successfully demonstrated monolingualism *first*. Similarly, access to literariness through its primary means of production—print publishing—is in the main reserved for those who have acquired legitimacy in aesthetic monolingualism before branching out into translingual experimentalism. I stress these claims not because I wish to merely object to this state of things, but rather because it is important to be clear about which underlying structures are amplifying certain practices and muting others.

I have also suggested that, although monolingualism indeed caught the variously opportunistic winds of national rancor over the course of political modernity (in France, Turkey, and more recently in Germany, the United Kingdom, and the Balkans), the structure of monolingualism itself is independent and prior to nationalism, in both theory and practice. This is a particularly important disambiguation in the current age of disenchantment with the overall explanatory logic and organizational power of nationalism and nationhood. Such general disenchantment may tempt us to anticipate that, alongside nationalism, monolingualism is apt to soon fall into disrepair or disrepute—that it is only a matter of time and a few successive generations of translingual speakers. The literary, linguistic, and political data collected in this book suggest that it is not a sound speculative hypothesis to presume a precipitous fall of monolingualism in the wake of postnational developments. Such a stance rests not on analysis but on several kinds of unsubstantiated hope: first, the hope that the globalization of data, capital, and meaning-making will have held at least a modest emancipatory promise, a way out of monolingualism for speakers and institutions, whether they wish it or not; and secondly, the hope that these profound changes in geopolitical structures will accelerate fruitful and critical paradigm shifts in research method, institutional behavior, and cultural production.

This second hope imagines that a multilingual methodology is always right around the corner for social sciences and humanities research, waiting for courageous innovators to guide its implementation. Soon, we hope, multilinguals who research multilingualism will find more and more reason and opportunity to research and compose multilingually—making meaning in languages they are learning, have learned well or less well, or indeed in combinations of languages. Non-native speakers of languages will seize the critical "privilege" we understand we are endowed with (Kramsch 1997), making scholarly sense in languages we did not grow up in. Anthony Pym's assertion that later-stage language learners make better translators than those who acquired multiple languages in early childhood (2013), because they have a more defamiliarized sense of the potentials of the language, will find a corollary in scholarly production. Critique will cease being a monolingual affair.

The general and obvious promise of multilingual knowing and being indeed convinces us, again and again, and in every context that matters, that all of this must be possible and imminent, and we wonder what the hold-up is, exactly. Ultimately, though, the hope that the multilingualization of societies, literatures, and institutions may be the silver lining of global convulsions in finance, data harvesting, refugee displacement, time–space compression, and precaritized mass labor migration turns out not only to be a "cruel optimism" (Berlant 2011), but also a histrionic one. Histrionic is a strong but appropriate word here, and we shouldn't shy away from using it in discussions about monolingualism and multilingualism.

Disciplines from translation studies to anthropology, from English to applied linguistics have entertained variously formulated "turns" toward multilingual inquiry, based in the realization that their research axia must *in the age of globalization* embrace a broader, many-languaged horizon upon culture, sociality, justice, politics, and aesthetics. This reorientation has routinely included a desire to listen to scholars working in a broader spectrum of language repertoires, home territories, and research traditions. We converse with one another about which normative aspects of scholarly genre, habitus, network, and format pre-empt such allolingual researchers from gaining the ear of their U.S. and European colleagues—whether in English or in another language. Most often, the process of interdisciplinary broadening has seemed to require a lingua franca in order to function communicatively, and that language has recently been English, following Philippe van Parijs's theory that the lingua franca or "maximal minimal language" of English provides Europe with the best platform for a "justificatory community" or "transnational demos" (2011).

Whereas national philologies like Germanistics and French Studies used to make do, quite contentedly, with multilingual output platforms for their scholarly conversations (Bonfiglio 2013), those disciplinary journals that seek to traffic internationally have turned to an Anglophone publishing model since 1990, appealing to a logic of broader appeal, audience access, and shared conversation. The International Association of Applied Linguistics (a bilingual French/English organization since its inception) quietly let go of French as a conference language in the 1970s. German Studies journals in the United States have seen a steady decline in German-language submissions since the 1980s, as native German speakers seek to dialogue with more interdisciplinary colleagues. Most major university presses in the United States will not publish research articles in languages other than English, again appealing to a maxi-min physics of optimal reach.

As Kees de Bot (2015) notes in his short history of applied linguistics, many scholars in that field divide their research time between publishing for smaller research audiences in their heritage languages of Portuguese, Dutch, Finnish, or Spanish, and then reformulating their broader research findings for the greater interdisciplinary good in English. Foregoing English for a less commonly read language of scholarly composition means objective disadvantages for connectivity and posterity in transnational spaces of scholarship. As is the case with literary publishing, it is often only established elites who can afford the flexibility and wherewithal to risk translingual offroading, when monolingualism offers so much promise and practicality.

It would be possible to see all of this as a temporary structural contradiction arising between current circumstances and emerging aspirations, on the pathway to new multilingual paradigms. Change takes time, and old habits die hard. Just as it took decades for the Proceedings of the Modern Language Association to stop publishing in languages other than English, it will take decades for that monolingualism to be superseded by something new and more capacious. Alternatively, we might attribute the incessant and overweening Anglophone supply chain in research production quite simply to American imperialism as such. Under this explanatory volley, major economic and political shifts will need to take hold in Asia, Latin America, and Africa before the linguistic winds begin to change.

Each of these approaches to explaining the de-multilingualization of research production in the postnational age however underestimates, I contend, the structuring power of monolingualism as such. Monolingualism, as suggested in Chapter 1, is indifferent to the particular language, nation, or society that manifests it. It holds no opinion on the cultural superiority or pragmatic advantages of English, Mandarin, or French, and it honors no history of linguistic development.

Monolingualism wishes only to be the elegant and simple form that makes "other languages" contextually superfluous or additional, such that everything that need be said in a given context may be said in one language alone, pending efficient translation or naturalization.

This organizational principle of sufficiency and plentitude in one language has meanwhile become crucial for software development, international linguistics, shipping, air traffic control, global studies curricula, superdiverse securitarian societies, liberal market economies functioning transnationally, and indeed world literature. This translational monolingualism is the primary characteristic of a new era, beginning in the 1990s, which I term the *linguacene*. In this period, machine translation broke with rules-based approximations of human language and began developing corpus-based algorithms that now, in their ever advancing returns-on-investment, guide cross-linguistic data retrieval at every turn. If early modern thinkers like Antoine Arnauld and Thomas Sprat envisioned "a language" as an extensive, exhaustive grid of propositional possibility, the civic and infrastrutural maturity of that vision is the linguacene.

Scholars have located the rise of the anthropocene, the era in which human action has profoundly reshaped geological development, with the invention of the coal-powered engine in the early 1700s. It is argued that, since this threshold moment, carbon-producing human institutions have irrevocably altered what the planet is and is becoming, where previous civilizational ages had only exerted topical, local, and aesthetic effects on the planet itself. Machine translation, in its incipient rule-based forms and its more advanced corpus-based forms, has helped to amplify and multiply the phenomena of anthropocene. Nuclear waste management, fracking, waterway rerouting, petroleum extraction, geostationary technology all rely on translingual discourses, often classified, patented, or otherwise proprietary ones, for their implementation. Whereas *anthropocene* designates an era of human *action* that alters the planet, *linguacene* accounts for an era in which large-scale discourse—translingually mediated—alters the planet in intensities and scalar trajectories unimaginable in the mid-twentieth century. Whereas Taylorism functioned on the procedure of opening new factories sequentially in new emerging markets, twenty-first-century protocols for industrial distribution in the linguacene first project global saturation, and deal with the logistical and linguistic hurdles as a matter of course. Multilingualism is then the field of symbolic extraction upon which these protocols must necessarily succeed, by way of efficiently managed, increasingly auto-correcting translational monolingualism.

This means several things simultaneously. First, it means that struggles to envision or manifest a multilingual poetics, a multilingual literature, an ethics of multilingual justice, or new modes of multilingual scholarly work for the twenty-first century are not being deterred or delayed primarily by institutional ill will, individual lack of knowledge, general disinterest, or misunderstanding. Enthusiasm for multiple-language inquiry indeed abounds and flourishes all around us. The desire to translate, and to translate beautifully and justly, abounds and flourishes too, upon pathways often considered untranslatable—and all the more so when we insist on calling them untranslatable. More people than ever wish to pronounce and use one another's words, songs, prayers, knowledges, and meanings to the betterment of their communities. Cassin et al.'s *Dictionnaire européen des intraduisibles* has gone far in raising consciousness about the manifest role of semiodiversity in scholarly pursuit. Its contribution is, among other things, an insistence on allowing foreign-language meanings to be an incitement to further, higher, and more complex discourse, rather than a mere incitement to equivalency-finding. Researchers wish to collaborate well and honorably with colleagues who know languages they do not, languages that they need, languages that they consider relevant despite their inaccessibility. This is an age of unprecedented willingness to listen multilingually, to become linguistically altered in the course of any given day, or lifetime.

This stance of openness is, however, in direct conflict with the logic of the linguacene, which requires the marshaling of controlled, proprietary content from language to language and from market to market without logistical interference. Optimization protocols in computer engineering and GILT (globalization, internationalization, localization, and translation) services stake their market claim upon their ability to deliver hassle-free translingual IP (intellectual property) conduits that can flex and learn in the face of new input. Vernacular multilingual behavior among individuals—making meaning in variously anational, hybrid, and mutating contexts—epitomizes logistical interference in the course of automated or otherwise mediated translingual transactions. As the explanatory promise of nation and ethnicity fails, these two modi operandi of language use—of strategic optimization on the one hand and ecological vernacularity on the other—will shape the core symbolic antagonisms of the twenty-first century. Accordingly, novels like Terézia Mora's *Day In Day Out,* James Kelman's *Translated Accounts,* and Chetan Bhagat's *One Night @ the Call Center* are indices of the emergence of a critical literature of the linguacene.

The relationship between embodied multilingual practice and algorithmic translingual transaction may be aptly illustrated with the metaphor of an interstate highway system, like that which was developed in the armament period of World War II in the United States. Designed to ensure efficient, scheduled delivery of goods and resources from one position on a national grid to another, the highway system sought to mitigate geological formations, terrestrial byways, and local viscosities of tradition. Funding the effort of course were stakeholders from various local communities, who leveraged the system toward their material and spatial interests. Municipalities and exurbs grew, throughout the 1960s and 1970s, in relation to their proximity to the grid system, while cities that were passed over in the construction phase for one reason or another experienced profound effects of deindustrialization, depopulation, and cultural obscurity. The system required unprecedented endeavors of demolition and displacement—both of human and non-human communities—while parallel infrastructural systems grew up in tandem or in compliance with the highway.

Such a schema helps us picture the potential transformation of cultural, literary, and linguistic practice in the advent of the linguacene. An interlingual highway system, confluent with the normative results of fuzzy cross-language retrieval ontologies based in vast and growing corpora of recorded language use, provides initial access pathways for potential simultaneous translation of content. Just as highway systems are built according to the needs of those who design, lobby, and pay for them, any interlingual highway is bound to cluster around already existing interests, who are invested in trafficking particular sets of meanings. These clusters of translatable language, like the industrial centers of the mid-twentieth-century United States when the interstate highway system was built, also tend to get more exits and onramps, more McDonalds, more malls, more rest stops, more Trader Joes. With time, communities tend to gravitate toward the highway and orient their interests around its interests. Meanings that are too large, heavy, awkward, unruly, unlicensed, or hazardous to fit into the highway traffic are indeed still allowed to make their way, in occasional sequential fashion, into other languages through creative, illicit, or otherwise alternative routes. As the interlanguage system accrues its own history of hubs and stakeholders, previously high-traffic sites that now find themselves at a prohibitive distance from the system's entry points will struggle to maintain the capacity for reiteration and reproduction. Newly designed high-traffic zones will be commissioned, peremptorily dispersing problems of translational logistics that had previously been assumed to be the defining pragmatic characteristic of languages and linguistic difference. Yasujiro Niwa's 1962 vision during his tenure as president of the Institute of Radio Engineers believed this interlanguage system would be fully in place by 2012.

Meanwhile, speakers in whatever relation to the interlanguage system they may find themselves are free and entitled to use "their" languages in whatever way they see fit, if one believes in the rational-actor approach to human language use. One only seldom experiences direct pressure, in the form of censorship, to alter one's linguistic reper-toire and the habits through which it is expressed. Indirect pressure, however, arises in all interactions that are mediated by the interlan-guage system, even when these interactions appear to be restricted to local, familiar participants. Messages to friends, in which one chooses to code-switch or use dialectal or sociolectal formulations, are auto-corrected. Texts that are written in too local a fashion are described as needing adherence to plain-language statements. "Non-native" compo-sitions or texts that celebrate aesthetic experimentation are categorized as too expensive to translate, and as contributing to the problem of "accidental content" in multilingual institutions like the European Parliament. Refusal to participate in compulsory code-switching—for instance, the insistence on referring to the Islamic deity as Allah rather than God/Gott/Dieu—meets with equally aphasic reactions, as the selective incorporation of certain code-switching practices ensures that domestic/foreign designations are maintained within a given systemic instance of monolingualism. The logistical hindrances that previ-ously obtained in large-scale commercial and diplomatic endeavors at crossing language barriers are thus devolved to individual vernacular users, who find their language use increasingly subject to contingent and irregular methods of disciplining and policing. House style guides at trade and university publishers respond to the intensification of translingual usages with more effective normative measures.

I suggested in Chapter 1 that monolingualism has become an ascribed social trait that plays a role in the way people understand each other's position in society and in global exchanges, and that it is no longer merely a clinical term for use at universities and among demographers. As Deborah Cameron observed about the general investment in linguistic assessments in recent decades as a defen-sible replacement for ethnic/characterological modes of assessing citizenship, monolinngualism has become the new civic solecism, the new way of being the wrong kind of world citizen. Those who find themselves competent in only one recognized linguistic repertoire soon also find themselves ranked lower in potential schemata of global participatory culture than they would have been in the early 1980s. Striving for translingual competence, a value vigorously endorsed by the Modern Language Association since 2007, corresponds also, however, to contemporary extractive logics of transnational corporations poised to access ever new commercial markets imagined to be monolingual. Speakers, subject to multiply convergent technologies of orthography on the one hand and institutional affirmations of multilingual competence on the other, will find themselves less competent than they had been decades ago, though their language repertoires and use have changed little. Drawing on Blommaert's work, the applied linguist Chantelle Warner (2014) considers this a phenomenon of scalar de-competencing.

Scholars in the linguacene, or at least those who are eager to compose or promote research in more than one language, face a difficulty that is a matter of structure rather than a matter of will. That is, researching multilingually isn't merely a matter of upping one's game, taking a risk, or trying something "out of the box." Such rationales for resisting the monolingual paradigm in scholarship will always place too onerous a burden on individual culture-and-knowledge workers, asking them to overcome yet another neoliberal hurdle in their self-flexibilization process. Researchers publish in English (when they well might have done so in Tikra, Mandarin, Sami, or Welsh) not merely because they wish to be heard by as wide an audience as possible, and because they don't want to restrict themselves to their own local audiences. Rather, the world of publishing and interdisciplinary research has come to comply with the requirements of the linguacene: a flexible, translational functionality that decommissions agentive, creative, and critical multilingualism. The linguacene is a network of related distributional structures and transactional processes that cannot entertain the need for other language, or language that cannot be incorporated through algorithmic translation. Most of our disciplines—whether translation studies, applied linguistics, or the national philologies—have done little to curtail the organizing principles of the linguacene. We have vociferously deconstructed linguistic imperialism and linguistic purism, we have renounced cultural chauvinism, and we have worried about the predominance of English as a language-of-instruction and a language-of-dialogue about multilingualism and translation. These objections, however, have had little to say about the modest, gradual, incremental advancements in the linguacene and its translingual interdiscursive

systems—advancements pursued by well-funded, positivistic technicians around the globe.

In the linguacene, languages themselves are being asked to change,
to lay themselves bare to translation and systematic translatability.
Under these conditions, we may ask whether languages themselves
are growing richer or poorer? Are certain languages and not others
are taking on certain forms of debt, labor, responsibility, flexibility,
rights, privileges, and value that other languages lack, or are unbur-
dened of. Under what conditions is it prudent, just, or progressive for
human beings to reorient their speaking practices toward the needs of
algorithms, toward the cross-linguistic highway systems of the digital
age?

Most of the meaningful interactions I now have with my students,
my family, my community, and my world are profoundly mediated
by the language of Base 2, a language in which I am an outsider. This
"monolingualism of the other" is the translational highway upon which
my most intimate meanings are converted and conveyed and—like an
organic heirloom tomato—routed back to me. If, as Marilyn Chandler
McIntyre proposes, we must "car[e] for words in a culture of lies"
(2009), that task has grown in import, urgency, and complexity amid
the global ascension of translational monolingualism. We remember
Kafka's Karl Rossmann, sitting at his equal-tempered piano, wondering
why it is that the soldier's song sung on the street, or remembered from
his homeland, doesn't sound quite as sonorous, quite as passionate,
quite as meaningful on his new equal-tempered instrument. As a
meaning-maker in the emergent linguacene, he is tempted to attribute
this dysphoria to nostalgia, or sentimentality, or his own lack of talent.
It has been the task of this book to suggest that Karl was right to step
away from the technocratic instrument of monolingualism and realize,
for the first time perhaps, that "no one could have pointed out the
tiniest item in the interior design that would have in any way spoiled
the overall effect of complete comfort and ease" (2008: 39). When,
however, he finds that "it certainly sounded strange whenever he
stood in front of the windows opening out onto the noisy street," (40)
this is the fissure in the linguacene where a new critique may begin
untempered.

WORKS CITED

Acosta, Abraham. 2014. "The Wager of Critical Multilingualism Studies." *Critical Multilingualism Studies* 2.1: 20–37.

Adelson, Leslie A. 2005. *The Turkish Turn in Contemporary German Literature: Toward a New Critical Grammar of Migration*. London: Palgrave Macmillan.

Adorno, Theodor W. and Walter Benjamin. 1999. *The Complete Correspondence 1928–1940*. Cambridge, MA: Harvard University Press.

Adorno, Theodor W. and Max Horkheimer. 2003 [1944]. *Dialektik der Aufklärung*. Frankfurt am Main: Suhrkamp.

Agamben, Giorgio. 1995. "We Refugees," translated by Michael Rocke. *Symposium*. 49.2: 114–19.

Agha, Asif. 2003. "The Social Life of Cultural Value." *Language and Communication* 23: 231–73.

Al-Issa, Ahmad and Laila S. Dahan, eds. 2011. *Global English and Arabic: Issues of Language, Culture, and Identity*. Bern: Peter Lang.

Alvarado, Isaias. 2015. "'Inglés sin Fronteras', la estafa a migrantes en EEUU que opera en Perú." *La Opinion*. 13 May.

Anderson, Benedict. 2006 [1983]. *Imagined Communities: Reflections on the Origin and Spread of Nationalism*. London: Verso.

Apter, Emily. 2005. "Translation after 9/11." *Transit* 2.1: 1–8.

Apter, Emily. 2013. *Against World Literature: On the Politics of Untranslatability*. London: Verso.

Arciniega, Víctor and Adriana López Téllez, eds. 1997. *Chiapas para la historia: antología hemerográfica, 1o de enero de 1994 al 10 de abril de 1995*. 1st ed. Vol. 3. México: Universidad Autónoma Metropolitana-Azcapotzalco.

Arendt, Hannah. 1996 [1943]. 'We Refugees.' In *Altogether Elsewhere: Writers on Exile*, edited by Marc Robinson. New York: Harvest Books.

Aschenberg, Heidi. 1998. "Il faut que je parle au nom des choses qui sont arrivés ... Zur Übertragung von Konnotation und Aposiopese in Texten zu Lager und Shoah." *Jahrbuch Deutsch als Fremdsprache* 24: 137–58.

Auer, Peter. 2007. *Style and Social Identities: Alternative Approaches to Linguistic Heterogeneity*. Berlin: Walter de Gruyter

Bach, Johann Sebastian. 2006 [1722–42]. *The Well-Tempered Clavier, Part I*, translated by Willard Palmer. Los Angeles: Alfred Music.

Baghat, Chetan. 2005. *One Night @ the Call Center*. Kolkata: Rupa Publications Private Limited.

Bakhtin, Mikhail. 1981. *The Dialogic Imagination,* edited by Caryl Emerson, translated by Caryl Emerson and Michael Holquist. Austin: University of Texas Press.

Bakhtin, Mikhail. 1994 [1940–65]. *Rabelais and His World*, translated by Hélène Iswolsky. Bloomington: Indiana University Press.

Bakhtin, Mikhail. 1996. "The Problem of Speech Genres." In *Speech Genres & Other Late Essays*, edited by Caryl Emerson and Michael Holquist. Austin: University of Texas Press, 60–102.

Bakhtin, Mikhail, Michael Holquist, and Vadim Liapunov. 1990 [1919]. *Art and Answerability: Early Philosophical Essays*. Austin: University of Texas Press.

Baldwin, Sandy. 2015. *The Internet Unconscious: On the Subject of Electronic Literature*. New York: Bloomsbury.

Barbour, J. Murray. 2004 [1951]. *Tuning and Temperament: A Historical Survey*. Mineola, NY: Dover.

Barthes, Roland. 1957. *Mythologies*. Paris: Éditions du Seuil.

Barthes, Roland. 1964. *La Tour Eiffel*. Paris: Delpire Éditeur.

Barthes, Roland. 1982 [1964]. "The Eiffel Tower." In *A Barthes Reader,* edited by Susan Sontag. New York: Hill and Wang, 36–50.

Barthes, Roland. 2012 [1957]. *Mythologies. The Complete Edition. In a New Translation*, translated by Richard Howard and Annette Lavers. New York: Hill and Wang.

Batchelor, David. 2000. "In Bed with the Monochrome." In *From an Aesthetic Point of View,* edited by Peter Osborne. London: Serpent's Tail.

Baumgarten, Murray. 1982. *City Scriptures*. Cambridge, MA: Harvard University Press.

Bell, David. 1995. "Lingua Populi, Lingua Dei: Language, Religion, and the Origins of French Revolutionary Nationalism." *American Historical Review* 100.5: 1403–37.

Benjamin, Walter. 2010 [1940]. *Über den Begriff der Geschichte*. Frankfurt am Main: Suhrkamp.

Berlant, Lauren. 2011. *Cruel Optimism*. Durham, NC: Duke University Press.

Bhabha, Homi K. 2013 [2006]. "Cultural Diversity and Cultural Differences." In *The Post-Colonial Studies Reader*, edited by Bill Ashcroft, Gareth Griffiths, and Helen Tiffin, Routledge, New York. 155–7.

Bialystok, Ellen and Fergus Craik. 2010. "Cognitive and Linguistic Processing in the Bilingual Mind." *Current Directions in Psychological Science* 19.1: 19–23.

Billig, Michael. 1994. *Banal Nationalism*. London: Sage Publications.

Blommaert, Jan. 2007. "Sociolinguistic scales." *Intercultural Pragmatics* 4.1: 1–19.

Blommaert, Jan. 2010. *The Sociolinguistics of Globalization*. Cambridge: Cambridge University Press.

Blommaert, Jan and Ben Rampton. 2011. "Language and Superdiversity." *Diversities* 13.2: 1–21.

Boa, Elizabeth. 2005. "Karl Rossmann, or the Boy Who Wouldn't Grow Up: The Flight from Manhood in Kafka's *Der Verschollene*." In *From Goethe to*

Gide: Feminism, Aesthetics and the Literary Canon in France and Germany, 1770–1936, edited by Mary Orr and Lesley Sharpe. Exeter: University of Exeter Press.

Bonfiglio, Thomas Paul. 2010. *Mother Tongues and Languages: The Invention of the Native Speaker*. Berlin: De Gruyter.

Bonfiglio, Thomas Paul. 2013. *Why is English Literature? Language and Letters for the Twenty-first Century*. Basingstoke: Palgrave.

Bourdieu, Pierre. 1977. *Outline of a Theory of Practice*, translated by Richard Nice. Cambridge: Cambridge University Press.

Bourdieu, Pierre. 1989. "Social space and symbolic power." *Sociological Theory* 71.1: 14–25.

Bourdieu, Pierre. 1991. *Language and Symbolic Power*, translated by Gino Raymond and Matthew Adamson. Cambridge, MA: Harvard University Press.

Bourdieu, Pierre. 1993. *The Field of Cultural Production*, translated and edited by Randal Johnson. New York: Columbia University Press.

Bourdieu, Pierre and Jean-Claude Passeron. 1970. *La Reproduction: Éléments pour une théorie du système d'enseignement*. Paris: Éditions de Minuit.

Boyer, Dominic. 2016. "Revolutionary Infrastructure." In *Infrastructures and Social Complexity*, edited by Penny Harvey, Casper Bruun Jensen, and Atsuro Morita. London and New York: Routledge.

Brook-Rose, Christine. 2007 [1968]. *The Brook-Rose Omnibus*. Manchester: Carcanet Press Limited.

Brown, Laura. 2003. *Fables of Modernity: Literature and Culture in the English Eighteenth Century*. Ithaca: Cornell University Press.

Brown, Penelope and Stephen Levinson. 1987. *Politeness: Some Universals in Language Usage*. Cambridge: Cambridge University Press.

Bruce, Iris. 2007. *Kafka and Cultural Zionism: Dates in Palestine*. Madison: University of Wisconsin Press.

Brunton, Finn and Helen Nissenbaum. 2013. "Political and Ethical Perspectives on Data Obfuscation." In *Privacy, Due Process and the Computational Turn: The Philosophy of Law Meets the Philosophy of Technology*, edited by Mireille Hildebrandt and Katja De Vries. Routledge, 164–88.

Buck-Morss, Susan. 2000. "Hegel and Haiti." *Critical Inquiry* 26.4: 821–65.

Bundesregierung. 2007 [2005]. "Act to Control and Restrict Immigration and to Regulate the Residence and Integration of EU Citizens and Foreigners," translated by Tes Howell. In *Germany in Transit: Nation and Migration 1955–2005*, edited by Deniz Göktürk, David Gramling, and Anton Kaes. Berkeley: University of California Press.

Bundesverwaltungsamt. 2005. "Wichtige Information für Spät-aussiedlerbewerber." Berlin: Bundesverwaltungsamt.

Butler, Judith. 1997. *Excitable Speech: A Politics of the Performative*. New York: Routledge.

Butler, Judith. 2011 "Bodies in Alliance and the Politics of the Street."

European Institute for Progressive Cultural Policies. Online at eipcp.net. Accessed 6 January 2016.

Butzkamm, Wolfgang. 1973. *Aufgeklärte Einsprachigkeit. Zur Entdogmatisierung der Methode im Fremdsprachenunterricht.* Heidelberg: Quelle & Meyer.

Byram, Michael. 1997. *Teaching and Assessing Intercultural Communicative Competence.* Bristol: Multilingual Matters.

Byram, Michael and Lynne Parmenter, eds. 2012. *The Common European Framework of Reference: The Globalization of Language Education Policy.* Bristol: Multilingual Matters.

Calvet, Louis-Jean. 1974. *Linguistique et colonialisme: petit traité de glottophagie.* Paris: Payot.

Cameron, Deborah. 1995. *Verbal Hygiene.* London: Verso.

Cameron, Deborah. 2000. *Good to Talk? Living and Working in a Communication Culture.* New York: Sage.

Cameron, Deborah. 2013. "'The One, the Many and the Other': Representing Multi- and Mono-lingualism in Post-9/11 Verbal Hygiene." *Critical Multilingualism Studies* 1.2: 59–77.

Canagarajah, Suresh. 2007. "Lingua Franca, Multilingual Communities, and Language Acquisition." *Modern Language Journal* 91.1: 923–39.

Carstens, Peter and Markus Wehner. 2006. "Schäuble: 'Der Islam ist keine Bedrohung für uns': Bundesinnenminister Wolfgang Schäuble im Interview." *Frankfurter Allgemeine Sonntagszeitung,* 12 March.

Casanova, Pascale. 1999. *La République mondiale des lettres.* Paris: Éditions de Seuil.

Casanova, Pascale. 2007. *The World Republic of Letters,* translated by M. B. DeBevoise. Cambridge, MA: Harvard University Press.

Cassin, Barbara, ed. 2004. *Vocabulaire européen des philosophies: Dictionnaire des intraduisibles.* Paris: Le Seuil/Le Robert.

Cassin, Barbara. 2015. "The Energy of the Untranslatables: Translation as a Paradigm for the Human Sciences." *Paragraph* 38.2: 145–58.

Castellanos Moya, Horacio. 2008 [2005]. *Senselessness,* translated by K. Silver. New York: New Directions Books.

Cenoz, Jasone and Durk Gorter. 2011. "Introduction to the Special Issue. A Holistic Approach to Multilingual Education." *Modern Language Journal* 95.3: 339–43.

Čermák, Josef. 1994. "Franz Kafkas Sorgen mit der tschechischen Sprache." In *Kafka and Prag,* edited by Kurt Krolop and H. D. Zimmerman. Berlin: de Gruyter.

Chamberson, Robert. 2008. "On the Futurology of Linguistic Development." In *Globalization and Language Vitality,* edited by Cécile Vigouroux and Salikoko Mufwene. London: Continuum, 171–90

Chandler McIntyre, Marilyn. 2009. *Caring for Words in a Culture of Lies.* Grand Rapids, MI: Eerdmans.

Cheah, Pheng. 2014. "World against Globe: Toward a Normative Conception of World Literature." *New Literary History* 45: 303–29.

Chomsky, Noam. 2009 [1966]. *Cartesian Linguistics: A Chapter in the History of Rationalist Thought*. Cambridge: Cambridge University Press.

Chow, Kat. 2014. "What Happens when a Language's Last Monolingual Speaker Dies?" National Public Radio, 8 January.

Chow, Rey. 2014. *Not Like a Native Speaker: On Languaging as a Postcolonial Experience*. New York: Columbia University Press.

Clyne, Michael. 2008. "The monolingual mindset as an impediment to the development of plurilingual potential in Australia." *Sociolinguistic Studies* 2.3: 347–66.

CNN Turk. 2014. "Erdoğan: "Türkçe ile felsefe yapamazsınız." 24 December.

Combs, Mary Carol, Ana Christina da Silva Iddings, and Luis C. Moll. 2014. "21st Century Linguistic Apartheid: English Language Learners in Arizona Public Schools." In *Affirming Linguistic Diversity in Schools and Society: Beyond Linguistic Apartheid*, edited by Pierre Wilbert Orelus. London: Routledge.

Conyers, John. 2012. "Statement of the Honorable John Conyers, Jr.: Hearing on H.R. 997, the English Language Unity Act." Subcommittee on the Constitution. 2 August.

Cook, Vivian. 2007. "The Goals of ELT: Reproducing Native-speakers or Promoting Multi-competence among Second Language Users?" In *International Handbook on English Language Teaching*, edited by Jim Cummins and Chris Davison. Dordrecht: Kluwer, 237–48.

Corngold, Stanley. 2001. "Allotria and Excreta in 'In the Penal Colony': For Rachel Magshamhrain." *Modernism/Modernity* 8.2: 281–93.

Coulmas, Florian, ed. 2007. *Language Regimes in Transformation. Future Prospects for German and Japanese in Science, Economy, and Politics*. Berlin: Mouton de Gruyter.

Council of Europe. 2014. "The Common European Framework of Reference for Languages." Available online: http://www.coe.int/lang-CEFR. Accessed 28 July 2015.

Cowley, Stephen J., ed. 2011. *Distributed Language*. Amsterdam: John Benjamins.

Crépon, Marc. 2015. "The Invention of the Idiom: The Event of the Untranslatable." *Paragraph* 38.2: 189–203.

Cronin, Michael. 2013. *Translation in the Digital Age*. London: Routledge.

Cross, Valerie V. and Clare R. Voss. 2000. "Fuzzy Queries and Cross-Language Ontologies in Multilingual Document Exploitation." *IEEE International Conference on Fuzzy Systems* 2: 641–6.

Crozet, Chantal, Anthony Liddicoat, and Joseph Lo Bianco. 1999. "Intercultural Competence: From Language Policy to Language Education." In *Striving for the Third Place: Intercultural Competence through Language Education*, edited by Joseph Lo Bianco, Anthony J. Liddicoat, and Chantal Crozet. Melbourne: Language Australia. 1–20.

Damrosch, David. 2003. *What is World Literature?* Princeton: Princeton University Press.

Damrosch, David. 2005. "Death in Translation." In *Nation, Language, and the Ethics of Translation,* edited by Sandra Bermann and Michael Wood. Princeton: Princeton University Press, 180–98.

De Angelis, Gessica and Larry Selinker. 2001. "Interlanguage transfer and competing linguistic systems." In *Cross-linguistic influence in third language acquisition: Psycholinguistic perspectives,* edited by Jasone Cenoz, Britta Hufeisen, and Ulrike Jessner. Clevedon: Multilingual Matters, 42–58.

De Bot, Kees. 2004. "The Multilingual Lexicon: Modeling Selection and Control." *International Journal of Multilingualism* 1.1: 17–32.

De Bot, Kees. 2015. *A History of Applied Linguistics.* London: Routledge.

De Certeau, Michel. 2011 [1980]. *The Practice of Everyday Life,* translated by Steven Rendall. Berkeley: University of California Press.

De Certeau, Michel, Dominique Julia, and Jacques Revel. 1975. *Une politique de la langue: la Révolution française et les patois.* Paris: Gallimard.

Deleuze, Gilles and Félix Guattari. 1986 [1975]. *Kafka: Toward a Minor Literature,* translated by Dana Polan. Minneapolis: University of Minnesota Press.

Dembeck, Till. 2015. "Oberflächenübersetzung: The Poetics and Cultural Politics of Homophonic Translation." *Critical Multilingualism Studies* 3.1: 7–25.

Dembeck, Till and Georg Mein. 2014. "Philology's Jargon: How Can we Write Post-Monolingually?" In *Challenging the Myth of Monolingualism,* edited by Liesbeth Minnaard and Till Dembeck. Leiden: Brill.

Derrida, Jacques. 1986. *Memoires: for Paul de Mann,* translated by Cecile Lindsay, Jonathan Culler, and Eduardo Cadava. New York: Columbia University Press.

Derrida, Jacques. 1998 [1996]. *Monolingualism of the Other, or, The Prosthesis of Origin,* translated by Patrick Mensah. Stanford: Stanford University Press.

De Swaan, Abram. 2001. *Words of the World: The Global Language System.* Cambridge: Polity.

Deutsche Nationalstiftung. 2006a. "Nationalpreis 2006." Available online: http://www.nationalstiftung.de/nationalpreis2006.php. Accessed 14 August 2008.

Deutsche Nationalstiftung. 2006b. "Laudatio des Bundestagspräsidenten Dr. Norbert Lammert anlässlich der Preisverleihung des Nationalpreises an die Herbert-Hoover-Realschule in Berlin am 27. Juni 2006." Available online: http://www.nationalstiftung.de/national- preis2006.php. Accessed 14 August 2008.

Díaz, Junot. 2008. *The Brief, Wondrous Life of Oscar Wao.* New York: Faber and Faber.

Díaz, Junot. 2012. *This is How You Lose Her.* New York: Penguin.

Djité, Paulin G. 1994. *From Language Policy to Language Planning—an*

Overview of Languages other than English in Australian Education.
Canberra: National Languages and Literacy Institute of Australia Ltd.

Dobstadt, Michael and Renate Riedner. 2013. "Grundzüge einer Didaktik der Literarizität für Deutsch als Fremdsprache." In *Deutsch als Fremdsprache: Deutschunterricht in Theorie und Praxis, Handbuch in 11 Bänden*, Vol. 10, edited by Bernt Ahrenholz and Ingelore Oomen-Welke. Baltmannsweiler: Schneider.

Dorostkar, Niku. 2014. *(Mehr-)Sprachigkeit und Lingualismus. Die diskursive Konstruktion von Sprache im Kontext nationaler und supranationaler Sprachenpolitik am Beispiel Österreichs.* Vienna: Vienna University Press.

Dowden, Stephen. 1995. *Kafka's Castle and the Critical Imagination.* Columbia, SC: Camden House.

Droste, Wiglaf. 1998. "Elefant im Paul-Celan-Laden." *die tageszeitung.* 24 July.

Dryden, John. 1701. *The Comedies, Tragedies, and Operas Written by John Dryden, Esq. Vol II.* London.

Duchêne, Alexandre and Monica Heller, eds. 2012. *Language in Late Capitalism: Pride and Profit.* London: Routledge.

Duffin, Ross. 2008. *How Equal Temperament Ruined Harmony (and Why You Should Care).* New York: W. W. Norton.

Eades, Diana. 2003. "Participation of Second Language and Second Dialect Speakers in the Legal System." *Annual Review of Applied Linguistics* 23: 113–33.

Eades, Diana, Helen Fraser, Jeff Siegel, Tim McNamara, and Brett Baker. 2003. "Linguistic identification in the determination of nationality. A preliminary report." *Language Policy* 2.2: 179–99.

Ecke, Peter and Christopher Hall. 2013. "Tracking Tip-of-the-tongue States in a Multilingual Speaker: Evidence of Attrition or Instability in Lexical Systems?" *International Journal of Bilingualism* 17.6: 734–51.

Edmunds, Lowell. 2010. "Kafka on Minor Literature." *German Studies Review* 33.2: 351–74.

El Diario. 2014. "García reconoce que es monolingüe." 12 April.

Ellis, Elizabeth M. 2006. "Monolingualism: the unmarked case." *Estudios de Sociolingüística* 7.2: 173–96.

Ellis, Elizabeth M. 2008. "Defining and investigating monolingualism." *Sociolinguistic Studies* 2.3: 173–96.

Ellis, Elizabeth M., Ingrid Gogolin, and Michael Clyne. 2010. "The Janus face of monolingualism: a comparison of German and Australian language education policies." *Current Issues in Language Planning* 11.4: 1–22.

El-Tayeb, Fatima. 2011. *European Others: Queering Ethnicity in Postnational Europe.* Minneapolis: University of Minnesota Press.

Elyashev, Israel Isodore. 1992 [1918]. "Two Languages—Only One Literature," translated by Hana Wirth-Nesher. In *What is Jewish Literature*, edited by Hana Wirth-Nesher. Philadephia: Jewish Publication Society.

Erol, Sibel. 2007. "Reading Orhan Pamuk's Snow as Parody: Difference as Sameness." *Comparative Critical Studies* 4: 403–32.

European Commission. 2008. "A Rewarding Challenge. How the Multiplicity of Languages Could Strengthen Europe: Proposals from the Group of Intellectuals for Intercultural Dialogue Set up at the Initiative of the European Commission." (Report). Luxembourg: Office for Official Publications of the European Communities.

Evan-Zohar, Itamar. 1990. "Laws of Literary Interference." *Poetics Today* 11.1: 53–72.

Finch, Andrew. 2010. "Critical Incidents and Language Learning: Sensitivity to Initial Conditions." *System* 38: 422–31.

Forsdick, Charles. 2015. "Locating world literature: monolingualism, translingualism, multilingualism." Invited Lecture. The University of Melbourne-Parkville. 26 October.

Foucault, Michel. 1977. "What is an Author?" In *Language, Counter-Memory, Practice*, edited and translated by Donald Bouchard. Ithaca: Cornell University Press.

Foucault, Michel. 1978 [1976]. *The History of Sexuality, Part II*, translated by Robert Hurley. New York: Pantheon Books.

Foucault, Michel. 1984. "Of Other Spaces, Heterotopias." In *Architecture, Mouvement, Continuité* 5: 46–9.

Foucault, Michel. 1994 [1966]. *The Order of Things*. London: Vintage.

Fox, Killiam. 2011. "Ellen Bialystok: Bilingual Brains are more Healthy." *The Guardian*. 11 June.

Freeman, Christopher. 1974. *The Economics of Industrial Innovation*. Harmondsworth: Penguin Books.

Gal, Susan. 1993. "Diversity and Contestation in Linguistic Ideologies: German Speakers in Hungary." *Language in Society* 22.3: 337–59.

Gal, Susan. 2006. "Minorities, migration and multilingualism: Language ideologies in Europe." In *Language Ideologies, Practices and Polices: Language and the Future of Europe*, edited by Patrick Stevenson and Clare Mar-Molinaro. London: Palgrave.

Gal, Susan. 2012. "Sociolinguistic Regimes and the Management of 'Diversity.'" In *Language in Late Capitalism: Pride and Profit*, edited by Alexandre Duchêne and Monica Heller. London: Routledge, 22–37.

Gal, Susan and Kathryn Woolard. 1995. "Constructing Languages and Publics: Authority and Representation." *Pragmatics* 5.2: 129–38.

Gee, James, Glynda Hull, and Colin Lankshear. 1996. *The New Work Order: Behind the Language of the New Capitalism*. Boulder: Westview Press.

Genette, Gérard. 1997 [1982]. *Palimpsests: Reading the Second Degree*, translated by Channa Newman and Claude Doubinsky. Lincoln: University of Nebraska Press.

Gentzler, Edwin. 2012. *Translation and Identity in the Americas: New Directions in Translation Theory*. London: Routledge.

Gezen, Ela. 2012 [2015]. "Converging Realisms: Aras Ören, Nâzım Hikmet, and Bertolt Brecht." *Colloquia Germanica* 45.3/4: 377–93.

Gibb, Elias John Wilkinson. 1900. *A History of Ottoman Poetry, Vol. 1.* London: Luzac.

Gilman, Sander. 1995. *Kafka: The Jewish Patient.* New York: Routledge.

Gilroy, Paul. 1995. *The Black Atlantic: Modernity and Double Consciousness.* Cambridge, MA: Harvard University Press.

Ginsberg, Elaine K. 1996. *Passing and the Fictions of Identity.* Durham: Duke University Press.

Glassman, James. 1997. "Dihydrogen Monoxide: Unrecognized Killer." *The Orlando Sentinel.* 28 October. Accessed 28 July 2014.

Glissant, Édouard. 1995. *Introduction à une poétique du divers.* Paris: Gallimard.

Goatly, Andrew. 1996. "Green Grammar and Grammatical Metaphor." *Journal of Pragmatics* 25: 537–60.

GoEnglish! 2011. "GoEnglish ofrece algo muy novedoso." Available online: http://www.goenglish.com.mx/index.html. Accessed 8 September.

Goffman, Erving. 1967. "On Face-Work: An Analysis of Ritual Elements in Social Interactions." In *Interaction Ritual.* New York: Doubleday. 5–45.

Gogolin, Ingrid. 1994. *Der monolinguale Habitus der multilingualen Schule.* Münster: Waxmann.

Gohard-Radenkovic, Aline. 2012. "Le plurilinguisme, un nuveau champ, ou une nouvelle idéologie: Ou quand les discours politiquement corrects prônent la diversité." *alterstice: Revue Internationale de la Recherche interculturelle* 2.1: 1–14.

Göktürk, Deniz, David Gramling, and Anton Kaes. 2007. *Germany in Transit: Nation and Migration 1955–2005.* Berkeley: University of California Press.

Göktürk, Deniz, David Gramling, Anton Kaes, and Andreas Langenohl. 2011. *Transit Deutschland: Debatten zu Nation und Migration.* Konstanz: University of Konstanz Press.

Gordin, Michael D. 2015. *Scientific Babel: How Science was done before and after Global English.* Chicago: University of Chicago Press.

Gottschlich, Jürgen. 2007. "Bravo Almanya!" In *Germany in Transit: Nation and Migration 1955–2005,* edited by Deniz Göktürk, David Gramling, and Anton Kaes. Berkeley: University of California Press, 168–9.

Gramling, David. 2009. "The New Cosmopolitan Monolingualism: Linguistic Citizenship in Twenty-first Century Germany." *Die Unterrichtspraxis/ Teaching German* 42.2: 130–40.

Gramling, David. 2010. "The Caravanserai Turns Twenty: or, New German Literature—in Turkish?" *Alman Dili ve Edebiyati Dergisi / Studien zur deutschen Sprache und Literatur* 24: 55–83.

Gramling, David. 2013. "Zur Abwicklung des Mythos literarischer Einsprachigkeit," translated by Ekbert Birr. *kultuRRevolution: zeitschrift für angewandte diskurstheorie* 65.2: 11–16.

Gramling, David. 2014. "The Invention of Monolingualism from the Spirit of

Systematic Transposability." In *Philologie und Mehrsprachigkeit*, edited by Till Dembeck und Georg Mein. Winter Verlag, 113–34.

Green, Simon. 2012. "Much Ado about Not-very-much? Assessing Ten Years of German Citizenship Reform." *Citizenship Studies* 16.2: 173–88.

Griswold, Olga V. 2011. "The English You Need to Know: Language Ideology in a Citizenship Classroom." *Linguistics and Education* 22: 406–18.

Grosjean, François. 2010. *Bilingual: Life and Reality*. Cambridge, MA: Harvard University Press.

Habermas, Jürgen. 1997. *A Berlin Republic*, translated by Steven Rendall. Lincoln: University of Nebraska Press.

Habermas, Jürgen. 2011 [2008]. "Die Dialektik der Säkularisierung." In *Transit Deutschland: Debatten zu Nation und Migration*, edited by Deniz Göktürk, David Gramling, Anton Kaes, and Andreas Langenohl. Konstanz: Konstanz University Press, 334–43.

Hagemann, Susanne. 2005. "Postcolonial Translation Studies and James Kelman's *Translated Accounts*." *Scottish Studies Review* 6.1: 74–83.

Halliday, Michael. 2001. "New Ways of Meaning. The Challenge to Applied Linguistics." In *The Ecolinguistics Reader. Language, Ecology and Environment*, edited by Alwin Fill and Peter Mühlhäusler. London: Continuum, 175–202.

Halliday, Michael. 2002. "Applied Linguistics as an Evolving Theme." Plenary address to the Association Internationale de Linguistique Appliquée. Singapore.

Hancké, Bob. 2009. *Debating Varieties of Capitalism*. Oxford: Oxford University Press.

Hanks, William. 2010. *Converting Words: Maya in the Age of the Cross*. Berkeley: University of California Press.

Hanks, William. 2014. "The Space of Translation." *Hau: Journal of Ethnographic Theory* 4.2: 17–39.

Haque, Eve. 2012. *Multiculturalism within a Bilingual Framework: Language, Race, and Belonging in Canada*. Toronto: University of Toronto Press.

Haynes, Bruce. 2002. *A History of Performing Pitch: The Story of "A"*. Lanham, MD: Scarecrow Press.

Herdina, Philip and Ulrike Jessner. 2002. *A Dynamic Model of Multilingualism*. Bristol: Multilingual Matters.

Hill, Jane H. 1995. "Mock Spanish: A Site For The Indexical Reproduction Of Racism In American English." *Language & Culture, Symposium 2*. Available online: http://language-culture.binghamton.edu/symposia/2/part1/index.html. Accessed 11 November 2008.

Hirsch, Marianne. 2008. "The Generation of Postmemory." *Poetics Today* 29.1: 103–28.

Hobsbawm, Eric. 1991. *Nations and Nationalism Since 1780: Programme, Myth, Reality*. Cambridge: Cambridge University Press.

Hobsbawm, Eric and Terence Ranger. 1992. *The Invention of Tradition*. Cambridge: Cambridge University Press.

Hoffman, Eva. 1989. *Lost in Translation: A Life in a New Language*. New York: Dutton.

Hokenson, Jan Walsh and Marcella Munson. 2007. *The Bilingual Text: History and Theory of Literary Self-Translation*. Manchester: St. Jerome Press.

Holquist, Michael. 2014. "What Would Bakhtin Do?" *Critical Multilingualism Studies* 2.1: 6–19.

Honneth, Axel. 2008. *Reification: A New Look at an Old Idea*. Oxford: Oxford University Press.

Horners, Josiane and Michel Blanc. 2000. *Bilinguality and Bilingualism*. Cambridge: Cambridge University Press.

Hu, Adelheid. 2012. "Academic Perspectives from Germany." In *The Common European Framework of Reference: The Globalization of Language Education Policy*, edited by Michael Byram and Lynne Parmenter. Bristol: Multilingual Matters, 66–75.

Hunt, Samantha. 2009. *The Invention of Everything else*. New York: Mariner Books.

Hymes, Dell. 1965. "Some North Pacific Coast Poems: a Problem in Anthropological Philology." *American Anthropologist* 67.2: 316–41.

Hymes, Dell. 1981. *In Vain I Tried to Tell You: Essays in Native American Ethnopoetics*. Philadelphia: University of Pennsylvania Press.

Irshaid, Faisal. 2014. "How Isis is spreading its message online." *BBC Online*. June 19.

Isacoff, Stuart. 2001. *Temperament: How Music Became a Battleground for the Great Minds of Western Civilization*. New York: Vintage.

Jacir, Emily. "Translate Allah." Available online: http://www.ahmadyarts.com/exhibitions/tarjama. Accessed 28 July 2014.

Jackson, Tony E. 2009. *The Technology of the Novel: Writing and Narrative in British Fiction*. Baltimore: Johns Hopkins University Press.

Jacobson, Robin Dale. 2008. *The New Nativism: Proposition 187 and the Debate over Immigration*. Minneapolis: University of Minnesota Press.

Jagoda, Zenon, Kłodziński Stanisław, and Jan Masłowski. 1987. "'bauernfuss, goldzupa, himmelautostrada'. Zum 'Krematoriumsesperanto' der Sprache polnischer KZ-Häftlinge." *Die Auschwitz-Hefte*. Vol. 2. Weinheim and Basel: Beltz, 241–60.

Jakobson, Roman. 1960. "Closing Statement: Linguistics and Poetics." In *Style in Language*, edited by Thomas A. Sebeok. Cambridge, MA: MIT Press, 350–77.

Jameson, Frederic. 1986. "Third World Literature in the Age of Multinational Capitalism." *Social Text* 15: 65–88.

Jarman, Francis. 2012. *Intercultural Communication in Action*. Rockville, MD: Borgo Press.

Jaspers, Jürgen. 2005. "Linguistic Sabotage in a Context of Monolingualism and Standardization." *Language & Communication* 25: 279–97.

Jessen, Jens. 2005. "Du bist Werbeagentur: Die Deutschlandkampagne." *Die Zeit* [Hamburg]. 6 October.

Jessner, Ulrike. 2003. "The nature of cross-linguistic interaction in the multilingual system." In *The Multilingual Lexicon*, edited by Jasone Cenoz, Britta Hufeisen, and Ulrike Jessner. Dordrecht: Kluwer Academic Publishers.

Jessner-Schmid, Ulrike and Claire Kramsch, eds. 2015. *The Multilingual Challenge: Cross-Disciplinary Perspectives.* Berlin: de Gruyter Mouton.

Jira, Martin. 1997. *Musikalische Temperaturen in der Klaviermusik des 17. und frühen 18. Jahrhunderts.* Tutzing: Hans Schneider.

Jira, Martin. 2000. *Musikalische Temperaturen und Musikalischer Satz bei J. S. Bach.* Hohengehren: Schneider.

Jones, Richard D. P. 1997. "The Keyboard Works: Bach as Teacher and Virtuoso." In *The Cambridge Companion to Bach.* Cambridge: Cambridge University Press, 136–53.

Jones, William Jervis. 1995. *Sprachhelden und Sprachverderber: Dokumente zur Erforschung des Fremdwortpurismus im Deutschen (1478–1750).* Berlin: Walter de Gruyter.

Jones, William Jervis. 1999. *Images of Language: German Attitudes to European Languages from 1500 to 1800.* Amsterdam: John Benjamins.

Jostes, Brigitte. 2010. "Monolingualism: An Outline of an Unpopular Research Programme." *Language and History* 53.1: 27–47.

Judson, Pieter. 2006. *Guardians of the Nation: Activists on the Language Frontiers of Imperial Austria.* Cambridge, MA: Harvard University Press.

Kachru, Yamuna. 1994. "Monolingual bias in SLA Research." *TESOL Quarterly* 28.4: 795–800.

Kafka, Franz. 1982. *Das Schloß.* Frankfurt am Main: Fischer.

Kafka, Franz. 1983. *Der Verschollene.* Frankfurt am Main: Fischer.

Kafka, Franz. 1990. *Kritische Ausgabe: Tagebücher*, edited by Hans-Gerd Koch, Michael Müller, and Malcolm Pasley. Frankfurt am Main: Fischer.

Kafka, Franz. 1992a. "Heimkehr." In *Gesammelte Werke*, edited by Max Brod et al. 12 vols. Vol. V: *"Hochzeitsvorbereitungen auf dem Lande" und andere Prosa.* Frankfurt am Main: Fischer.

Kafka, Franz. 1992b. "[Das Schreiben versagt sich mir]." In *Gesammelte Werke*, edited by Max Brod et al. 12 vols. Vol. VII: *"Hochzeitsvorbereitungen auf dem Lande" und andere Prosa.* Frankfurt am Main: Fischer.

Kafka, Franz. 1994. *Kritische Ausgabe: Drucke zu Lebzeiten*, edited by Wolf Kittler, Hans-Gerd Koch, and Gerhard Neumann. Frankfurt am Main: Fischer, Vol. 1: 282–4.

Kafka, Franz. 1998. *The Castle: A New Translation, Based on the Restored Text*, translated by Mark Harman. New York: Schocken Books.

Kafka, Franz. 2008. *Amerika: The Missing Person*, translated by Mark Harman. New York: Shocken Books.

Kafka, Franz. 2014. *The Metamorphosis*, translated by Susan Bernofsky. New York: Norton.

Kant, Immanuel. 1983 [1784]. *Perceptual Peace and other Essays*, translated by Ted Humphrey. Indianapolis and Cambridge: Hackett Publishing Company, 41–8.

Karmani, Sohail. 2005. "TESOL in a Time of Terror: Toward an Islamic Perspective on Applied Linguistics." 39.4: 738–44.

Katada, Fusa. 2002. "The Linguistic Divide, Autolinguals, and the Notion of Education-For-All." Proceedings of the International Conference on Computers in Education. n.p.

Katz, Jonathan Ned. 2007 [1997]. *The Invention of Heterosexuality*. Chicago: University of Chicago Press.

Katz, Stephen T. 2013. *Comparative Mysticism: An Anthology of Original Sources*. Oxford: Oxford University Press.

Kellman, Steven. 2000. *The Translingual Imagination*. Lincoln: University of Nebraska Press.

Kellman, Steven. 2016. "Omnilingual Aspirations: The Case of the Universal Declaration of Human Rights." *Critical Multilingualism Studies* 4.1: 5–24.

Kelman, James. 2002. *Translated Accounts*. New York: Anchor Books.

Kelman, James. 2008. *'And the Judges Said ...': Essays*. Edinburgh: Polygon.

Kerrigan, John. 2008. *Archipelagic English: Literature, History, and Politics 1603–1707*. Oxford: Oxford University Press.

Kilchmann, Esther. 2014. "Monolingualism, Heterolingualism, and Poetic Innovation: On Contemporary German Literature, with a Side Glance to the Seventeenth Century." In *Challenging the Myth of Monolingualism*, edited by Liesbeth Minnaard and Till Dembeck. Leiden: Brill.

Kirkpatrick, Andy. 2000. "The Disadvantaged Monolingual: Why English Alone is not Enough." *Australian Language Matters* 8.3: 5–7.

Klein, Rolf. 1989. *Die Intervallehre in der deutschen Musiktheorie des 16. Jahrhunderts*. Cologne: Bosse.

Kohl, Helmut. 1984 [1982]. "Koalition der Mitte: Für eine Politik der Erneuerung." In *Bundeskanzler Helmut Kohl: Reden 1982–1984*. Cologne: Presse- und Informationsamt der Bundesregierung. 143–4.

Komedi Kral. 2010. "Google translate'den İngilizce'den Türkçe Çeviriyi Seçin ve 'eğitime' Kelimesini Yazın Bakalım Ne Çıkacak xD." [Facebook post]. 25 December. Available online: http://www.facebook.com/note.php?note_id=480580683801&id=158547270989. Accessed 22 March 2011.

Komska, Yuliya. 2015. "Conspicuous Multilingualism." Talk. German Studies Association, Washington, DC. October 1.

Kong, Shuyu. 2004. *Consuming Literature: Best Sellers and the Commercialization of Literary Production in Contemporary China*. Stanford: Stanford University Press.

Konstantinou, Lee. 2009. "The Brand as Cognitive Map in William Gibson's Pattern Recognition." *Boundary 2* 36.2: 67–97.

Kramsch, Claire. 1997. "The Privilege of the Non-Native Speaker." *PMLA* 112.3: 359–69.

Kramsch, Claire. 2006. "From Communicative Competence to Symbolic Competence." *The Modern Language Journal* 90.2: 249–52.

Kramsch, Claire. 2008. "Multilingual, Like Franz Kafka." *International Journal of Multilingualism* 5.4: 316–32.

Kramsch, Claire. 2009. *The Multilingual Subject: What Foreign Language Learners say about their Experience and Why it Matters*. Oxford: Oxford University Press.

Kramsch, Claire. 2011. "The Multilingualism of the Other." In *Towards Multilingualism and the Inclusion of Cultural Diversity*, edited by Inez De Florio-Hansen. Kassel: Kassel University Press.

Kramsch, Claire. 2012. "Authenticity and Legitimacy in Multilingual Second Language Acquisition." *Critical Multilingualism Studies* 1.1: 107–28.

Kremnitz, Georg. 2004. *Mehrsprachigkeit in der Literatur: Wie Autoren ihre Sprachen wählen*. Vienna: Praesens Verlag für Literatur und Sprachwissenschaft.

Kristeva, Julia. 1990. *Strangers to Ourselves*, translated by Leon S. Roudiez. New York: Columbia University Press.

Kroskrity, Paul V., ed. 2000. *Regimes of Language: Ideologies, Polities, and Identities*. Santa Fe, NM: School of American Research.

Kroskrity, Paul V. 2004. "Language Ideologies." In *A Companion to Linguistic Anthropology*, edited by Alessandro Duranti. Malden, MA: Blackwell, 496–517.

Kymlicka, Will. 2001. *Politics in the Vernacular. Nationalism, Multiculturalism and Citizenship*. Oxford: Oxford University Press.

Ladurie, Emmanuel Le Roy. 1975. *Montaillou, village occitan*. Paris: Gallimard.

Lakoff, George and Mark Johnson. 2003 [1980]. *Metaphors we Live by*. Chicago: University of Chicago Press.

Lambert, Richard. 1999. "Language and Intercultural Competence." In *Striving for the Third Place: Intercultural Competence through Language Education*, edited by Joseph Lo Bianco, Anthony J. Liddicoat, and Chantal Crozet. Melbourne: Language Australia, 65–71.

Latour, Bruno. 1986. "The Powers of Association." In *Power, Action, and Belief: A New Sociology of Knowledge*, edited by J. Law. London: Routledge.

Latour, Bruno. 1993 [1991]. *We Have Never Been Modern*, translated by Catherine Porter. Cambridge, MA: Harvard University Press.

Lau, Jürg. 2005. "Achte auf die Details des Lebens. Ein Interview mit Orhan Pamuk." *Die Zeit* Online. 14 April.

Lau, Jörg. 2006a. "Deutschstunden." *Die Zeit* [Hamburg]. 1 February.

Lau, Jörg. 2006b. "Selbstachtung und Selbstverbesserung: Der Patriotismus der Berliner Republik." *Merkur: Deutsche Zeitschrift für europäisches Denken*. 9 September.

Lawson, Henry. 1972. *Autobiographical and Other Writings 1887–1922*, edited by Colin Rodrick. Sydney: Angus & Robertson.

Lefebvre, Henri. 1987. *La pensée marxiste et la ville*. Tournai: Casterman.

Léglu, Catherine E. 2010. *Multilingualism and Mother Tongue in Medieval French, Occitan, and Catalan Narratives*. State College: The Pennsylvania State University Press.

Lehman, Bradley. 2005. "Bach's Extraordinary Temperament: Our Rosetta Stone—1." *Early Music* 33.1.

Lennon, Brian. 2008. "The Antinomy of Multilingual U.S. Literature." *Comparative American Studies* 6.3: 203–24.

Lennon, Brian. 2010. *In Babel's Shadow: Multilingual Literatures, Monolingual States*. Minneapolis: University of Minnesota Press.

Lennon, Brian. 2012. "Can Multilingualism be Simulated?" *Critical Multilingualism Studies* 1.1: 94–106.

Leonhardt, Jürgen. 2013. *Latin: Story of A World Language*, translated by Kenneth Kronenberg. Cambridge: Belknap Press.

Levine, Glenn S. 2014. "From Performance to Multilingual Being in Foreign Language Pedagogy: Lessons from L2 Students Abroad." *Critical Multilingualism Studies* 2.1: 74–105.

Liddicoat, Anthony J. 2002. "Static and dynamic views of culture and intercultural language acquisition." *Babel* 36.3: 4–11.

Liddicoat, Anthony J. 2004. "Language Planning for Literacy." *Current Issues in Language Planning* 5.1: 1–17.

Lippi-Green, Rosina. 1994. "Accent, standard language ideology and discriminatory pretext in the courts." *Language in Society* 23: 163–98.

Liu, Lydia H. 1995. *Translingual Practice: Literature, National Culture, and Translated Modernity: China, 1900–1937*. Palo Alto: Stanford University Press.

Lo Bianco, Joseph. 1999. "Policy Words: Talking Bilingual Education and ESL into English Literacy." *Prospect* 14.2: 40–51.

Lourau, René. 1974. *L'analyseur Lip*. Paris: Union générale d'éditions.

Lyotard, Jean-François. 1988 [1983]. *The Differend: Phrases in Dispute*, translated by George Van Den Abbeele. Minneapolis: University of Minnesota Press.

Mahmood, Saba. 2009. "Religious Reason and Secular Affect: An Incommensurable Divide?" In *Is Critique Secular? Blasphemy, Injury, and Free Speech*, edited by Talal Asad, Judith Butler, and Saba Mahmood. Berkeley: Townsend Center for the Humanities, 64–100.

Makoni, Sinfree and Alastair Pennycook. 2006. *Disinventing and Reconstituting Languages*. Bristol: Multilingual Matters.

Makoni, Sinfree and Barbara Trudell. 2006. "Complementary and Conflicting Discourses of Linguistic Diversity: Implications for Language Planning." *Per Linguam* 22.2: 14–28.

Makoni, Sinfree, Geneva Smitherman, Arnetha F. Ball, and Arthur K. Spears.

2003. "Toward Black Linguistics." In *Black Linguistics: Language, Society, and Politics in Africa and the Americas*. London: Routledge.

Martí-López, Elisa. 2002. *Borrowed Words: Translation, Imitation, and the Making of the Nineteenth-Century Novel in Spain*. Lewisburg, PA: Bucknell University Press.

Martyn, David. 2014. "Es gab keine Mehrsprachigkeit, bevor es nicht Einsprachigkeit gab: Ansätze zu einer Archäologie der Sprachigkeit (Herder, Luther, Tawada)." In *Philologie und Mehrsprachigkeit*, edited by Till Dembeck und Georg Mein. Heidelberg: Winter Verlag.

Marx, Karl. 2001 [1852]. *The Eighteenth Brumaire of Louis Bonaparte*, translated by Daniel De Leon. London: Electric Books.

Matsuda, Paul Kei. 2014. "The Lure of Translingual Writing," *PMLA* 129.3: 478–83.

May, Stephen. 2013. *The Multilingual Turn: Implications for SLA, TESOL, and Bilingual Education*. London: Routledge.

McGhee, George. 1999. *Theoretical Morphology*. New York: Columbia University Press.

McNamara, Tim. 2005. "21st Century Shibboleth: Language Tests, Identity and Intergroup Conflict." *Language Policy* 4: 351–70.

Metz, Joseph. 2004. "Zion in the West: Cultural Zionism, Diasporic Doubles, and the 'Direction' of Jewish Literary Identity in Kafka's *Der Verschollene*." *Deutsche Vierteljahrsschrift für Literaturwissenschaft und Geistesgeschichte* 78.4: 646–71.

Microsoft Corp. 2010. "Go Global Development Center." Available online: http://msdn.microsoft.com/en-us/goglobal/bb688161.aspx. Accessed 17 December 2010.

Migraine-George, Thérèse. 2013. *From Francophonie to World Literature in French*. Lincoln: University of Nebraska Press.

Milroy, James and Lesley Milroy. 1985. *Authority in Language: Investigating Language Prescription and Standardisation*. London: Routledge.

Modern Language Association. 2007. *Foreign Languages and Higher Education: New Structures for a Changed World*. MLA Commons.

Montemayor, Carlos. 1997. *Chiapas: la rebelión indígena de México*. México: J. Morti

Moore, Robert. 2015. "From Revolutionary Monolingualism to Reactionary Multilingualism: Top-down Discourses of Linguistic Diversity in Europe, 1794–present." *Language and Communication* 44: 19–30.

Mora, Terézia. 2003. *Alle Tage*. Berlin: Luchterhand Literaturverlag.

Mora, Terézia. 2009a. *Day in Day Out*, translated by Michael Henry Heim. New York: HarperCollins.

Mora, Terézia. 2009b. *Der einzige Mann auf dem Kontinent*. Berlin: Luchterhand Literaturverlag.

Moretti, Franco. 2000. "Conjectures on World Literature." *New Left Review* 1.1: 54–68.

Morson, Gary Saul. 1998. "Sideshadowing and Tempics." *New Literary History* 29.4: 599–624.

Morton, Timothy. 2013. *Hyperobjects: Philosophy and Ecology after the End of the World.* Minneapolis: University of Minnesota Press.

Moulier Boutang, Yann. 2011. *Cognitive Capitalism,* translated by Ed Emmery. Cambridge: Polity.

Muallem, David. 2010. *The Maqam Book: A Doorway to Arab Scales and Modes,* translated by Yoram Amon. Tel Aviv: OR-TAV Music Publications.

Mudimbe, Valentin-Yves. 1988. *The Invention of Africa: Gnosis, Philosophy, and the Order of Knowledge.* Bloomington: University of Indiana Press.

Mufwene, Salikoko and Cécile Vigouroux. 2008. "Colonization, Globalization and Language Vitality in Africa: An Introduction." In *Globalization and Language Vitality,* edited by Cécile Vigouroux and Salikoko Mufwene. London: Continuum.

Mugglestone, Lynda. 1995. *"Talking Proper": The Rise of Accent as Social Symbol.* Oxford: Clarendon Press.

Mughan, Terry. 1999. "Intercultural Competence for Foreign Languages Students in Higher Education." *Language Learning Journal* 20: 59–65.

Müller, Max. 1878. "On Henotheism, Polytheism, Monotheism, and Atheism." *The Contemporary Review* 33: 707–34.

Mungan, Murathan. 2010. *Kırk Oda.* Istanbul: Metis.

Nekula, Marek. 2003. *Franz Kafkas Sprachen: "...in einem Stockwerk des innern babylonischen Turmes...".* Tübingen: Max Niemeyer Verlag.

Nekula, Marek. 2007. "The Divided City: Prague's Public Space and Franz Kafka's Readings of Prague." In *Franz Kafka im sprachnationalen Kontext seiner Zeit. Sprache und nationale Identität in öffentlichen Institutionen der böhmischen Länder,* edited by Marek Nekula, Ingrid Fleischmann, Albrecht Greule. Weimar. Köln: Böhlau, 85–106.

Niwa, Yasujiro. 1962. "Multilingual Communication." *Proceedings of the Institute of Radio Engineers* 50.5: 596.

Nobel Foundation. 2006. "The Nobel Prize in Literature 2006." Available online: http://nobelprize.org/nobel_prizes/literature/laureates/2006/index. html. Accessed 15 August 2008.

Noorani, Yaseen. 2013. "'Hard and Soft Multilingualism." *Critical Multilingualism Studies* 1.2: 7–28.

Nord, Christiane. 1997. *Translating as a Purposeful Activity.* Manchester: St Jerome.

Oard, Douglas. 2006. "Transcending the Tower of Babel: Supporting Access to Multilingual Information with Cross-Language Information Retrieval." In *Emergent Information Technologies and Enabling Policies for Counter-Terrorism,* edited by Robert Popp and John Yen. IEEE Press Series on Computational Intelligence, 299–314.

Oller, John W. 1997. "Monoglottosis: What's Wrong with the Idea of the IQ Meritocracy and its Racy Cousins?" *Applied Linguistics* 18.4: 467–507.

Oonk, Gerrit Hendrik, Ralf Maslowski, and J. G. M Roth-van der Werf. 2011. *Internationalisation in secondary education in Europe: a European and international orientation in schools : policies, theories, and research.* Charlotte: Information Age Publishers.

Ören, Aras. 1973. *Was Will Niyazi in der Naunynstrasse. Ein Poem,* translated by H. Achmed Schmiede und Johannes Schenk in collaboration with the author. Berlin: Rotbuch.

Ören, Aras. 1980. *Berlin Üçlemesi.* İstanbul: Evrim Matbaacilik Ltd.

Ören, Aras. 2007. "Chamisso Prize Acceptance Speech." *Germany in Transit: Nation and Migration,* edited by Deniz Göktürk, David Gramling, and Anton Kaes. Berkeley: University of California Press.

Ortega, Lourdes. 2007. "Second language learning explained? SLA across nine contemporary theories." In *Theories in second language acquisition: An introduction,* edited by Bill Van Patten and Jessica Williams. Mahwah, NJ: Lawrence Erlbaum. 221–46.

Ortega, Lourdes. 2008. "Foreword." In *A Meta-Analysis Investigating the Effects of Reading on Second Language Vocabulary Learning,* by S. Wa-Mbaleka. Saarbrücken: VDM Verlag. iii–v.

Oschlies, Wolf. 1986. "Lagerszpracha: Soziolinguistische Bemerkungen zu KZ-Sprachkonventionen." *Muttersprache* 96: 98–109.

Öymen, Altan. 2006. "Yasak tartışılıyor: Almanya'da Almanca." *Radikal Internet Baskisi.* 31 January.

Palumbo-Liu, David. 2008. "The Occupation of Form: (Re)theorizing Literary History." *American Literary History* 20.4: 814–35.

Pamuk, Orhan. 1985. *Beyaz Kale.* Istanbul: Can Yayınları.

Pamuk, Orhan. 2002. *Kar.* Istanbul: Iletişim.

Pamuk, Orhan. 2004. *Snow,* translated by Maureen Freely. New York: Knopf.

Pamuk, Orhan. 2005. "In Kars and Frankfurt." *The Nation.* 17 November.

Pamuk, Orhan and Hubert Spiegel. 2005. "Ich werde sehr sorgfältig über meine Worte nachdenken." *Frankfurter Allgemeine Zeitung.* 6 July.

Parks, Tim. 2010. "The New Dull Global Novel." *The New York Review of Books.* 9 February.

Pavlenko, Aneta. 2005. *Emotions and Multilingualism.* Cambridge: Cambridge University Press.

Peel, Quentin. 2001. "The Monotony of Monoglots." *Language Learning Journal* 23: 13–14.

Pennycook, Alastair. 2008. "English as a Language always in Translation." *European Journal of English Studies* 12.1: 33–47.

Pennycook, Alastair. 2010. *Language as a Local Practice.* London: Routledge.

Pennycook, Alastair and Emi Otsuji. 2015. *Metrolingualism: Language in the City.* London: Routledge.

Phillipson, Robert. 1992. *Linguistic Imperialism.* Oxford: Oxford University Press.

Phipps, Alison. 2013a. "Unmoored: Language Pain, Porosity, and Poisonwood." *Critical Multilingualism Studies* 1.2: 96–118.

Phipps, Alison. 2013b. "Linguistic Incompetence: Giving an Account of Researching Multilingually." *International Journal of Applied Linguistics* 23.3: 329–41.

Piller, Ingrid. 2001. "Naturalization Language Testing and its Basis in Ideologies of National Identity." *International Journal of Bilingualism* 5.3: 259–77.

Pitkänen-Huhta, Anne and Marja Hujo. 2012. "Experiencing Multilingualism—the Elderly Becoming Marginalized?" In *Dangerous Multilingualism: Northern Perspectives on Order, Purity, and Normality*, edited by Jan Blommaert, Sirpa Leppänen, Päivi Pahta, and Tiina Räisänen. London: Palgrave McMillan.

Porter, Catherine. 2014. "The Expository Translator." In *A Companion to Translation Studies*, edited by Sandra Bermann and Catherine Porter. Oxford: Wiley.

Pratt, Mary Louise. 2002. "The Traffic in Meaning: Translation, Contagion, Infiltration." *Profession* 2002: 25–36.

Pratt, Mary Louise. 2003. "Building a New Public Idea about Language." *Profession* 2003: 110–19.

Pratt, Mary Louise. 2009. "Harm's Way: Language and the Contemporary Arts of War." *PMLA* 124.5: 1515–31.

Pratt, Mary Louise. 2012. "If English was Good Enough for Jesus: Monolinguismo y mala fe." *Critical Multilingualism Studies* 1.1: 12–30.

Price, Joshua. 2014. "Translation and Epistemicide." Talk. Canadian Association for Translation Studies. Brock University, Saint Catherines, Ontario, Canada, 23–26 May.

Pym, Anthony. 1998. *Method in Translation History*. Manchester: St. Jerome.

Pym, Anthony. 2004. *The Moving Text: Localization, Translation and Distribution*. Philadelphia: John Benjamins.

Radaelli, Giulia. 2011. *Literarische Mehrsprachigkeit: Sprachwechsel bei Elias Canetti und Ingeborg Bachmann*. Berlin: Akademie Verlag.

Rafael, Vicente L. 2012. "Translation, American English, and the National Insecurities of Empire." In *The Translation Studies Reader*, edited by Lawrence Venuti. London: Routledge.

Rodriguez, Richard. 2004. *Hunger of Memory: The Education of Richard Rodriguez*. New York: Random House.

Rosello, Mireille. 2011. "Rudimentariness as Home." In *A Companion to Comparative Literature*, edited by Ali Behdad and Dominic Thomas. Chichester: Wiley.

Rothman, Jason. 2008. "Linguistic epistemology and the notion of monolingualism." *Sociolinguistic Studies* 2.3: 441–58.

Said, Edward. 1978. *Orientalism*. New York: Pantheon.

Said, Edward. 2007. *The Edward Said Reader*, edited by Moustafa Bayoumi and Andrew Rubin. New York: Vintage.

Saktanber, Ayse. 2002. "'We Pray Like You Have Fun': New Islamic Youth in Turkey between Intellectualism and Pop Culture." In *Fragments of Culture:*

The Everyday of Modern Turkey, edited by Deniz Kandiyoti and Ayse Saktanber. Camden, NJ: Rutgers University Press.

Samaniego Salinas, Malena. 2016. *Undergraduate translator education in Chile—an inquiry into teacher and student thinking, learning experiences and teaching practices.* PhD Dissertation, University of Arizona.

Schaap, Andrew. 2011. "Enacting the Right to have Rights: Jacques Rancière's Critique of Hannah Arendt." *European Journal of Political Theory* 10.1: 22–45.

Schieffelin, Bambi. 2007. "Found in Translation: Reflexive Language across Time and Texts in Bosavi, Papua New Guinea." In *Consequences of Contact: Language Ideologies and Sociocultural Transformation in Pacific Societies,* edited by Miki Makihara and Bambi B. Schieffelin. Oxford: Oxford University Press, 140–65.

Schmeling, Manfred. 2004. "Multilingualität und Interkulturalität im Gegenwartsroman." In *Literatur und Vielsprachigkeit,* edited by Monika Schmitz-Emans. Heidelberg: Synchron, 221–35.

Schnitzler, Arthur. 1924. *Fräulein Else.* Berlin: Zsolnay.

Schütz, Hartmut. 1988. *Nothwendiger Unterricht in der musikalischen Temperature—Ein Abriss der Stimmungsarten vom 15. bis zum 18. Jahrhundert.* Blankenburg: Kultur- und Forschungsstätte Michaelstein.

Schwarz, Roberto. 1992. "The Importing of the Novel to Brazil and Its Contradictions in the Work of Roberto Alencar." In *Misplaced Ideas: Essays on Brazilian Culture,* edited by Roberto Schwarz and John Gledson. London: Verso.

Sedgwick, Eve Kosofsky. 2007 [1990]. *Epistemology of the Closet.* Berkeley: University of California Press.

Seidlhofer, Barbara. 2007. "Common Property: English as a Lingua Franca in Europe." In *International Handbook of English Language Teaching. Part 1,* edited by Jim Cummins and Chris Davison. New York: Springer, 137–53.

Semprún, Jorge. 2003. "Jorge Semprún über das deutsche Nationalbewusstsein: Gedenkveranstaltung für die Opfer des Nationalsozialismus 2003." Available online: https://www.bundestag.de/ausschuesse_video? Accessed 15 April 2016.

Seyhan, Azade. 2005. "Is Orientalism in Retreat or in for a New Treat? Halide Edip Adivar and Emine Sevgi Özdamar Write Back." *Seminar: A Journal of Germanic Studies* 41.3: 209–25.

Shohamy, Elana. 2006. *Language Policy: Hidden Agendas and New Approaches.* New York: Routledge.

Sieg, Katrin. 2002. *Ethnic Drag.* Ann Arbor: University of Michigan Press.

Silverstein, Michael. 1979. "Language Structure and Linguistic Ideology." In *The Elements: A Parasession on Linguistic Units and Levels,* edited by Paul R. Clyne, William F. Hanks, and Carol F. Hofbauer. Chicago: Chicago Linguistics Society, 193–247.

Silverstein, Michael. 1996. "Dynamics of Recent Linguistic Contact." In *Handbook of North American Indians, Vol. 17, Languages,* edited by Ives Goddard. Washington, DC: Smithsonian Institution Press. 117–36.

Skutnabb-Kangas, Tove. 2000. *Linguistic genocide in education: or worldwide diversity and human rights?* London: Taylor and Francis.

Skutnabb-Kangas, Tove and Robert Dunbar. 2010. "Indigenous Children's Education as Linguistic Genocide and a Crime Against Humanity? A Global View." *Gáldu Čála. Journal of Indigenous Peoples' Rights* 1.

Slobin, Dan I. 1996. "From 'Thought and Language' to 'Thinking for Speaking'." In *Rethinking Linguistic Relativity,* edited by John Gumperz and Stephen Levinson. Cambridge: Cambridge University Press, 17–70.

Smith, Anthony D. 1998. *Nationalism and Modernism.* London: Routledge.

Smith, Barbara Ellen, Marcela Mendoza, and David H. Ciscel. 2005. "The World on Time: Flexible Labor, New Immigrants, and Global Logistics." In *The American South in a Global World,* edited by James L. Peacock, Harry L. Watson, and Carrie R. Matthews. Chapel Hill: The University of North Carolina Press, 23–36.

Smith, Rogers. 1999. *Civic Ideals: Conflicting Visions of Citizenship in U.S. History.* New Haven: Yale University Press.

Smyth, John Vignaux. 1998. "Music theory in Late Kafka." *Angelaki: Journal of the Theoretical Humanities* 3.2: 169–81.

Soja, Edward. 1980. "The Socio-Spatial Dialectic."*Annals of the Association of American Geographers* 70.2: 207–25.

Sollors, Werner. 1998. *Multilingual America: Transnationalism, Ethnicity, and the Languages of American Literature.* New York: New York University Press.

Sommer, Doris. 2003. *Bilingual Games: Some Literary Investigations.* New York: Palgrave Macmillan.

Sommer, Doris. 2004. *Bilingual Aesthetics: A New Sentimental Education.* Durham: Duke University Press.

Spector, Scott. 2002. *Prague Territories: National Conflict and Cultural Innovation in Franz Kafka's Fin de Siècle.* Berkeley: University of California Press.

The Spectator. 1879. "The Intellectual Status of the Aborigines Of Victoria." 29 March.

Sridhar, Shikaripur N. 1994. "A Reality Check for SLA Theories." *TESOL Quarterly* 8.4: 800–5.

Standing, Guy. 2011. *The Precariat: The New Dangerous Class.* London: Bloomsbury.

Stavans, Ilan. 2002. *On Borrowed Words: A Memoir of Language.* New York: Penguin Books.

Staworska, Beata. 2015. *Saussure's Philosophy of Language as Phenomenology: Undoing the Doctrine of the* Course in General Linguistics. Oxford: Oxford University Press.

Steffensen, Sune Vork. 2015. "Distributed Language and Dialogism: Notes on Non-locality, Sense-making and Interactivity." *Language Sciences 50:* 105–19.

Sternberg, Meir. 1981. "Polylingualism as Reality and Translation as Mimesis." *Poetics Today* 2.4: 221–39.

Steude, Wolfram. 2001. "Zur Rolle der Musik in der Fruchtbringenden Gesellschaft unter Fürst Ludwig von Anhalt-Köthen." In *Die Fruchtbringer—Eine Teutschhertzige Gesellschaft*, edited by Klaus Manger. Winter: Heidelberg, 155–70.

Steyerl, Hito. 2008. "Can The Subaltern Speak German?" translated by Aileen Derieg. Available online: http://translate.eipcp.net/strands/03/steyerl-strands01en. Accessed 18 August.

Steyerl, Hito, Encarnación Gutiérrez Rodríguez, and Nghi Ha Kien. 2003. *Spricht die Subalterne deutsch?: Migration und postkoloniale Kritik.* Münster: Unrast.

Stiegler, Bernard. 2010. "Memory." In *Critical Terms for Media Studies*, edited by William J. T. Mitchell and Mark B. N. Hansen. Chicago: University of Chicago Press, 64–87.

Stockhammer, Robert. 2014. *Grammatik: Wissen und Macht in der Geschichte einer sprachlichen Institution.* Berlin: Suhrkamp.

Suchoff, David B. 2003. "Kafka's Languages: Hebrew and Yiddish in *The Trial* and *Amerika*." In *Bilingual Games: Some Literary Investigations*, edited by Doris Sommer. New York: Palgrave Macmillan, 251–74.

Sugiharto, Setiono. 2015. "The Multilingual Turn in Applied Linguistics? A Perspective from the Periphery." *International Journal of Applied Linguistics* 25.3: 414–21.

Summers, Lawrence. 2012. "What You (Really) Need to Know." *The New York Times.* 20 January.

Süssmuth, Rita. 2007. "Report of the Independent Commission on Immigration," translated by Hilary Menges. In *Germany in Transit: Nation and Migration 1955–2005*, edited by Deniz Göktürk, David Gramling, and Anton Kaes. Berkeley: University of California Press.

Swensen, Cole. 2014. "Friendling Translation." *Critical Multilingualism Studies* 2.1: 148–61.

Taterka, Thomas. 1995. "Zur Sprachsituation im deutschen Konzentrationslager." *Magazin für Literatur und Politik* 21: 37–54.

Thomas, Jenny. 1983. "Cross-Cultural Pragmatic Failure." *Applied Linguistics* 4.2: 91–112.

Thompson, John B. 2010. *Merchants of Culture: The Publishing Business in the Twenty-First Century.* Cambridge: Polity.

Trabant, Jürgen. 2003. *Mithridates im Paradies: Kleine Geschichte des Sprachdenkens.* Munich: Beck.

Trudgill, Peter. 1986. *Dialects in Context.* Oxford: Blackwell.

UNESCO. 2014. *Universal Declaration of Language Rights.* Available online:

http://www.unesco.org/cpp/uk/declarations/linguistic.pdf. Accessed 14 July 2015.

Urciuoli, Bonnie. 2010. "Neoliberal Education: Preparing the Student for the New Workplace." In *Ethnographies of Neoliberalism*, edited by Carol Greenhouse. Philadelphia: University of Pennsylvania Press, 162–76.

Valdés, Guadalupe. 2005. "Bilingualism, Heritage Language Learners, and SLA Research: Opportunities Lost or Seized?" *Modern Language Journal* 89: 410–34.

Van Parijs, Philippe. 2011. *Linguistic Justice for Europe and For the World*. Oxford: Oxford University Press.

Varli, Ali. 2007. "Dil yasaği İşlemiyor." *Hürriyet* [Istanbul]. 22 January.

Venuti, Lawrence. 2016. "Hijacking Translation: How Comp Lit Continues to Suppress Translated Texts." *boundary 2* 43.2: 194–204.

Vericat, Fabio L. 2011. "Letting the Writing do the Talking: Denationalising English and James Kelman's Translated Accounts." *Scottish Literary Review* 3.1: 129–52.

Vertovec, Steven. 2007. "Super-diversity and its Implications." *Ethnic and Racial Studies* 30.6: 1024–54.

Vertovec, Steven. 2010. "Towards Post-multiculturalism? Changing Communities, Contexts and Conditions of Diversity." *International Social Science Journal* 61.199: 83–95.

Wagenbach, Klaus. 1991. *Franz Kafka*. Reinbek bei Hamburg: Rowohlt.

Warner, Chantelle. 2015. "Linguistic Vulnerability and Language Learning on the Periphery." Talk. Researching Multilingually at the Borders of Language, the Body, Law and the State. Brussels, Belgium.

Warner, Chantelle and Hsin-I Chen (forthcoming). "Translingual Conversationality in Facebook: Designing Talk in Social Network Spaces." *Language Learning & Technology*.

Waterhouse, Peter. 2003. "Das Klangtal." *Neue deutsche Literatur* 51: 66–80.

Waterhouse, Peter. "The Sound Valley," translated by Andrew Ziesig et al. *TRANSIT* 9.2: 1–13.

Wernicke, Christian. 2011 [1989]. "Langer Weg zum deutschen Pass." In *Transit Deutschland: Debatten zu Nation und Migration*, edited by Deniz Göktürk, David Gramling, Anton Kaes, and Andreas Langenohl. Konstanz: University of Konstanz Press.

Wimsatt, William K. and Monroe C. Beardsley. 1946. "The Intentional Fallacy." *Sewanee Review* 54: 468–88.

Wirth-Nesher, Hana. 1990. "Between Mother Tongue and Native Language in *Call it Sleep*." *Prooftexts: A Journal of Jewish Literary History* 10: 297–312.

Wirth-Nesher, Hana. 2008. *Call it English: The Languages of Jewish American Literature*. Princeton: Princeton University Press.

Woods, Michelle. 2014. *Kafka Translated: How Translators have Shaped our Reading of Kafka*. New York: Bloomsbury.

Wright, Roger. 1995. "La sociolingüística del monolingüismo." *Atti del XXI Congresso Internazionale di Linguistica e Filologia Romanza*: 483–6.

Yildiz, Yasemin. 2012. *Beyond the Mother Tongue: The Postmonolingual Condition*. New York: Fordham University Press.

Yngve, Victor H. 1994. *From Grammar to Science: New Foundations for General Linguistics*. Philadelphia: John Benjamins.

Yngve, Victor H. 2004. "Issues in Hard-science Linguistics." In *Hard Science Linguistics*, edited by Victor H. Ygnve and Zdzislaw Wasik. London and New York: Continuum Books, 14–26.

Zhang, Sarah. 2015. "The Pitfalls of Using Google NGram to Study Language." *wired.com*. 12 October.

Žižek, Slavoj. 1991. *Looking Awry: An Introduction to Jacques Lacan through Popular Culture*. Cambridge, MA: MIT Press.

Žižek, Slavoj. 1993. *Tarrying with the Negative: Kant, Hegel and the Critique of Ideology*. Durham: Duke University Press.

INDEX

Index